NATION, STATE AND MARGINAL PEOPLE

Perspectives and Dimensions

The Editors

Anil Kumar Sarkar is a Professor of History, University of Kalyani, Nadia, West Bengal. Earlier he had worked as Head and Associate Professor of History, University of Gour Banga. He is a founder-editor, *Journal of People's History and Culture* from 2015. His recent publications are:

1. *British Paramountcy and the Cooch Behar State (A Study of the Anatomy of Indirect Rule in Cooch Behar).*
2. *Ethnicity and Regional Politics of Eastern and North East India.*
3. *Historians and Historiography of Bengal and North East India: Dimensions and Perspectives.*
4. *Reflections on the History of North Bengal.*
5. *History of North Bengal: Colonial Ideology, Entrepreneurship, Society and Culture.*
6. *Women in Indian Society: Essays on Historiography and Politics.*
7. *Tribes of Sub-Himalayan Region: Meches, Rabhas, Totos and Garos.*

He has published more than 40 articles in National, International and Regional Academic Journals and Edited Books. At present, he is engaged in the studies on Princely states, Ethnicity, Dalits and Regional History of North Bengal and North East India.

Dr. Akhil Sarkar is an Assistant Professor of History, Nabadwip Vidyasagar College, Nadia, West Bengal. He obtained his Master's Degree from the University of North Bengal. He obtained his Ph.D. Degree (2020) "Impact of Vaisnavism in Colonial and Post-Colonial Nadia" from University of Kalyani, Nadia. He has published more than 10 articles in National, International and Regional Academic Journals and Edited Books. At present, he is engaged in the studies on Vaisnavism in Bengal.

Nation, State and Marginal People

Perspectives and Dimensions

Edited by

Anil Kumar Sarkar

Akhil Sarkar

CONCEPT PUBLISHING COMPANY PVT. LTD.

NEW DELHI - 110 059

ISBN: 978-93-5594-489-4

First Published 2022

Published and Printed by

Concept Since 1974

Concept Publishing Company Pvt. Ltd.
A/15-16, Commercial Block, Mohan Garden
New Delhi-110059 (India)
T: +91 11 4110 1460
E: publishing@conceptpub.com, W: www.conceptpub.com

Cataloging in Publication Data--Courtesy: D.K. Agencies (P) Ltd. <docinfo@dkagencies.com>

Nation, state and marginal people : perspectives and dimensions / edited by Anil Kumar Sarkar, Akhil Sarkar.

pages cm
Contributed articles.
Includes bibliographical references and index.
ISBN 9789355944894

1. People with social disabilities--India--West Bengal--Social conditions. 2. People with social disabilities--India--West Bengal--Economic conditions. 3. Marginality, Social--India--West Bengal. 4. Marginality, Social--Political aspects--India--West Bengal. 5. Women in development--India--West Bengal. I. Sarkar, Anil Kumar, 1973- editor. II. Sarkar, Akhil, editor.

LCC HN690.W47N38 2022 | DDC 305.568095414 23

Dedicated

to

All Marginal People in India

ACKNOWLEDGEMENTS

The present book focuses on the *Nation, State and Marginal People: Perspectives and Dimensions*. This work is mainly the collection of articles. We have great pleasure in recording our indebtedness to those who helped us in the pursuit of our work. First of all, we wish to record sincere gratitude to all contributors who have contributed their valuable article for publishing as a book. We are benefited from their scholarly suggestions, academic skills and scientific vision. The broad objective of the book is to evolve a fresh understanding of the issues and problems that beset this part of the country.

We sincerely remember Professor I. Sarkar (former professor), Department of History, University of North Bengal for his valuable criticism and suggestions time and again. We are also very much indebted to Professor Ananda Gopal Ghosh (former professor), Department of History, University of North Bengal, who helped us whenever required. We are grateful to Professor Anil Bhuimali, Hon'ble Vice-Chancellor, University of Raiganj, benefited from his scholarly suggestions, academic skills and scientific vision. We are also indebted to Professor Tapan Kumar Biswas, Hon'ble Vice-Chancellor, Harichand Guruchand University. We are also grateful to Professor Ali Athar, Department of History, Aligarh Muslim University for his valuable suggestions.

We are also very much indebted to Professor Chittabrata Palit (former) Professor of History, Jadavpur University and presently Director, Institute of Historical Studies, Kolkata, who have ever shown his interest and extended academic help whatever possible for us. We gratefully remember with all humility the counsel, help, and encouragement we have received from our colleagues, friends and students, like Rupkumar Barman, Pradip Chattopadhyay, Sudas Lama, Koushiki Dasgupta, Hosneara Khatun, Chhawang Subba, Chanchal Mandal, Amal Ch. Barman, Anil Biswas, Tapas Sarkar, Jaydip Sarkar, Koushik Chakraborty, Babulal Bala, Bipul Mandal, Parimal Bepari, Gouranga Roy, Sankar Biswas, Naresh Ch. Sarkar, Amitava Chatterjee, Subhas Biswas, Sabyasachi Chattopadhyay, Anirudha Das, Sutapa Sengupta, Manosanta Biswas, Mrinal Debnath, Manoj Kr. Haldar, Rajesh Biswas,

India is a signatory to several international instruments under the United Nations and is bound to take care of the provisions as agreed. However, despite these commitments, India continues to be a country with scores of marginalized people. A good number of people in India are deprived of food, shelter, education and access to healthcare facilities. Scheduled Castes and Tribes suffer most from hunger and malnutrition, making up 25 per cent of the rural population but 42 per cent of the poor. As a result of discrimination, many low-caste SCs and STs are expected to work as agricultural labourers without being paid, many held in debt bondage by their higher-caste employers. These marginalized sections need to be identified and there is an urgent need to restore their human rights. Then there are other groups like the domestic workers, those who work in *dhabas* and such unorganized sectors who are working in pitiable conditions and at a wage which is much less than the minimum and are discriminated against. Thus, as a country, India is home to a considerable number of vulnerable and discriminated sections of the population.

There are various reasons for marginalization and it is an outcome of socio-economic and cultural and historical factors. Human history is a story of dominance by the influential group over the weak and the meek. The dominant group always dominated the other group and exploitation used to continue over centuries. However, democracy took roots in most of the countries and by suitable legislation, this exploitation was done away with by enacting laws but in the developing countries due to the slow changing of the policies, the winds of change are yet to take place and this transition from exploitation to social justice is slow.

Marginalization about society is the exclusion of certain categories of people from society. In this exclusion, certain sections of the people are excluded or are deprived of normal activities. Social stigma is another aspect of this social exclusion from the dominant sections of society. These deprived sections also face other kinds of problems like lack of opportunities; the society keeps them away from the mainstream, they have very few social networks and interaction — and these are particularly the lower castes or those constitute the ethnic groups in the society. Even after seventy-four years of independence and the Constitutional guarantees, many sections of people particularly those belonging to the lower castes are still facing discrimination and they are still subject to atrocities and stand excluded from the social mainstream. They are attacked, their houses are set on fire and they are still isolated and many people refuse to mix with those people considering them as outcastes even today. Thus, even in the 21st century, they live as an isolated section within society. The identifiable marginalized groups include — women, people with disabilities, LGBT community, people suffering from HIV/AIDS etc.

A marginalized person believes that he has no importance in society. They have no participation in the economic activities of the State. They have no voice of their own and they continue to live as worthless members of society. They have no access to resources and they remain away from the rest of the society. All these will have a detrimental effect on their existence as human beings and members of society. Women may be excluded from certain jobs and occupations, incorporated into certain others, and marginalized in others. In general, they are always marginalized relative to men, in every country and culture. Women (or, men) do not present a homogeneous category where members have common interests, abilities, or practices. Women belonging to lower classes, lower castes, illiterate, and the poorest region have different levels of marginalization than their better-off counterparts.

The present book contains 19 articles on *Nation, State and Marginal People: Perspectives and Dimensions*. This volume analyses different aspects and provides an opportunity to address the changes and challenges faced by the marginal people. All the contributors have tried to highlight every nook and corner and explained the matters without bias picked up the right history.

Garia, Kolkata

Anil Kumar Sarkar
Akhil Sarkar

CONTENTS

PART – II
Women: Religion, Emancipation and Partition Sufferings

PART – III
Marginal People: Sports, Environment and Politics

CONTRIBUTORS

Agnita Pal, Research Scholar of History, University of North Bengal, Siliguri, Darjeeling, West Bengal, *Email:* agnitapal @gmail.com

Dr. Akhil Sarkar, Assistant Professor of History, Nabadwip Vidyasagar College, Nabadwip, Nadia, West Bengal, *Email:* akhil@nvc.ac.in

Ananta Das, Research Scholar of History, Sikkim University, Gangtok, Sikkim, *Email:* anantadas38@gmail.com

Dr. Anil Kumar Sarkar, Professor of History, Kalyani University, Kalyani, Nadia, West Bengal, *Email:* anilcob.2012@gmail.com

Apurba Ghosh, Research Scholar of History, University of Kalyani, Kalyani, Nadia, West Bengal, *Email:* apurbaghosh041995@gmail.com

Arindam Ghosh, Research Scholar of History, Rabindra Bharati University, Kolkata, West Bengal, *Email:* arindam.prithivi@gmail.com

Bablu Mallick, Research Scholar of History, Kalyani University, Kalyani, Nadia, West Bengal, *Email:* bablumallick571@gmail.com

Dr. Bipul Mandal, Assistant Professor of History, Kaliyaganj College, Kaliyaganj, Uttar Dinajpur, West Bengal, *Email:* bipulmandalklg@gmail.com

Gopal Chandra Das, Research Scholar of History, Kazi Nazrul University, Asansol, West Bengal, *Email:* gopalchandra4042@gmail.com

Kalikrishna Sutradhar, Freelance writer, Kaliyaganj, Uttar Dinajpur, West Bengal, *Email:* kali993348@gmail.com

Kausar Ali, Research Scholar of History, Raiganj University, Raiganj, Uttar Dinajpur, West Bengal, *Email:* kausaraliugb @gmail.com

Krishna Kanta Dhali, Assistant Professor of History, Gobardanga Hindu College, Gobardanga, North 24 Pargana, West Bengal, *Email:* rkd.caluniv@gmail.com

Md. Mainul Islam, Assistant Professor of History, Brahmananda Keshab Chandra College, Kolkata, West Bengal, *Email:* mainu 13484@gmail.com

Mohan Haldar, Research Scholar of History, University of Kalyani, Kalyani, Nadia, West Bengal, *Email:* mohan.haldar.1993@gmail.com

Mrinal Chandra Das, Research Scholar of History, Raiganj University, Raiganj, Uttar Dinajpur, West Bengal, *Email:* mrinalnbu1962@gmail.com

Payel Saha, Research Scholar of Political Science, University of Gour Banga, Malda, West Bengal, *Email:* payelsaha8989@gmail.com

Prasenjit Sarkar, Research Scholar of History, University of North Bengal, *Email:* psarkarp601@gmail.com

Sahel Bepari, Research Scholar of History, Cooch Behar Panchanan Barma University, Cooch Behar, West Bengal.

Suvasish Chakraborty, Research Scholar of International Relations, Jadavpur University, Kolkata, West Bengal, *Email:* suvasishchakraborty2011@gmail.com

Dr. Tridib Mandal, Assistant Professor of History, Gobardanga Hindu College, Gobardanga, North 24 Pargana, West Bengal, *Email:* tridibmandalghc@gmail.com

PART – I

Marginal Communities: Changes and Challenges

1

Dalits and Land Reforms in West Bengal

Anil Kumar Sarkar

There is no doubt that land reforms are not only for promoting land productivity but also for achieving equity in a highly unequal society. That is why the transfer of land from the land-owning to the landless is considered as an effective measure of both reducing economic inequalities and inequalities regarding social and political power in rural society. The agrarian societies are given more emphasis on land. According to Peter Robb, "for much of human history what mattered is 'how land is controlled — that is, under local power, rural property or taxation and agriculture'." In the Indian context the control of the land to a large extent brings in the caste dimension — the landowning dominant castes and the landless agricultural labourers dominated castes — thus, making land-based hierarchies intertwined with caste-based hierarchies.[1] Gyan Prakash has written in his book that the numerous village studies that point out the interdependent relationship between various caste groups in self-sufficient villages.[2] Gyan Prakash also explained that there seems to have been some continuity of the existing caste-based and land-based hierarchies from pre-colonial times to colonial times. Such a transition would have been made easier by the fact that the dominant-dominated caste relationship was also evident in the cultural domain — cosmological beliefs, rites and cults, ritual ranking and other aspects.[3]

If we scrutinize the scenario of the last phase of colonialism then the significant changes for the underprivileged classes/castes. There were many self-respect and secular movements among some specific castes in Kerala, Maharashtra, Bengal, Tamil Nadu and other parts of the country. And they obtained a legal status because of the Government of India (GoI) Act, 1919. Identifying depressed classes, GoI Act, 1935 notifies about Scheduled Castes (SCs) and temple entry Acts in the

1930s by various State Governments.[4] The land reform and distribution of land is not only enhanced production and reduces poverty but is also a part of a democratic revolution that frees the people of the countryside from the fetters of landlordism.[5] Traditionally, social classes and groups have not had access to land and free these classes from social and economic oppression.

The village economy determines the economic position and power relations between different social groups in the village. According to Ghosh and Chakrabarty, on ownership holdings of land, showed that in most States of India the proportion of land owned by Scheduled Caste households was much lower than their share in total population. However, in rural India, the proportion of land owned by SC households had increased in the period between 1982 and 1992.[6] Sukhadeo Thorat noted that in 1993-94 only 19 per cent of all Dalit households were self-employed in agriculture while the comparable statistics for non-Dalit/ Adivasi households was 42 per cent. He also pointed out "the limited access to agricultural land and capital assets is both due to the historical legacy associated with restrictions imposed by the caste system and the ongoing discrimination in the land market and capital market and other related economic spheres."[7]

This article is an analytical study on land ownership structure among Dalits in rural West Bengal. It proposes to analyze the attempts to do away with the land-based hierarchies through agrarian reforms. Some questions arise that the Dalits of West Bengal are benefited from the land reforms. Is there reduction in the inequalities? Dalits of West Bengal are more benefited with comparison to other states. Will land reforms alone can provide social justice and demolish the structure of subordination for the Scheduled Castes without grassroots mobilization and peasant movement? Why do the Scheduled Castes participate in the peasant movement? The main objective of this chapter is to search the queries and try to critically analyze the focal points.

If we look back on the history of the agrarian society of West Bengal then we see that it became extremely poverty-ridden, stratified and disintegrated on the eve of the departure of the colonial power from the Indian subcontinent. The Permanent Settlement Act of 1793, which opened in Bengal throughout British rule in India, introduced a series of intermediaries between the tiller and the real owner of the land. A large number of small cultivators lost their land in the process of emergence of such intermediaries like Zamindars, Talukdars, Izaradars, Patnidars, Jotedars etc. The deteriorating economic conditions of the lowest strata was reflected in the rapid expansion of the number of the sharecroppers and the agricultural labours.[8]

Table 1.1: Rayati Area Transferred during the Last 12 Years (1940)

District	*Total area enquired into*	*Transferred during last 12 years*		*Transferred area cultivated*			
		Area	*Per-centage*	*By purchaser's family*	*By Barga-dars*	*By Labourers*	*By under-tenants*
Bakarganj	1752.66	99.97	5.7	56.09	43.88	—	—
Bankura	5479.86	308.05	6.7	48.47	77.06	36.99	205.53
Birbhum	5375.58	228.34	6.7	46.32	92.82	87.20	—
Bogra	1984.45	59.23	3.0	28.37	18.60	0.50	11.76
Burdwan	4759.15	185.83	3.8	82.32	65.36	38.15	—
Chittagong	1693.95	164.90	9.7	79.97	20.50	5.42	59.01
Dacca	1082.27	53.46	4.9	23.31	22.86	5.99	1.30
Dinajpur	6512.22	260.84	3.8	147.31	87.23	16.13	0.17
Faridpur	1796.54	120.19	6.6	90.79	24.53	—	4.87
Hooghly	2228.09	60.83	2.7	29.93	25.72	5.18	—
Howrah	1186.30	24.29	2.0	7.29	16.80	0.20	—
Jalpaiguri	4645.06	439.96	9.4	66.06	185.59	14.93	173.38
Jessore	5133.74	431.05	8.3	102.14	136.35	13.32	179.24
Khulna	1701.68	72.63	4.2	31.56	41.07	—	—
Malda	1107.93	77.02	6.9	48.51	17.95	—	10.56
Midnapore	4693.64	349.64	7.4	120.03	175.81	39.14	14.66
Murshidabad	5070.62	638.74	12.5	127.95	152.65	1.00	357.14
Mymensingh	3597.53	201.93	5.5	88.78	105.33	—	7.82
Nadia	4008.57	877.50	21.8	570.24	172.00	27.60	107.66
Noakhali	1208.43	65.74	5.5	63.42	2.06	0.26	—
Pabna	1673.28	63.76	3.8	51.23	14.03	—	—
Rajshahi	5617.84	196.78	3.5	68.62	37.85	—	90.31
Rangpur	7964.30	380.60	4.7	80.60	144.92	10.73	144.35
Tippera	2112.91	99.39	4.2	59.65	10.41	13.61	15.72
24-Parganas	5083.42	412.65	8.1	133.15	190.41	25.05	64.07
Total	**85470.04**	**5923.35**	**6.9**	**2252.11 Or 38%**	**1882.29 Or 31.7%**	**341.40 Or 5.7%**	**1447.55 Or 24.6%**

Source: Land Revenue Commission's Report, 1940, Vol. 2, pp. 120-121.

Table 1.1 shows that the Land Revenue Commission's report observed that of 85470.04 inquired acres all over the province of Bengal 5923.35 acres were transferred, of which 31.7 per cent was turned over to Barga (sharecropping) and 24.6 per cent to the under-tenants. The increase of sharecroppers was interlinked with the indebtedness of the small cultivators who were mostly from the Scheduled Castes, Scheduled Tribes, or Muslim background to the village money lenders and other intermediaries (mostly come from the upper castes). When the poor peasant unable to repay the debt lost his land to the lenders and he was resettled on the same land on the condition to pay half of the produce of the creditor. Peasants who lost their land but were not settled on it as sharecroppers became landless agricultural labourers. They constituted 22.5 per cent of the total number of families of Bengal in late 1940.[9] Floud Commission, the Land Revenue Commission appointed by the British Government submitted their report in 1942, which recommended abolition of the intermediary system in the land administration in Bengal. As a result, on demands from the people of the state, the West Bengal Estates Acquisition Act of 1953 was enacted.

Tebhaga Movement (1946-47) was the first organized peasant movement of undivided Bengal which initiated the large-scale mobilization of the peasantry under the leadership of the Bengal Kisan Sabha (dominated by CPI). In this movement, the sharecroppers demanded to retain Tebhaga (two-third) share of the produce for themselves and thereby to reduce the share of the produce of the landowners from one-half to one-third a demand recommended by the Land Revenue Commission.[10] The process of mobilization of the agricultural labourers, sharecroppers, poor peasants, tenants of various categories became the driving force against the intermediary class of landowners, money lenders, traders and the British bureaucracy.[11] The Tebhaga movement spread rapidly in the northern part of Bengal and mainly Scheduled Caste-dominated villages. The landowners, the sharecroppers predominantly represented by the Scheduled Castes and the Scheduled Tribes collected paddy in their courtyard to retain one-third of the produce. The British Government looked at the Tebhaga movement as a law and order problem, instead of implementing the recommendation of the Land Revenue Commission. The organized peasants' resistance against the police and the landlords combine. But this movement collapsed in the face of strong police oppression, organizational weakness of the movement and change in the political climate of the state in the wake of attainment of independence and partition of Bengal in 1947. The Bargadar means a person who under the system generally known as *Adhi barga*, or *bhag* cultivates the land of another person on condition of delivering a share of the produce of such land to that person includes a person who under the system generally known as *kisani*, who cultivates the land of another person on condition of receiving a share of the produce of such land from that person.

After independence, the land laws in the State of West Bengal have gone through various changes. Land reforms in post-independence West Bengal began with the enactment of The West Bengal Non-Agricultural

Tenancy Act, 1949 and The West Bengal Bargadars Act, 1950. Then came The West Bengal Estates Acquisition Act, 1953 which came into force on February 12, 1954, and which principally abolished the Zamindari or intermediary system and all estates and all rent receiving interests in each estate. All the estates in the State of West Bengal vested in the State free from all encumbrances and a ceiling were imposed on the holding of land. The comprehensive measures of land reforms were introduced by the West Bengal Land Reforms Act, 1955 which came into force in February 1956 and the said Act has undergone quite many significant amendments until now. All kinds of land have been brought within the purview of the said Act and a family ceiling has been imposed on holding of land. This Act has also been subsequently amended in 1957, 1960, 1962, 1965, 1966.

Table 1.2: A Raiyat is Entitled to Hold Land to the Extent (Ceiling Limit)

Raiyat	*Irrigated area*	*Non-irrigated area*
An adult unmarried person or a sole surviving member of the family	2.5 standard hectors (6.18 acres)	3.50 standard hectors (8.65 acres)
A family consisting of 2 to 5 members	5 standard hectors (12.35 acres)	7 standard hectors (17.30 acres)
Family of more than five members	5 standard hectors + 0.5 standard hectors (1.24 acres) for each member above five subject to 7 standard hectors	7 standard hectors + 0.7 standard hectors (1.73 acres) for each member above five subject to 9.80 standard hectors (24.22 acres)
Family of 9 or more members	7 standard hectors	9.80 standard hectors
Any other rayat (which *inter alia* includes a company)	7 standard hectors	9.80 standard hector

Source: The Bengal Chamber, *A Handbook of Land in West Bengal*, p. 8.

The rural society of West Bengal visualized a gap between the land reforms ideology and the implementation of the same till the late sixties. The landowners in alliance with the local police and reforms administration could in most effectively deny the tenant his rights.[12] The tenants were aware of their rights, they were generally in too weak a position both socially and economically to insist on their rights. As a result of this gap-termination of a sharecropper from land by the landowners, *mala fide* land transfer (losing of land by the poor peasants) and increasing unemployment became rampant in rural West Bengal. The sharecropper who constituted 20.5 per cent of the household in 1952-53 reduced to 10.8 per cent of the rural household by 1970-71.[13]

Table 1.3: Percentage of Cultivators and Agricultural Labourers in West Bengal by the Scheduled Castes and General Categories

	Cultivators		*Agricultural labourers*	
	Scheduled Castes	*General categories*	*Scheduled Castes*	*General categories*
1961	—	38.5	—	15.30
1971	33.4	32.00	42.6	26.00
1981	30.2	29.76	42.7	25.23
1991	31.29	28.42	46.04	24.83

Source: Census of India 1961, 1971, 1981, 1981.

Table 1.3 shows the agrarian population's sharp division to the lower strata of the agrarian hierarchy. The agriculture labourers are always high position on the other. In 1971, 81, 91 reported 42.6, 42.7, 46.04 respectively. The All India Rural Credit Review Committee in its report in 1968 also pointed out that there has been the "emergence of sharp polarization between the more privileged and less privileged classes in the rural areas."[14] The distribution of surplus vested land has not been able to ensure the economic security of the marginal cultivators and hereby a vast majority of these cultivators have opted for agricultural wage-earning as the main means of their livelihood.

Table 1.4: Land Distribution, Operation Barga and Homestead of Scheduled Castes and Scheduled Tribes of West Bengal — June 30, 1992

Sl.No.	*Items*	*Total*	*Scheduled Castes*	*Scheduled Tribes*
1.	Distribution of surplus vested lands	(100) (20.43 lakhs)	37.20% (7.60 lakhs)	19.18% (3.92 lakhs)
2.	Operation Barga	(100) (14.39 lakhs)	30.99% (4.46 lakhs)	12.09% (1.74 lakhs)
3.	Homstead distribution	(100) (2.58 lakhs)	41.8% (1.08 lakhs)	15.50% (0.40 lakhs)

Source: Government of West Bengal, Tabulated from Dasgupta, 1995.

According to a Government of West Bengal Report, till June 30, 1992, a total of 12.69 lakh acres of agricultural land are declared surplus vested of which 9.36 lakh acres are distributed among 20.43 lakh of beneficiaries. The percentage of the Scheduled Castes and the Scheduled Tribes to the total number of beneficiaries are given in Table 1.4. Fixed-rent leasing is prohibited, but sharecropping is allowed and subjects to protection. A person lawfully cultivating other's land is presumed to be a sharecropper and is given permanent and heritable rights with a fixed level of rent if the landlord shares in inputs.

Table 1.5: Distribution of Ownership Holding among Weaker Sections

Size class	*Scheduled Caste*		*Scheduled Tribe*		*Others*	
	1982	*1992*	*1982*	*1992*	*1982*	*1992*
Marginal (less than 1 ha)	26.6	30.2	12.0	18.7	10.9	14.9
Small (1 to 2 ha)	22.71	22.2	18.8	22.7	15.6	17.5
Medium (2 to 4 ha)	24.0	20.4	29.2	27.7	22.6	24.7
Large (above 4 ha)	26.8	27.2	40.0	30.9	50.9	42.9
Total	**100.0**	**100.0**	**100.0**	**100.0**	**100.0**	**100.0**

Source: NSS report relevant years.

Table 1.5 shows the distribution of ownership of the land of Scheduled Castes (SC) from 1982 to 1992 increased all over India for the marginal ownership of land that is less than 1 hectare and small distribution of the land of SC shows more or less same. But the medium ownership of land distribution of the SC shows decreased and the large distribution of land ownership is increased.

West Bengal is one of the few states in India where land reform was implemented on a large scale. Land reform implemented in West Bengal had three components: (a) Operation Barga involved registration of the names of the *bargadars* (sharecroppers) land records, (b) redistribution of ceiling surplus land to the landless and marginal farmers, and (c) distribution of homestead land.[15] The major beneficiaries of land reform in West Bengal have Scheduled Castes (SC) and Scheduled Tribes (ST). Till 2008, of the total beneficiaries of agricultural land through land reform, 56 per cent were Scheduled Castes and Scheduled Tribes which were almost double the proportion of Scheduled Caste (SC) and Scheduled Tribe (ST) population in the state.[16] Thus, the main beneficiaries of land reform were the rural poor, primarily the small and marginal peasants and agricultural labourers. Land reform brought the land to sections of the peasantry that were hitherto denied access to land. Whatever little gains were achieved by the agrarian economy of West Bengal in the 1980s were reversed with the initiation of a market-oriented reform programme. These policies had an adverse impact on all sections of the peasantry, except for a very few at the top. The sections of the peasantry who had benefited from land reform, cultivated on small plots of land and usually belonged to the category of rural poor — Scheduled Castes, Scheduled Tribes and Muslims — were most adversely affected. Table 1.6 shows that almost two-thbird of Scheduled Caste and Scheduled Tribe households and three-fourth Muslim households did not cultivate land in rural West Bengal in 2011-12. The corresponding figure for Hindu-others was high at 52.1 per cent but lower than the other three.

Table 1.6: Proportion of Households that did not Cultivate Land, Social and Religious Groups, West Bengal, 1987-88 to 2011-12

Year	*Scheduled Castes*	*Scheduled Tribes*	*Muslims*	*Hindu-Others*
1987-88	46.5	32.2	41.9	33.3
1999-00	55.4	44.0	56.5	38.1
2009-10	65.3	74.6	69.6	51.0
2011-12	65.4	65.3	75.4	52.1

Source: NSS, 43rd round (1987-88) and Scheduled Castes, Scheduled Tribes and OBCs in 55th (1999-00), 66th (2009-10) and 68th (2011-12) rounds.

Table 1.7: Households that do not Own Any Land Other than Homesteads as a Proportion of all Households, by Social Group, Rural India, 2003 in per cent

States	*Adivasi*	*Dalit*	*Non-Dalit/Adivasi*	*All*
Andhra Pradesh	48.7	64.5	49.6	53.2
Arunachal Pradesh	4.5	53.6	93.8	23.5
Assam	27.6	49.8	40.9	40.3
Bihar	22.1	72.3	35.3	43.7
Chhattisgarh	18.4	31.5	31.0	26.2
Delhi	100.0	99.7	97.3	98.1
Goa	0.0	—	59.0	57.1
Gujarat	34.3	67.0	43.1	44.1
Haryana	100.0	84.1	34.9	49.5
Himachal Pradesh	14.5	22.7	23.5	22.7
Jammu & Kashmir	44.1	21.8	8.9	11.0
Jharkhand	18.7	41.7	24.9	24.7
Karnataka	54.0	57.5	34.7	40.4
Kerala	66.1	85.4	66.1	68.3
Madhya Pradesh	41.1	35.6	30.8	34.0
Maharashtra	61.2	69.6	35.5	44.8
Manipur	11.0	41.6	45.6	30.2
Meghalaya	25.4	59.2	60.9	29.0
Mizoram	15.0	100.0	6.0	14.9
Nagaland	9.3	—	100.0	15.5
Odisha	33.3	52.8	35.9	38.5
Punjab	98.9	88.9	36.5	56.9
Rajasthan	6.8	39.3	17.0	19.6
Sikkim	35.5	65.1	46.7	44.4
Tamil Nadu	66.7	78.7	59.5	64.5
Tripura	48.5	67.4	62.1	59.4
Uttar Pradesh	51.8	33.9	23.2	26.3
Uttarakhand	60.9	33.7	25.2	27.7
West Bengal	48.8	54.1	42.8	46.5
India	**35.5**	**56.5**	**37.8**	**41.6**

Source: Computed from unit-level data, *NSS Land and Livestock Holdings Survey*, 59th Round.

Table 1.7 shows data on the proportion of households that do not hold any land other than homesteads by States and social groups in 2003. By NSS 2003 data, 41.6 per cent of rural households in rural India did not own any land other than homesteads. The incidence of landlessness was higher among Dalit households than among Adivasi households and non-Dalit/Adivasi households. While 56.5 per cent of Dalit households did not own non-homestead land, 35.5 per cent of Adivasi households and 37.8 per cent non-Dalit/Adivasi households did not own non-homestead land. In West Bengal, 46.5 per cent of households do not own land other than homesteads. This is slightly higher than the national average. However, the proportion of landless Dalit households is below the national average in West Bengal by both definitions of landholdings.

Table 1.8: Growth in the Proportion of Households that do not Cultivate Land, by Social Group, Rural India, 1993-94 to 2004-05 in per cent

States	*Adivasi*	*Dalit*	*Non-Dalit/Adivasi*	*All*
Kerala	– 40.7	– 32.2	– 50.7	– 47.6
Jammu & Kashmir	– 100.0	– 34.1	– 20.2	– 35.2
Bihar & Jharkhand	– 0.1	– 6.2	24.7	9.6
Assam	– 29.3	– 38.7	– 8.8	– 17.3
Gujarat	– 8.4	4.5	13.0	9.3
Tripura	– 7.2	– 0.2	14.4	3.8
Karnataka	12.1	20.5	19.9	20.4
Madhya Pradesh & Chhattisgarh	23.9	13.4	35.3	26.1
Maharashtra	3.7	13.2	7.8	11.6
Punjab	25.0	– 0.8	25.2	11.1
Tamil Nadu	40.8	9.7	14.7	13.2
Uttar Pradesh & Uttarakhand	20.3	22.6	23.6	23.4
Andhra Pradesh	54.7	23.7	19.9	22.6
West Bengal	38.0	3.2	18.2	13.9
Haryana	-56.4	6.7	21.7	15.1
Odisha	6.1	3.7	30.2	17.2
Rajasthan	23.3	61.6	22.8	37.6
Himachal Pradesh	128.0	60.7	32.0	42.1
India	**11.6**	**8.7**	**10.8**	**10.6**

Source: Computed from (i) NSS Report No. 425, Employment and Unemployment Situation among Social Groups in India, 1993-94; (ii) NSS Report No. 516, Employment and Unemployment Situation among Social Groups in India, 2004-05.

The increase in the share of households without access to land for cultivation in India between 1992-93 and 2004-05 is higher for Adivasi households (11.6%) and non-SC/ST households (10.8%) than for

Dalit households (8.7%). The increase in landlessness among Dalits is very low in West Bengal. It is mostly the Adivasi households and non-Dalit/Adivasi households who have lost land in West Bengal in this period.

The percentage of landless households has been declined among the Scheduled Castes over the years in West Bengal and marginal landholding patterns are increased. The marginal cultivators are more among the SC community, that is 81.22 per cent and we have calculated small, marginal and landless together is 96.78 per cent. The Scheduled Caste people occupy the bottom of the agrarian society. The source of power, privilege and dominance are land in rural areas and marginal landholders have never been a source of power and privilege. There is no doubt that these SC communities become marginalized in the agrarian society. It :s also very important that the United Left Front government has been successful in implementing the land reform laws but these land reforms in West Bengal have not been able to eradicate poverty and to provide economic security to the Scheduled Castes and Scheduled Tribes. It has also been seen that after 1967, left political parties radically mobilized the rural poor for speedy implementation of the land reforms. The Naxalbari movement 1967-1971 gave extra energy to the process of radical mobilization of rural poor.

After 1977, CPIM adopted the strategic path of ideological revisionism and have resorted to institutionalized mass mobilization. The local left political leaders had mobilized the poor for the distribution of surplus vested lands implementation of Operation Barga, institutional credit to the rural poor, implementation of Minimum Wage Act for the agricultural labourers, pressuring government officials for initiating food for work and other relief programmes, against usury, against feudal obligations to the big landowners etc. One thing is very much true, this mobilization was strengthened the local-based party politics. Indeed, the collective mobilizations, ideological orientations, organizations and the leadership of the peasant movements in West Bengal have been phenomenal changes. We find significant pre-election year spikes in land reform activity throughout the 1970s and 1980s. Moreover, we cannot reject the hypothesis that the reforms implemented five years before 1978 were comparable to those in the post-1978 period. This adds to the evidence of the importance of electoral competition motives in the land reforms, which operated equally for both the Left and Congress parties. Because of all the evidences, we are, therefore, inclined in favour of the view that electoral competitiveness rather than ideological differences played a significant role in the West Bengal land reforms.

A massive mass-mobilization campaign involving party leaders, local activists and the administrators was mounted to identify surplus or *barga* land, and distribute (or register) them. Election to local governments (panchayats) was mandated from 1978 onwards, and the active cooperation of the newly elected bodies was sought in this process. The panchayats set up land reform committees (Bhumi Sanskar Sthayee Samiti) with the state government's junior land reform officer acting as a convenor, which was empowered to form 'lists' of surplus lands and suitable beneficiaries. Settlement camps were set up, with follow-up re-orientation camps, to create an open and participatory process for the preparation of these lists, in which tenants and poor farmers participated widely.[17] The Left Front government subsequently made Operation Barga the centrepiece of its mass mobilization effort of poorer peasants throughout the state. Membership in the Kisan Sabha swelled from 1.3 million in 1977-78 to 8.5 million by 1990. While the initial drive in 1979 was interrupted by the floods, the operation was mounted again in 1980, with the active cooperation of the Panchayati institutions. Over a million *bargadars* were registered by 1981, up from 242,000 in 1978 and increasing to almost one and a half million by 1990.[18]

West Bengal is one State in India where efforts have been made to grant land rights to landless households, especially Dalit and Adivasi households. The impact of land reforms in West Bengal is reflected at the national-level statistics on land holdings. Secondary data show that Dalit households in West Bengal have better access to land compared to other States. This is indicated by the fact that the proportion of landless Dalit households in terms of ownership holdings is lower in West Bengal than the national average and the Index of Access to agricultural land is higher than the national average. There has been very little increase in the incidence of landlessness among Dalits in West Bengal between 1993-94 and 2004-05. Village level data show that Dalit, Adivasi and Muslim households have been major beneficiaries of land reforms in West Bengal. These social groups have gained access to agricultural and homestead land through the process of land reforms. The policy of land reform implemented by the Government of West Bengal has thus contributed though in a limited way to lowering inequalities across social groups in the State.

NOTES AND REFERENCES

1. Peter Robb, *Ancient Rights and Future Comforts: Bihar, The Bengal Tenancy Act of 1885, and British Rule in India*, Curzon Press, 1997, p. xi.
2. Gyan Prakash, *The History and Historiography of Rural Labourers in Colonial India*, Oxford, 1992, pp. 1-46.
3. Gyan Prakash, *Reproducing Inequality: Spirit Cults and Labour Relations in Colonial Eastern India*, Modern Asian Studies, 1992, pp. 282-304.
4. Hiroyali Kotani (ed.), *Caste System, Untouchability and the Depressed*, Manohar, 1999, p. 42.
5. Ramachandran and Swaminathan, Madhura (eds.), *Agrarian Studies: Essays on Agrarian Relations in Less Developed Countries*, Tulika Books, 2002.
6. G. Chakrabarty and P.K. Ghosh, *Human Development Profile of SCs and STs in Rural India*, NCAER, New Delhi, 2000, p. 32.
7. Sukhadeo Thorat, "Oppression and Denial: Dalit Discrimination in the 1990s", *Economic and Political Weekly*, 39, 6, February 9, 2002.
8. Sanjib K. Behera (ed.), *Dalits and Land Reforms in India*, Indian Social Institute, 1999, pp. 35-36.
9. *Report of the Land Revenue Commission*, 1940, Vol. 2, pp. 120-121.
10. D.N. Dhanagare, "Peasant Protest and Politics — The Tebhaga Movements in Bengal (India) 1946-67" in *Journal of Peasant Studies*, 3(3), 1976, p. 616.
11. A.R. Desai (ed.), *Peasant struggles in India*, Bombay: Oxford University Press, 1979, p. 419.
12. B. Dasgupta, "Sharecropping in West Bengal: From Independence to Operation Barga", *EPW*, XIX (26): A 85-96.
13. Please see *NSS Report 1955-56, 1970-71.*
14. Please see *All India Rural Credit Review Committee Report, 1968.*
15. S. De Roy, "Impact of Fish Farming on Land Relations: Evidence from a Village Study in West Bengal", *Indian Journal of Agricultural Economics*, Vol. 68, No. 2, April-June 2013, pp. 222-239.
16. Government of India, "Employment and Unemployment Situation in India 1999-2000 (Part 1)", *NSS Report Number 458*, 2001.
17. G.K. Lieten, *Continuity and Change in Rural West Bengal*, New Delhi: Sage Publications, 1992, pp. 135-136.
18. *Ibid.*, p. 161.

2

Challenges and Changes of the Marginal Community in Bengal

A Study of the Namasudras

Bipul Mandal

Marginal people of Bengal can be seen that invariably the notified and denotified tribes, the Scheduled and Backward castes, the Dalits, are severely economically oppressed and culturally persecuted. We have seen that the Tribals are exploited in various ways. Their simplicity also ends up in the clutches of moneylenders. They have had to deal with the impacts of globalization as plastic and polythene shoes have replaced leather shoes and made their traditional occupation practically obsolete. Elders due to their illiteracy and poverty are no longer respected by their offsprings, yet the children remain impoverished due to their inadequate education. All of these tribes and castes have an ancient civilization and culture going back 2000 years. The legacy of exploitation of these beautiful, marginalized communities has culminated in the current conflict brought on by corporate land-grabbing under the euphemism of Special Economic Zones.

On the backdrop of social awakening and the introduction of various new facilities like education to specific class and caste groups and communities by the colonial government, a number of socio-religious movements had emerged among the low caste community, which took the shape of caste consolidation movement during the last quarter of the nineteenth and first half of the twentieth century. One of these movements was the movement of the Namasudras of Bengal. With the development of the history of its own and with enough indigenous culture which marked out Bengal from other parts of north India there developed in Bengal a system of caste which although very much a part of total

Indian civilization, bore certain elements which may be differentiated as being peculiarly Bengali.

The Chandalas, who were known after the 1911 Census as Namasudras, lived in the districts of undivided Bengal — Bakharganj, Faridpur, Dacca, Mymensingh, Jessore, Khulna, Dinajpur, Jalpaiguri, and Cooch Behar, which contained, in 1901, more than 76 per cent of this caste population. But these areas where they tilled the soil, the land was owned by the high caste Hindus and Muslims. As a result, in their case, their low ritual rank had, by and large, coincided with their subordinate class position. The lower caste Chandalas in these areas had a complex relationship with upper-caste Zamindars regarding their religious or social rights that had regulated by power and hierarchy. They had no religious, social, professional identity. The great majority of Namasudras, about 78 per cent of the actual earners in 1911, lived on agriculture, but of this agricultural population, only 1.5 per cent was in the rent receiving category, about 3.56 per cent were agricultural laboures, about 95.71 per cent were farmers with or without occupancy rights.[1] The rapid reclamation of the marshes and the forests in Eastern Bengal had transformed the Namasudras into a settled peasant community. After that low ritual rank, subordinate social class status of the Namasudras were completely changed its self-perception and underwent a radical transformation.

The Namasudra leaders realized the necessity of a more effective social organization that would both unite the community together and give them the self-confidence to claim themselves as a collective against the hegemonic elites of the local Hindu society. This realization of the community explains the growing popularity of the Matua sect, which had emerged and spread among the Namasudras in the 1870s.[2] This sect was started by Harichand Thakur (1812-1878) son of Jasobanta Thakur, was born in 1811 (or 1812) in a Vaishnava Namasudra family at Orakandi in Gopalganj Sub-division of Faridpur district. From childhood, he began to talk about the equality of all men and women. He took cultivation and small trade for a living but already know as a religious person endowed with magical healing power. He soon began to attract disciples from his village. He started gathering a following, one day he experienced *atmadarshan* or self-revelation, through which he realized that he was the incarnation of God himself, born on earth to bring salvation to the downtrodden. Immediately after this, he started organizing his sect based on a simple non-ritualistic doctrine of Bhakti 'all rituals, except devotion to God, faith in mankind and love for living creatures', are distortions.[3]

After his self-revelation, he started organizing his sect on bans of a simple ritualistic Matua doctrine of Bhakti *Hate Kam Mukhe nam* (doing worldly duties while chanting his holy name), *garhastya dharma* (duties of a householder), abolished the caste system, protested against the Vedic religious orthodox texts. He introduced the religion of Matua for the philosophic upliftment of the downtrodden castes. He explained that through the chanting of Harinamgan or *Nam Sangkirtan* (song) would possible the purification of soul and attainment of God.[4] The sect gradually grew in size as it became the rallying point for all the untouchables and lower caste peoples in the region. People began to believe that Harichand was gifted with supernatural power, not only to cure a disease, to give life to the dead or to tame a tiger but to punish the social offense less as well, he could overthrow an oppressive Brahman landlord or curse a cruel *Naib* with leprosy.[5]

The *Namsankirtan, Kirtan* was an essential feature of Matua religious life and performed several important social functions. As it was sung collectively, it gave the sect a congregational character and helped its predominantly Namasudra devotees to construct and continually reinforce their collective identity through a shared experience of devotion, it had a great levelling effect and was not, therefore, liked by the orthodox custodians of social hierarchy. It also fostered among the participants a sense of co-operation and courage, self-confidence which strength to stand up to the powerful adversaries who held them down in society.[6]

Harichand Thakur offered to his follower *Dwadash Agga* (Twelve Instructions) and sixteen commandments for the purity of soul which later became the religious duties of the people belonging to the Matua religion. The Matua poet Haribar Sarkar was the first to explain the 'Twelve Commandments'. Those who followed this *Dwadash Agga* of Harichand Thakur and engrossed themselves in the chanting *Harinam* came to be known as Matua. The etymological origin of Matua can be explained in various ways such as Tarak Chandra Sarkar's in 'Sri Sri Hari Lilamrita', 'Hari Dayal Hari Gan Harimam Sar', and 'Pramete Matoyara Matua Nam Tar'.[7] According to a recent version of 'Matua Mahasangha' journal's "Matua is a socio-economic religion with a spiritual outlook based on uplift of downtrodden class and for their salvation through eradicating the barriers of caste and untouchability, socio-economic disparities."[8]

Hari Chand Thakur could not tolerate false Vaishnavs or the religious practices and rituals of the Brahmins. He revolted against them and discovered the simple path of *Harinam*. Their salvation lies in the *nam*.

Ar Ek bakye chhilo sunya bani sone,
Sesh lila koriba ami Ishan kone.
Nich hoye kariba je nicher uddhar,
Ati nimne na namile kishe Avatar.[9]

(*English translation:* There was an aerial voice that God would make his just Lila in the Ishan Kone (North East Horizon) to save the downtrodden as being a downtrodden. If anyone could not come down to the bottom how he could claim as an *avatar*.)

Harichand Thakur took the first step to organize the Chandals (later to be called Namasudra under Harichand Thakur's initiative leading to the British administrative order of implementing the same) under the banner of the Matua Community. His *Kritan* (songs) were simple lyrics with no ragas or *gourchandrikas*. The songs were aimed at the social development of Namasudras and other social subaltern groups. Anybody from any caste and class was welcomed to the congregation. The identity of Harichand made the Namasudras all the more enthusiastic as here was a Brahmin with a lower caste wife, taking about social upliftment of the whole community and initiating reforms through simple *namgaans*. The accommodation of a Brahman in the Namasudra community gave a whole new inspiration to raise the awaited voice against social injustice upon them.[10] Acharya Mahananda Halder narrated in '*Sri Sri Guruchand Charit*',

Hin boli, nich boli je sab Janere,
Dur kari diyechilo Baner bhitare.
Sei sba Sarbahara Manusher Dal,
Avatar ale tara kiba pelo phal.[11]

(*English translation:* Those who were depressed or downtrodden threw to the forest, but coming to the *Avatar* (Gods) they overcome all the difficulties.)

For those people who are hatred, depressed and exploited by the upper castes in the society, religion must save them from social degradation. But none of the religions has spread their kind hands to establish them on human rights. For this reason, there exists untouchability in society and that is why there are depressed, downtrodden and untouchables in the society who are suffering from poverty. Unawareness and superstitions — to them the sermon of nationality, fairness or purity and unity are meaningless.

To raise the voice, Harichand knew that he was to organize the sporadic people of the caste in Bengal. Not only the concerned community followed him, a majority of the dominant Namasudras, from the educated middle class to the agriculture-based lower class, joined the Matua sect. *Kritan* played as a catalyst in bringing them under one common roof songs like, *Jar Dal Nei, Tar Bal Nei* (one who doesn't have a group, doesn't have any power) gave them the ideology by which they could protest. For the Namasudra devotees of Matua sect, *Kritan* was also a source of collective strength. The *namgaans* emphasized the superpower of the *gurus*, both Harichand Thakur and his son Guruchand Thakur, who could help their disciples to overcome all the crises of their lives.[12] The *namgaans* are formation which helped the Namasudras to assert their collective will and raise their voice against any injustice of the society.

Harichand Thakur gave the call to the oppressed class and wanted to establish a classless, casteless and equality in the society. He wanted inequality could be removed for ever and the lower class would not be addressed as low. He wanted his followers to give shape to his difficult ideals to reflect in the social system. The main task of his followers was to transform family life into a centre of one united force.[13]

The social movement of the Namasudra was started in 1872-73 when the high caste Hindus did not attend the '*Shradh*' (a respectful and wilful offering rite in reaction to this attitude of the high caste Hindus, the Namasudras began to boycott the movement which denied cooperating with the high caste people concerning prepare their houses (high caste Hindus) and cultivate in their fields etc. The social degradation of the Namasudras made them united against upper caste tyranny which helped them to develop a defiant attitude against social disabilities. To this must be added their agrarian discontent which manifested itself in the form of peasant resistance against Zamindary oppression. While the struggle between the Hindu landlords and Muslim peasants was perceived in religious terms, the Namasudras linked their struggle against higher caste Zamindars with movements for caste upliftment.[14] In the district of Dinajpur, Jalpaiguri, Cooch Behar, Khulna, Jessore the Namasudras were overwhelmingly employed as *bargadars* (sharecroppers) or agricultural labourers, that is to say, they were at the bottom of both economic and social hierarchies.[15] The Namasudra leaders became successful in channelizing agrarian discontent into a broader mass movement for social upliftment. The educated section of the Namasudras gradually drifted away from the mainstream of national movement for the socio-economic upliftment of their community.

When the Namasudra's social movement began, a lot of their energies were directed towards the elimination of sectional differences and construction of horizontal solidarity among the members of these various sub-castes. From time immemorial the Chandals have been despised by the upper-class Hindus and a Brahman thought himself defied by even treading the shadow cast by the body of Chandal. Their leaders, in their first conference in Khulna in 1881, stressed the need for unity and caste consciousness as the first step towards social improvement.[16] It was seen that after Census of 1881, W.C. Macpherson, Assistant Commissioner of Sylhet District hanged a notice, "that Namasudra must always be written and not Chang or Chandal for all persons of the said caste that Deputy Commissioner has ordered that any who does not write Namasudra shall be removed from employment."[17] F.B. Peacock, Commissioner, Presidency Division wrote to Bengal Government, "the improvement in the condition of the Chandals who are the chief agriculturist in Narail Subdivision, had led them, it is said, to aspire to a superior status in the Hindu Caste system. They now call themselves Namasudra and profess to be *Vaishnavs*."[18] According to Garret, "The Namasudra show a considerable aptitude for organization and it was at much pain they succeeded in getting their designation recognized in place of the term Chandal to which they objected."[19] The Bengal Government declared that "the Namasudras will write in place of Chandals, Census Reports of 1901, that it would not be, in the humble view of the memorialists, out of place here to mention that the memorialists had submitted a petition to your honour, and that your honour was pleased to grant them the permission on the 3 August, 1901, to be entered as Namasudra at the Census."[20] But surprisingly, the Chandals or Namasudras had to be written when the Census report was published in 1901. In the Census of 1911, Chandal was dropped, only Namasudra remained.

Like many other castes, the Namasudras also sent petitions, for the recognition of their new caste name. During the Census operations of 1891, they submitted several petitions, but their prayer was not fully granted. In the caste tables of the Census of 1891, the caste was shown as 'Namasudra or Chandal'. Hence in 1901, the Namasudras of the districts of Dacca, Faridpur, Bakharganj, Mymensingh, Jessore and Pabna once again appealed to the government. Bhishmadev Das[21] and several other members of the Namasudra Association of Orakandi,

Faridpur, sent a representation, praying that their caste should be designated as Namasudra and the old despising name 'Chandal' should be deleted. In support of their claim, they also submitted copies of the *Vyavasthas* or opinions of several Pandits of Bengal.[22] But even then, their request was not fully respected. The mobility was, therefore, renewed when the Census operations of 1911 were instituted and disturbance of peace at different banners.

In the second phase of the Matua movement, Sri Guruchand Thakur was given the responsibility to preach and propagate the Matua religion and the principle of his father Harichand Thakur. His historical appearance on the earth in the year of 1847 A.D. (1253 B.S.) on the day of *Dol Purnima* is a remarkable incident. He propagated the thought among his disciples to make them vibrant with the spirit of sincere labour and to make them fit for the present modern age. He thought that education is the ultimate root of all progress of the depressed and downtrodden people. Spiritual liberation was impossible unless they were liberated from the darkness of ignorance. Social bondage cannot be broken if there is no sign of spiritual liberation. Uneducated men are of no use and they are compelled to be exploited and deprived of their bare necessities of life. So they will have to attain the same height of education just as the upper caste or the Varna Hindus of the society. He also told to the depressed and the downtrodden people:

Vidya jadi Pao, Kahare darao,
Kar dware chao bhiksha.
Raj shakti pabe, Bedana ghuchibe
Kale habe se pariksha.[23]

(*English translation:* If they can acquire education, they can be partners in the administrative or governmental process and remove distress.)

Guruchand Thakur was a farsighted philosopher. He knew that the present age and life had to be comprehended to tear the servile bond of decades. For this, he directed his disciples to set up many educational institutions. He gave them financial assistance. He taught every depressed man to remove superstitions, blind faith and ignorance. He advised them to construct new roads, and repair their own houses themselves. But he gave top-most priority to education and enlightenment. With the starting of the British administration in Bengal, many Christian clergymen came here to preach their religion. Taking the opportunity of racial difference or diverse caste system, they tried to convert the depressed and downtrodden into Christianity. Among these clergymen, C.S. Mead, Australian clergymen, dwelt in Eastern Bengal to propagate Christianity. Yet for instance, the history of the lower caste Namasudra movement in the early twentieth century suggests that a degree of empowerment was possible through missionary presence even where that presence did not lead to significant conversions. As we have seen earlier, the metrical biography of Guruchand Thakur (1847-1937), leader of the dissident Vaishnava Matua sect which constituted the core of the Namasudra upthrust, explains in vivid detail the circumstances that led to the Matuas to seek the assistance of the C.S. Mead striking an alliance that proved very fruitful for the Namasudras in their quest for educational facilities, service jobs and eventually political advantages. The Namasudra wanted to start a high school at Orakandi, Faridpur. Guruchand accepts the offer of financial and other assistance from Mead, and it was also very careful to emphasize that the motives were entry pragmatic get money for the school and obtain access to British officials.[24] The Namasudras were quite satisfied with their Matua faith founded by Guruchand's father Harichand Thakur and very few of them turned Christian.[25] The questions of Brahman origin were less important than education, which immediately associated a call for economic improvement through prudence hard work, frugality, keeping away from idle amusement.[26] Guruchand Thakur then said to him that only the spread of education can make depressed and downtrodden people embrace Christianity.

This discriminatory treatment towards the Namasudras by the higher caste organization and the benevolent attitude of Christian Missionaries brought the Namasudras closer to the Christian Missionaries and the British rulers. The Guruchand Thakur, a social reformer of outstanding ability, brought about a renaissance among the members of his community. As a farsighted man, he realized that to be socially elevated the Namasudras must have education, for education brings wealth and without wealth, no caste can move up on a social scale. He stood firm against the suspicion of the elder Namasudras and there about the ulterior motive of the Christian missionaries.[27] He donated a piece of land where the Australian Baptist Mission was started. Besides, Mead began to run a charitable dispensary for their treatment. The elementary school was developed into a high school.

Realizing the importance of Western education Guruchand Thakur induced C.S. Mead, the Australian missionary, to visit Orakandi for spreading education among the Namasudras. The Namasudras of Orakandi were immensely indebted to him for his contribution to their all-round development. Though his main intention of preaching Christianity did not achieve much success, yet his contribution towards the social upliftment of the Namasudras was remarkable.[28] C.S. Mead fought against illiteracy and spread education among the Namasudras. Christian missionaries with their spirit of equality and liberal education system had attracted the depressed classes especially the Namasudras. The Christian missionaries opened schools for all children and importance was attached to merit and not to caste. They faced stiff opposition from the orthodox Hindus who vehemently opposed the activities of the Christian missionaries especially their public preaching against the caste system. The Missionaries indeed exalted the greatness of Christianity over Hinduism to baptize the lower caste Hindus. Before coming into direct contact with the Christian Missionaries, Namasudras were exposed to liberal influences of the Islamic faith and a large section of them embraced Islam[29] to get rid of Hindu tyranny. Although Indian social reformers like Raja Rammohun Roy and Dayananda Saraswati tried to protect Hinduism from the inroads of Christianity. Liberal reforms of these leaders, however, remained confined to urbanized upper-caste Hindus. The Namasudras of rural East Bengal and North Bengal remained almost untouched by these reforms. In the sphere of education, also, the initial beneficiary of the British education system was the urbanized Hindu upper castes. The lower caste Hindus found in this "new learning the fulfilment of a historic destiny."[30]

Guruchand Thakur was thus the savior of the depressed and down-trodden people of India. He tried to reach these unfortunate people to the modern age by concrete and fruitful steps. Indeed he was the real friend and philosopher of the poor and the ill-fated. He wanted them to come to the forefront of enlightened civilization. They would learn to question the validity of the existing values. Thus, he was constantly concerned with the idea of uplifting their caste and class. So he made arrangements with C.S. Mead regarding the spread of education and establishment of several institutions. He helped them to get Government services. Mr. Mead went back to his native land and addressed Guruchand Thakur as 'Great Leader' in his book, *The Namasudras and Other Addresses*.[31]

Mr. Mead wrote,

> "Guruchand Babu is a leader of outstanding ability and wide-spread influence. In the various activities of my missionary life he has made possible many things that without his backing could not have

been carried through. With a liberality of thought, a courage and far-sightedness uncommon among men of the older orthodox school. He has sought the uplift of the great Namasudra caste."[32]

Guruchand Thakur showed the Indian farmers the path of light only to save them from the age-long exploitation of the higher caste people and the depressed and downtrodden people by launching several movements against the existing social order. He said the Hindu society by reforming the social system. He also laid stress on female education and he set up a girl's school, 'Shanti Satyabhama Institution'. The political, economical and moral yardstick was to be raised for the advancement of the poor and distressed. So he requested Dr. Mead to change their economic standards by giving them government services:

Eai sab chehle jadi chakri na paie,
Lekha para keho nahi karibe hetai.
Eder baybastha tumi karo mahasay,
Era dhanya hok sabe tomar kripai.[33]

(*English translation:* Those who will not get service, then they will not be shown interest towards education. So you arranged something, they will become the success of your blessing.)

For this, in the first part of 1906, he went to meet the then Governor of East Bengal and appealed to him for the mass education and Government service to the depressed and downtrodden people. He narrated to the Governor regarding the ill-treatment of the Caste-Hindu bureaucrats of the government offices. He could realize that only Royal or British assistance was needed to raise their standard. The foundation of life had dried up — that stream of life had to be rejuvenated by kindling the source. Thus, he presented their tragic life stories of the downtrodden to the Governor with the help of C.S. Mead. This facilitated their service in government offices and also in education.[34] On 31 October, 1906 the Governor of Bengal Presidency, Sir Lanslate Hare recommended to Lord Minto, Governor-General of India a draft proposal with a list of 31 depressed and downtrodden castes for social uplifting them. According to the draft proposal, Lord Minto was accepted by the Morley-Minto Reform Act in 1909. In the year 1909 seats were reserved for them in the Bengal Legislative Assembly.[35] Reservation was created only for the Bengal Presidency which is narrated by Mahananda Halder in his book '*Sri Sri Guruchand Charit*':

Ehen prakare, Lat Darbare,
Patitere dilo gati.
Holo Jagaran, Namasudragan,
Raj karya pae Bange.[36]

(*English translation:* Down-trodden or the depressed who got the position to the Royal Court (Lat Darbar), By awakening Namasudras, were participating to royal activities.)

While C.S. Mead left India for ever, he remarked on his record date, December 1921, regarding Guruchand Thakur as follows:

> "Being about to leave India for good, I am glad to leave on record my gratitude to Babu Guru Charan Thakur of Orakandi for all that he has done for me. I come to live at Orakandi as being the most influential centre of Namasudra life in this district. Guru Charan Babu is a leader of outstanding ability and widespread influence. In the various activities of my missionary life, he has made possible many things that without his backing could not have been carried through with liberality of thought, an act of courage and a foresightedness uncommon among men of the older orthodox school he has sought the uplift of the great Namasudra caste. They owe a great deal to him, so do I."[37]

C.S. Mead was a great friend for the upliftment of the depressed and downtrodden people of Bengal than any other depressed class leaders of India. The present position of the backward class people of India may be attributed to the selfless efforts of Guruchand Thakur and the movement of the Matuas. In this regard one point mentioned here that Namasudra leaders or well-wishers of the backward classes like Babu Kamalakanta Das, Secretary, Namasudra Association, Orakandi, lodge a petition for the appointment of the District or Sub-Divisional Inspector of school on 5 May, 1927. He said, "the people of the Namasudra community in Bengal, is very backward especially in education and as education lies at the basis of all cultures, it is of high importance that suitable facilities, by way of special encouragement, should be afforded for the spread of education among them . . . ."[38]

As a result of this movement, the reservation for the Scheduled Caste was made possible. So, there is no other person of India who fought for the Reservation of the Scheduled Caste, the only means of their upliftment. Guruchand Thakur with Matua movement earned them the light of education and service and again their political right. It is recorded in Mahananda Halder's '*Sri Sri Guruchand Charit*':

Manab jiban jage jato prayojan,
Manab achare prabhu kare ta sadhan.
Tare nor bhabe nor thake tare dhare,
Adrishya kripar chhaya dhare rakhe tare.
Nor pakshe Raj shakti oti prayojan,
Sei shakti Guru Chande kare akarshan.[39]

(*English translation:* Lords have given everything whatever human needs. Royal power is a necessity in every human life. Guruchand Thakur attracted to this power.)

The *Rajshakti* or political power has attracted him and the untouchables were not recognized in the modern political system. Once they had their kingdom, they were attached to the politics of the country. But foreign religions with the help of their religious kings invaded Bengal, such as the Brahmanas, Buddhist and Islam religions. They captured the throne of Bengal and destroyed all documents and records of their past activities from the pages of history. So, the original people or the Adivasi people of Bengal are not Dalit, but they are *Patit* (compelled to fall below). Harichand Thakur and Guruchand Thakur knew the age-long sufferings of the *Patit* or the Depressed. So upliftment is necessary.

Raj parichito era na chhilo kakhan.
Patit rayechhe era sudhu se karan.
Ami boli raj karya ei jatike dao.
'Samo drishti rakhe raja' e-niti dekhao.[40]

(*English translation:* Namasudras had no royal identity. For this reason, they became *Patit* (downtrodden or depressed community). So give them royal power and see everyone in equal eyes.)

The main causes of the downfall of the Chandals were they are being not recognized by the British rulers. For this reason, Guruchand Thakur started a movement with his followers or disciples and reservation was introduced in education, employment and representation in the legislature. In earlier pages of this chapter also mention in 1909 a list of reserved caste with thirty-one communities was created only in Bengal under the Morley-Minto Act of 1909. Still, then no such reservation was created in any other Indian provinces or presidencies. In 1919, this reservation provision under Montego-Chelmsford Act was spreaded in other Indian provinces of presidencies.[41] This has been mentioned in '*Sri Sri Guruchand Charit*' of Acharya Mahananda Halder,

Tapashili Jati madhey ja kichhu hoiachhe
Hari Chand Kalpa Brekshay shakali fallechhe.[42]

(*English translation:* As a result, a large number of Scheduled Caste people of India have been recognized as man and all these were for the Matua movement.)

Guruchand Thakur expressed his pathos regarding the downtrodden people:

Biswer savay jara peyechhe ashan,
Tara ki karechhe mane se chinta kakhan.
Ke se saktidhar jar charan parase,
Jagiye uthila pran nabin harashe.[43]

(*English translation:* Whatever achievements have been obtained so far, have been done by the untiring efforts and movements under the leadership of distinguished personality, versatile genius and prophetic vision, which are yet to be realized by the concerned people and the worked with respect and honour.)

Guruchand Thakur wanted to evolve a great force by uniting *Karma* (Works) with *Dharma* (Religion). The main thing behind this great force is *Raj-shakti* (Royal Power), which will build-up a religious state (*Dharma-Rajya*) where the Matua disciples will remain in front of the state.

Jei dharma Raja aachhe sei dharma taja,
Dharma Rajye bas kare dharmasil Praja.[44]

(*English translation:* No religion can be great, unless, religion is united with Raj-shakti. Only religious people can live peacefully in that 'Dharma-Rajya'. Guruchand Thakur advised the Matuas to hold the key of the politics.)

Aaein sabhay jio, Aami boli Raja hao,
Dur karo e-jatir byatha.[45]

(*English translation:* To become a King and overcome all the difficulties of the community.)

When India Administrative Act was enforced in 1935, Guruchand Thakur advised the Matua sect to get entry into the Legislative Assembly.

The Matua sect was inspired by his advice, the Scheduled Castes contested in the election independently and won most of the seats in the Bengal Legislative Assembly, according to this Act. He could foresee the future of the Indian scenario. He could visualize in his eye that the oppressed and the backward class people had great opportunity to exert their authority and power in the field of Government services. There can be an opportunity for liberation in the last phase of the twentieth century. Acharya Mahananda Halder says in his '*Sri Sri Guruchand Charit*':

Panchas bachhar pubbe Guru Chand koy,
Vote diye sab kaj haibe nirnoy.
Votea Raja-Praja haibe prithibi bhoria,
Krome krome sei bakya esechhe pholia.[46]

(*English translation:* Fifty years ago Sri Sri Guruchand Thakur said that a task will be completed by way of the electoral process. A view of Guruchand Thakur is true in the present time.)

Thus our great seer prophesied that there would be democracies throughout the world, based on the voting system. Today world shows the reflection of his prophecy and vision. Even this warning regarding class conflict (struggle) has also come true in the present day and that is mentioned in '*Sri Sri Guruchand Charit*'.

Jatir unnati lagi, Hao sabe swartha tyagi,
Diba-ratri chinta koro tai,
Jati dharma, Jati man, Jati mor bhagaban
Jati chhara annya chinta nai.
Kiba vidya, kiba dhane, Kiba shilpe, ki bigyane
Rashtra niti kshetre Raj-kaje.
Sabkhane thaka chai, Ta bhinnya upan nai
Raj-beshe 'sajo' Raj-saje.
Nara-Nari dui jane, Prati karye prati-kshane
Tale tale hao agrashar.
Alasata deo chhere, Balo sabe bajrasware
Aage chalo nahi abasar.[47]

The above quotation reflects a new era in the lives of the Matua people. They must organize all the depressed and downtrodden people under one banner to capture political power and politics is the key to all progress in the society. One point must be remembered in this context that India is caste oriented country. There is always a continuous clash among different castes and creeds. So caste is religion, caste is honour. No other thinking except the development of own caste. Guruchand Thakur could visualize in his eyes that they would have to think of their own social and political future and their development. The caste Hindu-people, who hates the depressed and backward class people, cannot be their real friends. They will have to separate themselves from the social and cultural bondage of the Caste Hindus, until and unless they leave their supremacy over the society and cultural domination.

In 1920 when Mahatma Gandhi called upon the non-co-operation movement against the British Raj but the peasantry was far away from this movement. This movement was limited to the higher-caste Zamindars and the middle-class people. This time the British Government had planned to uplift the oppressed and the backward class people due to the movement of the Matua sect. The non-co-operation movement did not spread among the common people or the peasantry. For the success of the Non-co-operation movement, Gandhiji enquired to Deshabandhu Chitta Ranjan Das about the leaders of the oppressed and the backward class people. Deshabandhu Chitta Ranjan Das told Gandhiji about Guruchand Thakur and his overall influence on the lower castes. Gandhiji expressed his willingness to meet Guruchand Thakur and directed Deshabandhu to communicate with him.[48] After getting a letter from Deshabandhu Guruchand Thakur faced a great dilemma. On one side, the country was Independent, but on the other hand, the millions of oppressed and the backwards who are ignorant, uneducated and neglected in the society. Their development had just begun. After deep thinking, Guruchand Thakur wrote a letter to Deshabandhu Chitta Ranjan Das. He described in his letter the overall situation and pathetic condition of his community and peasants who are being hatred and neglected by Caste-Hindus. Lastly, he concluded in his letter with the following version,

Bharat pallir desh pallite paran,
Sahar chhere sabe palligrame jan.
Palli jadi Jage tabe jagibe Bharat
Abashya sugam habe swadhinatar path.
Mahatma Gandhike Tai janai barata,
Bhabai dekhen jen tini mor katha.[49]

(*English translation:* India is a country of Pally (Village). According to Guruchand Thakur life exists in the village. By awakening of rural people through India will awake and smooth the way to get Independence.

Though Thakur send a message to Mahatma Gandhi for considering the matter.)

After receiving the letter from Guruchand Thakur, it touched the heart of Mahatma Gandhi and he saw the ever true picture of their life. Mahatma Gandhi expressed his desire to visit Orakandi to meet Guruchand Thakur. In the meantime, in September 1920 Gandhiji was arrested his visit to Orakandi remained unfulfilled. But, he declared the 'Gram Swaraj' and 'Harijan' movement in this context. If the divergent ways of religion and politics can be harmonized, the oppressed and the backward class will not remain stamped as under-developed. Guruchand Thakur wished that there would be no domination or untouchability in the society or the country. No one should put faith in such evils. It is the exhibition of man's inhumanity to man. According to Guruchand Thakur, all the inhabitants of this globe will seem to be one and equal. He also said to his disciples:

> *Jei shakti Hari Chand diye gechhe sabe,*
> *Sei shakti Hindugan grahan karibe.*
> *Sarbajati samannyay habe tar mate,*
> *Bahi bahi hoye sabe chalibe se pathe.*[50]

(*English translation:* That power has been given by Harichand Thakur to the Hindus is acceptable. According to him all the communities combined and follow the same way.)

Guruchand Thakur directed the Matua sect, to progress in life with the sole aim of establishing universal harmony among all other sects. The unification and assimilation of 'religion' and 'work' can prove to be a rejuvenating spirit in human society. This harmonizing can give birth to a renaissance. Thus the main motives of the Matua religion are mainly based on the assimilation of *Sattwick* (Truth) and *Rajasik* (Political) thoughts. Guruchand Thakur has, therefore, directed his disciples to follow the principles and establish those principles and ideals in reality. The then President of Indian National Congress, Netaji Subhas Chandra Bose spoke on the occasion of the first death anniversary of Guruchand Thakur, the extract from the *Hindustan Standard* (March 1938) is as follows:

> "The first-anniversary meeting of his holiness the late Sri Sri Guru Chand Thakur of Orakandi, Faridpur was held at Albert Hall,15, College Square on Sunday last, under the Presidentship of Mr. J.C. Gupta, Bar-at-law, M.L.A. Subhas Chandra Bose, President of Indian

> National Congress paid a glowing tribute to the memory of the late Guru Chand Thakur. During his speech, he remarked that the late Thakur was a superman. He regenerated the Hindus of Bengal by infusing new life into them. He started a movement with his two lakhs of disciples which elected the status of the Scheduled Caste who have able to fall in line with the caste Hindus in social and political life."[51]

This feeling of attachment to the colonial rule was also to a large extent due to the influence of the Christian missionaries, who had long been trying through their noble-minded activities to win over such lower communities, the 'human debris of India', as the Bishop of Madras described them.[52] As the upper caste educated people to mature their hopes of an expansion of Christianity, it was 'the pariah community, and not the Brahmin', that began to occupy 'the position of highest strategic value for such missionary activities.[53] In eastern Bengal, during the famine of 1906, the areas which were most affected were the swampy regions of Faridpur and Bakharganj. The worst sufferers were the poorer classes of peasants who had no plows or land of their own and the poorer high caste *bhadraloks* who depended for their livelihood entirely upon a small patrimony or inheritance.

The Swadesh Bandhab Samiti under the direction or guidance of Aswini Kumar Dutta organized relief work in the famine-stricken areas. But while the swadeshi relief fund, as it has been alleged, 'was largely used for the benefit of the 'bhadralok classes', the Christian missionaries both Catholic and Protestant, did excellent work among the distressed Namasudra peasants of the bill tracts, in co-operation with the government officials.[54] This naturally brought the missionaries closer to the Namasudras. But closest to them was perhaps a particular Australian Baptist missionary, Dr. C.S. Mead. The Orakandi School which had been started with unpretentious resources on a plot of land, donated by Guru Chand himself, needed further financial assistance for nourishment, as the Kayasthas of the locality refused to help. Appeals were, therefore, sent to Head, then stationed at the district headquarters of Faridpur. Orakandi being 'the most influential centre of the Namasudra world', the missionary felt that 'this artistic centre should be occupied'.[55] In a meeting held at Orakandi in early 1905, Mead promised to help and pleaded for a piece of land, both for opening a school and a mission. Although the elder Namasudras and their priests were hesitant and dubious about the ulterior motives of this missionary, the leader stood firm, and himself donated a piece of land on which Mead started his mission in 1906, initially in a tent.[56]

Christian missionaries with their spirit of equality and liberal education system had attracted the depressed classes especially the Namasudras. The Christian missionaries opened schools for all children and importance was attached to merit and not to caste. They faced stiff opposition from the orthodox Hindus who vehemently opposed the activities of the Christian missionaries especially their public preaching against the caste system. The missionaries indeed exalted the greatness of Christianity over Hinduism to baptize the lower caste Hindus. Before coming into direct contact with the Christian missionaries, Namasudras were exposed to liberal influences of the Islamic faith and a large section of them embraced Islam[57] to get rid of Hindu tyranny.

In this regard one point mentioned here that Namasudra leaders or well-wishers of the backward classes like Babu Kamalakanta Das, Secretary, Namasudra Association, Orakandi, lodged a petition for the appointment of the District or Sub-Divisional Inspector of School on 5 May, 1927. He said, "the people of the Namasudra community in Bengal, are very backward especially in education and as education lies at the basis of all culture, it is of high importance that suitable facilities, by way of special encouragement, should be afforded for the spread of education among them . . . ."[58]

Apart from teaching the gospel to the Namasudras with the assistance of Rev. H. Sutton, Mead also began to run a charitable dispensary The elementary school for boys was raised to the status of a High School, where about 200 ladies came to study from different villages across rivers and Marshes. A day school and a Sunday school for girls were opened under the supervision of Miss Tuck. The Widows' Home at Orakandi, looked after by Nurse Thomson, provided shelter to many destitute Namasudra widows, while Miss Kamala Bose a Christian Bengali young lady, started working for the upliftment of the Namasudra women at Gopalganj, about 20 miles away from Orakandi.[59] All these activities were made possible by the local support that Mead received from Guru Chand and his followers, which gave him a strong base in an area predominantly inhabited by the members of a disgruntled but ambitious untouchable caste. Before his departure from India, Mead, therefore, openly acknowledged, "in the various activities of the missionary life he (Guru Chand), has made possible many things that without his backing could not have been carried through . . . ."[60] Expression of gratitude was, however, reciprocal. As a Namasudras paper put it, "... the Christians (are) lifting the rock from off us, and we are getting a chance to rise, but we do not know how to express the gratitude we so deeply feel."[61] But as Mead realized, the Namasudras had only learned to "lift their heads but refused to turn their heads to behold the Lamp of God and then . . . to bow their heads in living and lowly homage at his pierced feet."[62] The Faridpur Mission could convert only two Namasudra families before 1911.[63]

What the missionaries could, however, more or less successfully achieve, was to widen the cleavage between the nationalists and this ambitious social group.[64] Political agitations were as much a problem of the missionaries, as it was of the government, for they "widened the gulf between Indians and Europeans, thus setting the missionary in a very difficult position."[65] Mead, therefore, projected himself as the benefactor of the Namasudras, won their gratitude, tried to ensure their loyalty to the government and on some occasions, acted as a liaison between the two. Similarly, in other districts as well, the Namasudra leaders sought the counsel and assistance of the missionaries in establishing schools and hostels and in organizing other methods of uplifting their community. That help was readily given by Rev. P. Noble in Dacca, Rev. Sutton at Mymensingh, Hr. Burry at Comilla, Mr. J. Read at Jessore and Mr. W. Carey at Barisal.[66] The missionaries, as a result, gained considerable influence among them. When the nationalist movement started and pressures were brought to bear upon the Namasudras to join it, as Rev. P. Noble of Dacca Baptist Mission observed, "the missionaries were able to exercise a steadying influence and helped the masses to maintain their loyalty to Government."[67] There was, of course, a tiny group opposed to the Christian missionaries, but the majorities were friendly and "thoroughly loyal to Government."[68] Rev. Noble became the Vice President of the Dacca Namasudra Samiti. This organization, along with its counterpart in Faridpur, to which Dr. Mead was associated with, sent deputations to the government expressing the unflinching loyalty of the Namasudra community to the British Raj.

After Guru Chand Thakur, under the leadership of Pramath Ranjan Thakur Namasudra movement looks a new turn. At the beginning of 1938, a number of prominent Namasudra legislators, including P.R. Thakur agreed to join Congress and fight for India's freedom.[69] Matua Mahasangha is to bring salvation to the downtrodden through a 'religion-based modernity', which would mean not just spiritual salvation, but overcoming the 'natural, social and the psychological barriers that hinder the process of the oppressed. It is thus presented as a reformist religion that proposes to fight against casteism and superstitions, as well as social and economic backwardness. True to the universalism, of the gurus, its membership remains open to everyone, irrespective of caste, religion, or gender and all members enjoy the same right within the organization. Sekhar Bandopadhyay stated that "with the death of Guru Chand in March 1937, the major influence that had kept the Namasudra movement away from Congress politics was removed."[70] Then the Calcutta Scheduled Caste League, formed later that year, emerged as a new and vital link between the Congress and the Namasudra leaders those who were associated with the new organization included such prominent personalities as P.R. Thakur, Rashik Lal Mandal etc.

The Namasudras providing their movement with crucial organizational base Guru Chand Thakur told his followers, *Jar dal nei tar bal nei* (one who doesn't have a group, doesn't have any power). He conveyed the message of organizing for collective action. To bring the sect under a centralized organizational network, Matua Mahasangha started and worked even before 1915, through the initiative of Tarak Gosain. In 1931, under the presidentship of P.R. Thakur Matua Mahasangha was permanently set up. He also was connected with the other socio-political organization like Namasudra Samiti, 'Bengal Namasudra Association'. and 'Bengal Depressed Classes Federation' as these offered the most convenient means for mass contacts. He protested vehemently when Bengal was decided to be partitioned by the Independence of India Act, 1947. He submitted a deputation to the Boundary Commission the partition of Bengal that had made in a meeting in Dhaka on 22 June, 1947.[71] When this attempt eventually failed, he left East Bengal and permanently settled in Thakurnagar of West Bengal.

The partition of Bengal destroyed the strong unity of Matua as well as the Namasudra movement. Lakhs of people of the Namasudra community of East Bengal had settled in different regions of India as a refugee. To foster unity among them, P.R. Thakur established a colony in Thakurnagar in North 24 Pargana, West Bengal by his initiative and started the annual *Baruni Mela* (Matua Mela) so that the people of the same community could meet each other. At the same time branches of Matua Mahasangha were established in different places of Bengal. Besides Matua Mahasngha, Hariguru Chand Seva Sangha, Matua Seva Sangha and Matua Mission are still carrying on their socio-religious reformation and programme of educational activities.[72]

The study of the Namasudra caste, the second largest community in undivided Bengal, is essential to trace the historical development of the caste struggle in Bengal. Indeed, without the organized movements of the Namasudras and few other caste fulfilment of the mission of the depressed classes would have been a difficult task. The deep-seated grievances of the Namasudras found expression in the form of caste struggle which influenced the course of the National movement. The present work seeks to explain the sources of grievances of the Namasudras which transformed them from their low social status into a new political force to reckon with. The true nature of this kind of movement cannot be explained by sheer Nationalist historiography where every manifestation of grievances of a section of the mass is explained in terms of colonial impact. Similarly, the grievances and protests of the Namasudras cannot be explained solely by colonial discourse where landlords and money lenders are identified as instruments of exploitation.[73] The true nature of their movement can be traced from various factors that shaped its course, viz. traditional domination of the upper castes, colonial impact and awakening of the Namasudras, their numerical strength and their clan fraternity. The Namasudras got religious and cultural nourishment through the formation of a socio-religious organization named Matua Mahasangha. It strengthened the bond among different classes of the community.

The British government had shown favours to the depressed classes to fulfil their twin objectives: (i) winning the support of these castes to curb the rising tide of nationalism, and (ii) playing the role of responsible government by removing the inequalities in the socio-economic sphere. The impact of the British rule was felt in every sphere of Namasudra life. It only made them aware of their numerical strength but also promoted social mobility and generated in them a spirit of defiance to the social authority of the higher castes. Under the British, the doors of education were opened for all which gave them a golden chance to become educated and enlightened in Western education. In the economic sphere, British policies made inroads into the traditional caste structure by developing the market economy. The British government introduced the element of competition in the Indian economic system which eliminated the occupational monopoly of different castes opening a new horizon for them. In the administrative sphere, the British policy of 'protective discrimination' widened the scope for employment opportunities for them.

In the national political scene, we find two parallel movements — one for achieving Swaraj and the other for removing social disabilities of the depressed classes. How far and to what extent the two streams of movements went hand in hand? During the period of the national movement, the Namasudras did not question the legitimacy of the British rule as they thought it would serve a providential purpose elevating them socially, economically, and politically. So they dissociated themselves from the national movement and opposed it on a number of occasions. Why did the nationalist leader fail to attract the Namasudras in the mainstream of the national movement? Was it due to organizational failure or highhandedness of the nationalist leaders who had shown sympathies to the cause of the Namasudras? Though they were not against the freedom struggle, they had a different perceptions about freedom. They realized that without the help of the British government they would not be able to fulfil their demands. The Namasudra leaders apprehended that if additional power was vested in the hands of a few caste Hindu leaders without giving any share of power to them it would hamper their future progress. The Britishers stimulated aspirations in the minds of the Namasudras by granting a separate electorate for the Muslims in the Morley-Minto Reforms Act of 1909. The demands and aspirations of the Namasudras have been studied in detail to identify their political mission.

It is interesting to note that the gradual transformation of the Namasudra movement from a socio-religious movement to a movement for separate political identity. Caste consciousness and political awareness of the Namasudras led them to form caste associations which later on turned into a political organ for extracting their demands. The electoral politics of the Namasudra leaders carried on relentless struggle on the floors of the Assembly of reservation of seats for the Scheduled Caste in the elective bodies like Union Boards, District Boards, Municipalities and Corporations.[74] The Poona Pact of 1932 opened up political prospects for the depressed classes, a separate political identity. Besides they tried to keep alive the issues for the coming election of 1937 to mobilize the masses. The mass base of the Namasudra leaders had indeed become eroded to a certain extent as they shifted their attention from rural socio-economic issues of constitutional concessions.

It is true that during the Namasudra Movement the resources were very meagre and the people were very scattered and approachability was very challenging. Harichand Thakur and his son Guru Chand Thakur struggled relentlessly to do away with social ills like untouchability, inequalities of the caste system, right to enter temples or shrines and overall development of rural Bengal as well as North Bengal in the last half of the nineteenth century and first half of the twentieth century.[75] They united the people of the lower community people and protected them from religious conversion. They established many educational institutions to step up the condition of the downtrodden of the society. Their relentless struggle for the upliftment of the downtrodden made them popular among thousands of persons.

Under the Matua movement Namasudra community tried to preserve its own indigenous rural culture and tradition and articulate new literature called 'Matua Literature' that was created against the caste-based orthodox text further reinforced by the fact of social mobility arising among the Matuas in particular and Namasudras in general. Tarak Sarkar, a pioneer of Matua literature wrote *Sri Sri Hari Lilamrita* published in 1916 and *Mahasangha Kirtan*, Mahananda Halder's *Sri Sri Guruchand Charit, Bicharan Pagals* and *Hari Sangeet* were the other primary important Matua literature. Besides the songs of Matua poets, *Hari Yatra, Hariloot, Harisabha, Santi Sabha* are also significant in Matua culture. This literature created consciousness among the Dalit communities and was given a significant influence on the literary movement of the Matuas. It is beyond question that the organization of the Matua sect provided opportunities for social mobilization and helped evolve and articulate community consciousness. But in course of time the movements gradually lost their radicalism and slipped as one more Hindu sect with its uniqueness minuscule into the acceptance of Hari Thakur as one of the many deities to be worshipped by the devotees.[76]

A study of the organized movements for social upliftment in Bengal in the late nineteenth and the early twentieth century inevitably suggests that caste was an important factor in the socio-religious life of this province. Bengal was no exception to the general rule, although problems of untouchability or social disability were not that acute here. Caste-consciousness was utilized for the social mobilization of a vast multitude, still largely untouched by secular culture or a more broad-based national politics. And it was the limited nature of the process of modernization under colonial rule that led to a rejuvenation of such caste sentiments in the cultural and social consciousness of the Bengali Hindus, gradually leading to their articulation in political life. But at the same time, the very forms of expression of such sentiments led to an erosion of the traditional society as well. Caste as a social institution was not new in Bengal, neither was the phenomenon of corporate social mobility. Indeed, the caste system could exist for such a long time because of this limited flexibility that allowed positional readjustments for ambitious groups coming up from the bottom from time to time. But under colonial rule, the whole phenomenon assumed new dimensions. The political and economic changes of this period led to a disintegration of the old, hierarchical, interdependent relationships between castes.

Hence these people, though conscious of their new secular status and aware of the existence of a market system, instead of demanding a levelling off of the society, went for Sanskritization and demanded higher ritual ranks, thus consciously endorsing the caste system. But the way they expressed their sentiments also weakened the structure of the traditional society and its behaviour pattern. The large-scale appropriation of symbols of higher ritual status signified a protest against the institution of caste, for it used to make those symbols an exclusive monopoly of the higher castes alone. And above all, the very idea of organizing movements for caste mobility, and that, too, by a number of castes at a time, threatened the hierarchical structure itself and challenged by implication the ideology of caste that made caste ranking theoretically immutable in the upward direction. Moreover, the marks of distinction between castes were fading out, because of Sanskritization and other forms of reference group behaviour. Colonial ethnographers in the late nineteenth century discovered two central contradictions in the pluralist society of Bengal: One between the Hindus and the Muslims and the others among the Hindus themselves, between the more advanced high caste *bhadraloks* at the one end and the under-privileged lower castes, eventually known as the 'depressed classes', at the other. This stereotype began to influence the colonial policy when the *bhadraloks* began to question the legitimacy of the Raj at the turn of the century.[77] To weaken their movement the British first tried to rally the Muslims and, then with equal consistency, sought to mobilize the depressed classes in support of the Raj. This they did by evolving a policy of 'protective discrimination, that sought to grant special, favour in matters of education, employment and constitutional rights, first, to the Muslims and, then, to the depressed classes, later called the 'Scheduled Castes'.

NOTES AND REFERENCES

1. Sekhar Bandopadhyay, "A Peasant Caste in Protest" in Sekhar Bandopadhyay and Suranjan Das (ed.), *Caste and Communal Politics in South Asia*, Calcutta: K.P. Bagchi & Company, 1993, p. 150.

2. "Emergence of Such Popular Religious Sects among the Protesting Lower Caste and Untouchables was not a very Unusual Phenomenon in Colonial India." Sekhar Bandopadhyay, *Caste Protest and Identity in Colonial India: The Namasudras of Bengal, 1872-1947*, New Delhi: Oxford University Press, 2011, p. 35.
3. *Ibid.*, also Tarak Chandra Sarkar, *Sri Sri Harileelamrita*, (An account of the life and teachings of Harichand), Faridpur, 1323 B.S. pp. 13ff.
4. *Sri Sri Harileelamrita*, Introduction.
5. Sekhar Bandopadhyay, "Popular Religion and Social Mobility in Colonial Bengal; The Matua Sect and the Namasudras" in Rajat Kanta Roy (ed.), *Mind, Body and Society*, New Delhi: Oxford University Press, 1995, p. 163.
6. *Ibid.*, pp. 167-68.
7. *Sri Sri Harileelamrita*, p. 94.
8. Tushar Chattopadhyay, *Introduction of Matua Sahitya Parikrama*, edited by Birat Bairagya, 1999, p. 47.
9. *Sri Sri Harileelamrita*, p. 107.
10. Sujay Thakur, "The Kritan of Resistance and a Divide Bengal: A Study of the Matua Community", *Bharatiya Pragna: An Interdisciplinary Journal of Indian Studies*, Vol. I, No. 1, 2016, pp. 13-17.
11. Mahananda Haldar, *Sri Sri Guruchand Charit*, Thakurnagar, 5th Reprinted, 2009, cited in Paramananda Halder, *Essence of the Matua Religion*, Sridham Thakurnagar: Thakurbari, 2003, p. 15.
12. *Sri Sri Harileelamrita*, p. 2.
13. Halder, *Essence of the Matua Religion*, p. 27.
14. *Ibid.*, p. 38.
15. *Ibid.*
16. Haldar, *Sri Sri Guruchand Charit*, pp. 119-20.
17. West Bengal State Archives (WBSA), General Department, Kolkata. Letter No. 87 J.G. Dated Alipur, 18th July, 1881, Annual Administration Report, Presidency Division for 1880-1881; Bhibhuti Bhusan Mandal, *Bangler Nabajagaran o Guruchand Thakur*, Kaliyaganj, 2013, pp. 27-28.
18. West Bengal State Archives (WBSA), General Department, Kolkata. Letter No. 87 J.G. Dated Alipur, 18th July, 1881, Annual Administration Report, Presidency Division for 1880-1881.
19. J.A.E. Garret, *The Gazetteer of Nadia District*, Calcutta, 1910, p. 46.
20. WBSA, Political Department, (Political), Letter No. 2796, Dated 3rd September, 1901, Annual Administration Report, Presidency Division.
21. WBSA, GB, Appointment (Appointment), File No. 18L-220, Progs. No. 262-263, August 1921.
22. WBSA, General (Miscellaneous), GB, File No. 100-4, B, August 1901, Prog. No. l; also Notes, pp. 1-2; two such Vyavasthas are quoted in Sitanath Biswas, *op. cit.*, pp. 89-95.
23. Haldar, *Sri Sri Guruchand Charit*, p. 130.
24. Sumit Sarkar, *Beyond Nationalist Frames: Relocating Post-Modernism, Hindutva, History*, Delhi: Permanent Black, 2002, pp. 235-37.
25. Halder, *Guruchand Charit*, p. 2.
26. Balaram Sarkar, *Namasudra Jnanabhandar* (Storehouse of Information on the Namasudras), Faridpur, 1911, p. 80.
27. Naresh Chandra Das, *Namasudra Sampraday O Bangladesh* (in Bengali), Calcutta, 1368 B.S., p. 44.

28. Jogesh Chandra Pal, "Banglar Hindu", *Bangabani* (2nd half), 4 Agrahayan, 1333 B.S., pp. 397-98.
29. William Ward, *A View of the History, Literature & Mythology of the Hindoos*, Vol. I, Serampore: Mission Press, 1818, p. 160.
30. C.S. Mead, *The Namasudras and Other Addresses*, Adelaide, 1911, p. 12.
31. Haldar, *Sri Sri Guruchand Charit*, Introduction, p. VIII; C.S. Mead, *The Namasudras*, p. 12.
32. Halder, *Essence of the Matua Religion*, p. 44.; Haldar, *Sri Sri Guruchand Charit*, pp. 100-23.
33. *Ibid.*, pp. 176ff.
34. *Ibid.*, Introduction, pp. VIII-IX.
35. *Ibid.*, p. 219.
36. Haldar, *Sri Sri Guruchand Charit*, p. 417.
37. WBSA, Government of Bengal, Education Department, Education Branch, File No. 2P-35. Progs No. 895-896, 5 May, 1927.
38. Halder, *Essence of the Matua Religion*, pp. 47-48.
39. *Ibid.*
40. Haldar, *Sri Sri Guruchand Charit*, Introduction, pp. VIII-IX.
41. Halder, *Essence of the Matua Religion*, pp. 47-48.
42. *Ibid.*, p. 49.
43. *Ibid.*, p. 50.
44. *Ibid.*
45. Haldar, *Sri Sri Guruchand Charit*, p. 574.
46. *Ibid.*, p. 443.
47. *Ibid.*, pp. 413-15.
48. *Ibid.*, p. 415; Halder, *Essence of the Matua Religion*, p. 56.
49. Haldar, *Sri Sri Guruchand Charit*, Introduction, p. XII.
50. "Hindustan Standard", 27 March, 1938 cited in Halder's *Essance of the Matua Religion*, pp. 46-47.
51. Mead, *The Namasudras*, p. 27.
52. *Ibid.*
53. Sekhar Bandopadhyay, *Caste, Protest*, p. 55.
54. Mead, *The Namasudras*, p. 8.
55. Haldar, *Sri Sri Guruchand Charit*, pp. 142-63.
56. Jogesh Chandra Pal, "Banglar Hindu", *Bangabani* 5 (2nd half), 4 Agrahayan, 1333 B.S., pp. 397-98.
57. WBSA, Government of Bengal, Education Department, Education Branch, File No. 2P-35. Progs No. 895- 896, 5th May, 1927.
58. Mead, *The Namasudras*, pp. 9ff.
59. *Ibid.*, p. 9.
60. *Ibid.*, p. 110.
61. *Ibid.*, p. 76.
62. *Ibid.*, pp. 24-60.
63. *Ibid.*, pp. 24-30.
64. *Ibid.*, p. 31.
65. Sekhar Bandhopadhyay, *Caste, Protest*, p. 55.
66. Rev. P. Noble, Baptist Mission, to F.C. French, Commissioner of Dacca Division, 15 October, 1917, Political (Political), GB, File No. 8a-10, E November 1917, Prog. No. 65.
67. *Ibid.*

68. Biswas, *Matua Religious Movement*, p. 331.
69. Bandopadhyay, *Social Protest or Politics of Backwardness?*, pp. 189-90.
70. *Matua Mahasangha*, 57th Edition, Chaitra, 1412 B.S., p. 8.
71. Nandadulal Mahanta, *Matua Andolan O Banglar Dalit Jagaran*, Calcutta: Annapurna Prakasani, 2002, pp. 340-41.
72. Partha Chatterjee, "For an Indian History of Peasant Struggle", *Social Scientist*, Vol. 16, No. 11, November 1988, pp. 11-14.
73. Sekhar Bandhopadhay, *Caste, Protest*, p. 55.
74. Ratan Kumar Biswas, *Caste Movements in Bengal (1872-1947)*, Kolkata: Progressive Book Forum, pp. 19-24.
75. Halder, *Essence of Matua Religion*, p. 45.
76. Bandopadhyay, *Caste Protest*, p. 59.
77. *Ibid.*

3

The Local Deities and Subalterns of Sundarbans

A Historical Analysis

Tridib Mandal

Philosophy begins, where science ends and religion takes over, where philosophy ends. This well-versed saying is a perfect manifestation of the livelihood struggle of the fatalist people, residing adjacent to the forests and marshy lands of Sundarban. They live on, with total submission and deep-rooted faith in local deities and depend solely on the magic of *mantra*, *tantra* for their lives and living. Local belief strongly holds that the almighty God has neither a beginning nor an end. He has no form or deformation. The making or dissolution of matter, the ups and downs in life, every tit bits of the Universe are only the expressions of his illusionary whims.

The fatalist people of the area, with their local belief used to worship idols of human or superhuman figures as a god. They were imagined as a god, possessed with supernatural eminent power. Some of the examples are cited here as — Dakshin Roy, Bastu Thakur, Laxmidevi, Sitala Mata, Panchananda, Banbibi and so on. All of them imagined as deities are chiefly expected to fulfil the wishes of the worshippers. As they hear the prayers of the devotees and bestow upon them welfare and happiness, they are considered as '*devata*'. The inner meaning being "I will give you (*deba-ta*) everything you pray for, to me, with full submission and faith."

The subalterns of Sundarban had only those openings for sustenance, which were directly connected to nature and were strongly motivated by their unfathomed faith in local deities, which reinforced their very hazardous ways, to earn a living. Their life and livelihood were based on the forest resources life wood, golepata, honey, resin, the huge storage of fish in the shallow water of the numerous creeks and rivers and also the crop fields protected by earthen dams.

Geographical Set-up

'Banga' is a land situated in the eastern corner of 'Bharatvarsha'. The land has been named after Banga, who was one of the eminent sons of Boli Raja. Incidentally, Boli Raja did compose the '*Rig Veda* about 2500 BC. The land of 'Banga' was situated on the flood plain of Padma-Meghna rivers. As this low-lying tract was protected by embankments (*a-al*) for human habitation, the land derived its name as Banga+Al — Bangladesh. The Portuguese pronunciation was 'Bengala' which was reshaped in English as 'Bengal'.

In its geographical entity, 24 Parganas was under the jurisdiction of Poundra Vardhan. The then great king Sasanka used to reign this territory from its capital Karna Subarna. During the middle age, Pratapaditya, the great hero of Bengal, established an independent Jessore state, including 24-Parganas, Jessore and Khulna. The Mughal troops were repeatedly defeated by him. This land was under the jurisdiction of the Santgaon Government during Pathan's reign. When Mirjafar became the Nawab of Bengal, he gifted the Jaigeer (Mandal) of 24 Parganas to Clive in 1757 A.D.[1] The deed of gift had has been inscribed on a marble plaque on the bank of the Hughli river.

The 24-Parganas according to this jurisdiction are: (1) Akbarpur, (2) Ahirpur, (3) Ajimabad, (4) Balia, (5) Baridhati, (6) Madan-Malla, (7) Magura, (8) Pyekan, (9) Ektiarpur, (10) Bamundhara, (11) Dakhinsagar, (12) Khaspur, (13) Sahangarh, (14) Garh, (15) Hatiagarh, (16) Ektiarpur, (17) Penchakul, (18) Malda, (19) Latani, (20) Muragachha, (21) Uttar Pargana, (22) Sahandarh, (23) Ghatijuri, and (24) Kolkata. These 24 Parganas formed the district of 24 Parganas during the British rule.[2]

However, the greater Sundarban used to mean an extensive land between the Hooghly and the Meghna rivers, comprising almost entire Barisal, Bakharganj, Khulna and undivided 24 Parganas covering an area of about 14 thousand sq.miles. The areal extent of the present-day Sundarban has dwindled after independence, following the partition of Bengal in 1947. The greater portion of the Sundarban has ceded to Bangladesh. The Sundarban of West Bengal is bounded by the eastern bank of the Vidyadhari river on the north, the West banks of the

Ichhamati-Kalindi rivers, and fifty-five islands along the eastern bank of the Piyali river in the south. The entire stretch was situated in the undivided district of 24 Parganas stretching from Diamond Harbour, Alipore, and Basirhat, sub-divisions. The islands are located in Kakdwips, Sagar, Namkhana, Patharpratima, Mathurapur, Jainagar, Kultali, Canning, Basanti, Gosaba, Minakhan, Haroa, Hasnabad, Sandeshkhali. The total stretch of Sundarban in 24 Parganas is 9630 sq.kilometre.[3] For administrative convenience the district has been divided as North and South 24 Parganas on 1st March, 1986.

Nomenclature

It has not been recorded in history, as to how and when the name Sundarban evolved. Myriad numbers of Sundari (Heretiera Phyron) or 'Sundri' trees used to grow on this land, which might have a reason for such a nomenclature of the tract. Few people believed that from 'Sundarban' or 'Chandradwipban' the name Sundarbans has derived. Still, others believe that the name took after the 'Chandavanda' tribe who once used to abode this land. This forest land goes underwater during high tide and again emerges from underwater during low tide. As such this land was also called the 'Vatidesh' (emerging with ebb). This name was in vogue even before the 17th century. The present-day extensive area recognized as Sundarban once used to be a very rich human settlement and civilization.[4] This rich settlement and the reserved forest has a deep invisible symbiotic relationship, which protects the human settlement of the area from the surges of the southern seas and the severe cyclonic outburst.

A Perusal of the Sundarban Area

Sundarban is a land, silt clay and brine water, earth, forest and mangroves. Canals, bills, creeks, rivers, *nalas* have shaped the curious forms of the 55 islands. The socio-morphological characteristics of Sundarban are unique with huge river estuaries, sea beaches seashores, pastures, reserved forests, birds sanctuaries, huge cultivated fields, villages, hamlets, markets and rural markets, small ports, mokam, and the highly revered pilgrimage of Ganga Sagar lying close to the Maharshi Kapilmuni's hermitage. The beauty of the forest area has become more owe inspiring, with the existence of a variety of crocodiles, Kamat, fish-eater crocodiles, sharks, dolphins in the water, the forest invaded by world-famous Royal Bengal Tigers, Bagroles, wild cats, wild boars, chital deer, foxes and venomous snakes of different species. Besides, there are numerous native and foreign migratory birds.[5]

People

The majority of the population of Sundarban belong to Hindu and Muslim sects. Besides, there is a handful of Buddhists and Christians. During the Middle ages, adventurous fortune-seekers migrated to this area. For example, when the eminent 12 landlords (Baro Bhuias) were defeated in the hands of the Mughals, the aristocrats thriving under their protection were, eager for a hideout and a new shelter. They crossed the Western Sundarban and started to settle in many areas along the Adi Ganga of 24 Parganas. Similarly, some of the exasperated aristocrats of Southern Bengal, who were ousted from their land by continuous Bargi attacks also migrated to Sundarban. The large and small Jamindaris of 24 Parganas evolved from the migratory landlords of the north and east districts of Bengal. The Roys of Rajpur, Baruipur, Dutta's Mitra and Motilal of Majilpur, Singha's of Mathurapur, Haldar of Budge Budge and Pututundu of Laxmi Kantapur may be cited as an example. All of them were aristocrats, Brahmins or Kayasthas.[6]

Most of the common people of the area socially belonged to subaltern groups. The Census of India, 1881, has recorded 266 *jatis* residing in 24 Parganas inclusive of Sundarban. Total population was 10,03,110. Amongst this population, Pundras outnumbered others, accounting for 22 per cent of the total population. The second in this racial order was Kaibartas who formed 14.6 per cent of the population, followed by Bagdi and goals, accounting for 8 per cent and 6 per cent respectively. Chandal or Namasudra only constituted 2 per cent of the population in 24 Parganas.[7] But they accounted for a larger share of the population in East Sundarban. W.W. Hunter in his "Account of Sundarian" has classified Hindus of Sundarban according to their occupation. The classes[8] are as follows:

Poundra/Pode: In ancient books, the reference of Paundra has been made, side by side with ancient warrior classes or Khastriyas, like Oudra, Dravir, Dard, Kirat, Khas, Mahisak etc. This Paundra civilization was seated on in long the lower Ganga valley as an extended part of the Pundra bhumi and was familiar as Gangaridi Civilization. The blood of Pundra Jati not only runs through the veins of the Pod or the Bengalee Paundra Khastriya but has been mingled with different races and communities of extended India, just like Austric and Dravidian history. The Gangetic Paundras often ventured for lands in the east and west for business or war and gradually settled there and by proliferating scattered all over, in many directions of the country.

During this glorious period, 'Gangridi Confederation' or a federal nation was formulated under the aegis of Magadh Emperor Dhanananda. So, the greater Ganga plain and the great jati of Gangaridi imply the entire extended Bengal and its ancient people. As it now transpires, the present farmers, toilers and the underdeveloped people who are treated in sheer negligence at present, had ancestors who used to be once vibrant with velour and prosperity and were the lord of fortune of the independent Gangona dwip.[9]

The Pods are sub-classed as

(a) *Dheno Pod*— mainly attached to agriculture.
(b) *Mechho Pod*— devoted to fishing essentially.

But, both the sects perform cultivation, fishing and wood cutting. The average economic status is of medium standard.

Chandal or Chanral (Outcaste): This is by caste Namasudra. They are involved in the cultivation and seasonal wood cutting. Recently many of them have become educated and have improved their economic standard.

Napit (Barber): They are hair cutters and shave also. They have attached to cultivation also. Most of them are poor.

Kaibarata (Fishermen): They are principally fishermen, but also perform cultivation. Few of them are middle class, but most are poor.

Kapali: They are attached to cultivation and are small shopkeepers. They belong to the middle class.

Jelia (Fishermen): They are both farmers and fishermen. Few of them are middle-classed.

Bagdi: Both farmers and fishermen. Most of them are poor.

Tior: Farmers, labourers and fishermen. They are generally poor.

Dhoba (Washerman): Their chief occupation is to wash cloths.

Kaora and Kahar: Their occupations are farming, swine husbandry, playing band in marriage and ceremonies and carrying Pulky (hand-carried cart).

Sunri: They prepare wine and sell it.

Jugi/Jogi: They are mainly weaver but also involved in farming.

Cobbler (Shoemaker): They are very poor and outcast in society. They scrape out animal hides and dry them with salt, for selling in the market. The hide is used for shoemaking and also to play drums in marriage or *puja* festivals.

Some Scheduled Tribes are residing in this area, viz. ***Scheduled Tribes:*** Sardar, Buno, Munda. Their occupation involves farming, wood cutting, fish and crab catching, catching rats and molasses. They are fond of 'Hanria' made from rotten rice and wine. ***Malangi:*** They have come from Odisha to settle in Sagardwip and Namkhana. Their occupation is to make salt out of seawater as also wood cutting. ***Meer Shikari:*** They are involved in preying in the forest also catch fish for selling out in the localities. ***Sanpure (Shakecharmer):*** They earn a living by snake charming. ***Bede:*** They are involved in black magic like *Jharfuk* and *Tantra-mantra*. ***Mogh Bauddha:*** They are settled in the Bhangar area of Hashnabad. They came from Arakan. ***Native Christians:*** They mainly being too Scheduled Tribe and Scheduled Caste population. Stressed by socio-economic pressure, they were converted to Christianity in the lure of a better economic changeover. Their occupation involves business and farming. ***Muslims:*** They principally from three classes: (a) Shiekh — They are involved in farming and wood-cutting. (b) Said — They are cultivators. (c) Pathan Muslims — They are few. Some of the Muslims of the society are rich, though the majority faced sheer poverty.

Other Occupations

The subaltern classes were divided into a few sub-classes, depending upon their occupations. Their social respect and standard used to depend on their occupations. There is no denying the fact that cultivation held pride of position and many from other social sects had an urge to leave their petty job for farming. The same feeling incited the subaltern who had an eagerness to leave the *varna*-based Hinduism for Vaishnabites. They cherished that this will bring them social prestige. For example, the Bagdis of Tentulia embraced the Vaishnab religion at the beginning of the 19th century and was placed in a higher social order of prestige. The Ajluff Muslims of the lower order also tended the higher order of transmigrating to the higher order of Seikhism.[10]

A few poor and subalterns from outside Bengal took shelter in 24 Parganas for various reasons out of Malangis, who were salt makers came from Odisha in the 18th-19th century. They were noted as Malangis. Their occupation has earlier been discussed. Another group of Scheduled Tribe people came from the Chotanagpur area. They were Santals, Mundas, and Oraons. They are known as 'Bunos' in 24 Parganas. The agents used to appoint them in the hard task of forest clearing during the decades of 1980.[11] The other opportunities, the subalterns used to enjoy were directly related to nature. Numerous creeks, *nalas* and river bound and salt-rich tide inflected sloping land, presence of extensive forest were conducive to easy nature-related occupation apart from farming. Fishing, Salt brine, honey, resin and wood collection became the inherent occupation of the common people.

Housing

The houses of the farmers and agricultural labourers had mud walls and thatched roofs. The rooms had either two or eight such roofs. The rooms had veranda either on one side and in some other cases on four sides. Each house had rooms for cowshed and threshing (*dhenki ghar*). The houses were made of poles of Sundari, Garan, Keora trees, animal staff, bamboo etc. The roofs in many cases were made of thatches of Golpata, Hogla pata and Hetal pata. However, as with time many of the inhabitants of the area became solvent, which resulted in the construction of pucca houses. The furniture of the houses is not worth mentioning. There used to be some utensils like plates and other such utensils, cooking pot etc. A few possessed some brass utensils. There was no electricity. Recently in some localities, government-aided solar energy has been installed.

Colloquial Language

The colloquial language is generally that language which the rural people use, for their general conversations. The difference between the urban and rural or colloquial language or that between the language used in Kolkata or Sundarban area depends mainly on the nature and character of the language. This language does not bear any literary evidence. In Sundarban, people of different ethnic groups cohabit and each of them has its own and original local dialect. After they had settled in this locality and exchanged ideals, gradually there was the exchange of language too. Thus an extensive area gave birth to a new language. Examples of the new areal language of this region can be traced from literary works like, "Majhii (Boatmen) by Paresh Bhattacharya, 'Chaitali Ghurni' (the spring whirlpool) by Tarashankar Bandyopadhya, 'Banbibir Jahura Namo' (Praise of Banbibi) by Munsi Boiruddin and 'Ganga' by Samaresh Basu. An example from the local language may be cited — "Ami tomago badi jabo bullam, kintu jati parini, choto pailir edda chabal hoyechhe. Chabalda bes bhalo dekhit hoyechhe."[12] (I told you, that I would go to your house. But couldn't, as my little daughter has delivered a son. The boy is rather good-looking). However, with the change of time and extension of education, the influence of language used in Kolkata can be traced in rural areas of the locality.

Festivals

The main festivals of Sundarban are observed without any religious taboo. There is no religious conservation amongst the hard-working people of Sundarban. The Hindus join Muslim festivals. The Muslims in return do the same. There are deities, who are worshipped both by Hindus and Muslims, e.g. Bon Bibir Mela, Gaji Mela, Charak Mela, Gangadevi Puja.

The Charak Mela of Sundarban is highly acclaimed as the 'Gajan Festival'. The devotees who have a 'Manasik' (Promise to God), embrace a *Uttara* (neck girdle) in the name of the Lord Siva on the 1st day of Chaitra. People believe that if they can appease Lord Siva, their families will remain free from all types of diseases and the economic affluence of the family will flourish. The festival continues for one month from the 1st day of Chaitra, and on Chaitra Sankranti (the last day of Chaitra month) it is consummated.

The subaltern Hindus of different localities of this area principally belong to the Vaishnav sect. The majority of pods, fishermen, Bagdi, Kaora, Bairagi, Vasa sects are the worshippers of Hari (Lord Vishnu). They imbibe 'Tulsi mala' on the neck. On the full Monday of Magha Month (Maghi Purnima Tithi), they celebrate the birthday of Sri 'Chaitanya' with great grandeur. Besides, worship of Hari, Kirtan (Pala) is also observed during Kartika month.

Local Deities

The initial origin of local deities cropped up from outside world of the traditional and aristocratic Puranas. They were born initially out of fear of people's minds, who imagined the existence of some super-powered gods and deities. The origin of local deities emerged more from an urge for getting relief from diseases and oppressions. They were nurtured by home-centric mindset-ups of people for their necessities. Their prayers to gods reveal the deep-rooted inter-connection of their religious beliefs and their local behaviours. They prayed for escape from danger, material properties, begetting of a child, to get back their lost possession, saving of life from the attack of tiger, snake, smallpox and cholera. The part and parcel of this worship were more related to local beliefs and age-old folk culture rather than direction instructed in a religious book. Like many other places of Bengal, there are many local deities scattered all over 24 Parganas, who are harmonious with life, livelihood, relief and necessities of people residing on the land.[13] The deities like, Dharma Thakur, Panchu Thakur, Bara Thakur, Ateswar, Makal Thakur, Tatli Gaji, Kalu Roy, Manikpir, Jwarasur, Barakhan Gaji, Satya Pir, Basuli, Narayani, Harijhi Chandi, Satbibi, Olabibi, Beraki, Alakshmi, and the festivals like Gajan, Gamvira, Charak and Holi are the true examples of non-Aryan influences on Aryan culture.

People of this area believe that the *Banadevata* (lord of the forest) would be in a rage if they chop *Pabitra Kunja* (sacred groves). A brief discussion has been made hereunder, on the aspects of Banabibi, Dakshin Roy, Bada Khan Gaji and few other local deities.

Banabibi

Banabibi is one of the Muslim goddesses, who raise the fear of the tiger. Irrespective of Hindu or Muslim, all put their *naibedya* (offerings) to her. The image of the deity has impressions of both Hindu and Muslim religions. In Sajnekhali, Netadhopani, Pathar Pratima, Samsernagore, Parghumti areas the idols of Banabibi resemble that of the goddess Saraswati. The image is pleasant looking, of golden or yellow colour with two hands and a huge *mukut* on the head (head gear). She does not bear an *asabari* (Scepter). In many other places, specific Islamic influence on the idol is reflected. The idol wears *ghagra* (skirt) or *pyjama* with shocks and shoes. There is a *tikli* (forehead pendant) and a small hat with colourful flowery embroidery. Her long hair is braided. In some idols, she holds a child on her lap. The child is Dukhe, according to local belief. The foresters before entering the forest, arrange for worshipping this deity. About a week before entering forests, the women folks of the household begin to perform various rituals. They strictly follow the verdicts of cleanliness and purity and keep *manat* (wish, which will be rewarded to the deity when fulfilled) to her. At the time of worship, hens are released in the name of mother Banbibi. So long, the husband is off to the forest the wife puts off her conch and iron bangles (*Sankho hoa*), does not wear vermilion (*sindur*) on her head and keeps her door open at night. This ceremony is mainly performed in March, April and May (Chaitra-Vaisak) and occasionally in December-January (Agrahan, Pausa & Magh). During the *Puja* ceremony, *Palagan* (musical acclamation for a deity) for Banabibi is arranged. This *Palagan* narrates the life history of Dukhe. The *Palagan* is titled 'Dukhe Yatra'.[14] Wajed Ali, a poet writes in his poem 'Banbibir Ban':

Prati bachhar Bosekh mase Mongolbare,
Dalbendhe sab Nauka nie ase baner dhare.
Banabibir name tara sara die jai,
Morog Kimba Murgi die manat metai.
Banbibir jangaler esab pratha achhe,
Sundorboner geon manush esab nie banche.
Gangaridi rajatwa to tai Banbibir ban,
Vayal Sabuj holeo ta mugdha kare mon.[15]

(On Tuesday of Baisakh every year, people in groups of boats come to the fringe of the forest. They hail in the name of Banbibi and keep their promise by offering cock or hen. These types of customs are in vogue in the forest of Banbibi. The rural folks of Sundarban live in them. The Banbibir ban is situated in the Kingdom of Gangaridi. Though awe-inspiring green, it enthralls the mind.)

Dakshin Roy

Dakshin Roy is the God Tiger on one hand and is also the lord of the harvest. Recent researches, however, have scribed Dakshin Roy as a tyrant king whereas Banabibi has been depicted as a saviour of the oppressed people. But, whatever may be the truth behind the ideas, people of the land of water and forest, worship Dakshin Roy as the highest order of forest lord. He is the true local deity of the people of this area. He is seated on a tiger and dressed as a warrior. He puts on armour on his arms and holds, sword, bow and arrow. In some of the idols, he is seen to carry a Mungerigun, for example, in Dhapdhapi village of Baruipur Police Station, Dakshin Roy in his temples seems to carry a Mungeari indigenous gun (*gada banduk*). In some localities, big carnivals (*mela*) are also arranged, for example in Vevia of Hasnabad, Dhapdhapi and Dhosa of Baruipur, Canning, Gosaba, Parghumti, Samsernagar, Kalitali etc. Both Hindus and Muslims like Mouli, Kathure and Jele (Honey collector, Woodcutter, Fisherman) and other people worship him. The arrangement for *puja* does not need any grandeur. A humble offering of fruit, flowers and *arghya* (leave, flower, grass and bunched together) serve the purpose. In some places tradition of hen, offerings prevail.[16]

In the Mangal Kavya of Haridev the Dakshin Roy says:

Ami to Jangal Raja Dakshin Iswar,
(Amar) Sebak bate hoy to dhibar.[17]

(I am Dakshin Iswar, the king of the jungles and the fishermen are my care givers.)

Bar Khan Gaji

In Sundarban, this festival is known as 'Gajir Mela' (Gaji's Carnival) or 'Gajir dorga'. Gaji means the conqueror. This deity is worshipped equally by the Hindus and the Muslims. The idols are made of earth. He is draped with a turban on his head, has a long beard and thick mustache and holds a sharply pointed sword. The offerings are fruits, flowers and Shirni with oversized sugar-made sweets (*batasa*) and *kodma*, *patali* (jaggery). Chicken is also offered. Earthen pots like pitchers and cooking vessels are sold in the carnivals held on the occasion of the worship.

Kalu Roy: The idol of this god has an entire human impression.

Pir Gaji: Pir Gaji has a strong influence on extensive areas of Sundarban along with other local deities. Hindus and Muslims offer *Sinni* to him.

Manik Pir: He is worshipped by the peasant families as a saviour of cows.

Manosa, the Goddess of Snakes: This goddess is worshipped twice — on the Sankrantis of (last days of) Sravana and Vadra. All the peasant families observe this worship. A huge menu of dishes is cooked on the eve of the worship day. The next day these are consumed after the ceremony is over. The main *Prasad — Kachu Sak* and *Panta Vaat* (green leaves of yam and stale rice). For the well-being of their families, people of locality float small boats made out of the banana tree and decorate them with red paper or cloth and keep in them, milk and banana throughout the entire Bhadra (August-September) month.

Sitala Puja: To get rid of pox, measles and other diseases that outbreak at the end of winter and beginning of spring, people worship goddess Sitala.

Satima: Few people of this locality have faith in Satima's worship. It is believed in society that Satima possesses some devotees and gives directions through them for medicines. People believe that very difficult and incurable diseases are cured by Satima's medicine.

Ola Bibi

According to human belief, Ola Bibi is the goddess of 'Olaotha' which is generally termed as Cholera. The name Ola Bibi has an Islamic connection. In folk belief, 'Ola' denotes nama (uncontrolled purges), which is the main symptom of the disease. The word 'bibi' denotes a noble Muslim woman. Ola with bibi denotes an image of a noble Islam lady. The goddess is worshipped for the disease after which, she has been named and with offerings, singing and *hajat* she is coaxed to be appeased.[18]

Before the advent of Muslim dominance over Bengal, Ola Bibi used to be worshipped by the Hindus as Olai Chandi. In Islamic culture, no Hindu god or goddess can be worshipped with Hajat. So, Ola Bibi in Islamic wrapper is worshipped with hajat instead of *puja*. The converted Islams worship Olai Chandi as Ola Bibi and make hajat in an Islamic culture instead of offering a *puja*. Olai Chandi and Ola bibi are the same, taking shape from the faith and belief of the people. In the same way Banachandi or Banadurga has become Banabibi, Shitala — Asmabibi; Saptamatrika as Satbibi. The palagan of Ola bibi is known as 'Khalnir Gan'.[19]

Crop Festival

The farmers of the area practice various functions in different parts of Sundarbans from Ambubachi held in Asad (May-June) to Nabanna of Pausa (December-January). The belief in the Hindu peasant families goes on like that, the earth remains in menstruation during the first week of Asada and gets piquant; as such become fertile for the production of crops. During this period the peasants stop ploughing or digging the earth and obey various rituals. The cooking in the households is forbidden on the first day and the diet consists of milk, mango, banana, jack fruit etc. After sowing the seeds in the field, they select an auspicious day for transplanting seven bunches of young seedlings of paddy to some other plots. Along with these seedlings they also plant young seedlings of yam, branches of Amra (sour fruit-bearing plant) and also some flowers. On this day they keep a curry of yam leaves and boiled Amra in their diet. During early Karttika (October-November), the paddy plants are imagined as pregnant women and peasant families arrange to marry them away. This function is known as Laxmi Mayer bia (marriage of mother Laxmi). On this occasion, the womenfolk of the family prepare *Prasad* (offerings) with green leaves of *neem* (green margo leaves), fresh turmeric, sun-baked a tap rice, banana, yam, *ghee* and honey and keep it on banana leaves within the paddy fields. They sing and utter:

Ma Laxmi go
Aswin gelo Kartik elo
Ma Laxmi garve porlo
Bandhe Bandhe ek gola dhan dao go.[20]

(Oh! mother Laxmi, Aswin has passed, and Kartik turns up. Mother Laxmi is running through a phase of pregnancy. Oh mother, please give us huge bunches of paddies that fill our granaries.)

After this, when the new harvest is raised, the first offer *puja* and *Sinni Prasad* to Laxmi and Narayan and then they consume their food themselves. This worship takes place in the bright half of the fortnight on some Thursday or Sunday.

Geeti Pala

In the Sundarban area one form of Geeti Pala (lyrical session) goes on, which is sung in Panchali Yatra style before the audience. For example, Jarina, Sagarvasan, Rupaban Yatra (the voyage of Rupaban), Rakhal Bandhu (the cowboy friend), Rumni-ghumni, the Dukher banabas (the forests going of Dukhe), Ramleela etc. Performance of their 'pala's move the heart of the commoners. It is still unknown as who wrote these 'pala's. The 'pala's are composed of numerous songs. The secular and open-hearted humane touch, enthrall the listeners. The female characters of this yatra pala are usually acted by males. However, in some cases, it has been noted that the females also take part in these occasions. These Yatra 'pala's used to be presented in colloquial local dialects in different villages. The musical instruments used, were flute, harmonium, *dhol* (drum). Each group comprised seven to eight participants. The duration of 'pala gan's used to be nonetheless two to three nights.[21]

Faith on Mantra-Tantra (Black Magic)

People dwellers of the land used to have unfathomed faith in *mantra* (hymns) and *tantra* (magics). *Mantra-tantra, dhulo para, jal para* (magic earth dust, magic water), *Charanamrita* (the water from idol's feet), earth from the open temple of god etc., might have saved a few, while many others died of diseases. It is rumored that when Cholera and Smallpox used to outbreak in villages, people from distant villages came to visit the Kali temple of Kaccharibari (office of landlords) of Malekan Ghumti. They used to collect water from the pond of Kalibari, with a deep-rooted faith that this will save the life of their near and dear ones. The fate-bound people in the woods and forests used to chant these magical powers to save themselves.

The name of these *mantra-tantras* are peculiar, e.g. *Nauka bandha* (boat protection), *ghar bandha* (house protection), *Para bandha* (locality protection), *bane nama* (forest entrance), *Khilen* (to shutter off), *Bagh bandi* (controlling tiger), *Jal para* (magic water), *tel para* (magic oil), *halud bandha* (magic turmeric), *Sarisha baan* (magic sarish for evil purpose), *bas kara* (to hypnotize), *Sindur Para* (magic vermilion), *pan para* (magic beetle leave), *Jhatar Kathi Para* (magic stick of broom) and more like this.

It has also been rumoured that this tract is infested by 6 species of snakes and the *gunins* (masters) know 64 separate remedial *mantras* waving off venoms from snake bites. Even *mantras*, for banishing ghosts are also heard of. An example of a *jalpara mantra* in cited here:

Jal Jal Jaleswari Ganga Bhagirath
Bhagirath Gangar marte to sarathi
Haste te koria jal dilum amuker gaye
Amuker ghar chhar, dore chhar, behali swamir kol chhar.
Amar ei jal para siggir lag
Kar dohai? Devi ma Ban bibir dohai lag.[22]

(Water water the goddess of water Ganga Bhagirathi. Bhagirath, the Charioter of Ganga on earth I sprinkle water by hand on one's body leave one's room, leave one's door, leave one's husband's intimacy this my magic water may work immediately whose order? Ma Banbibi's order.)

A group of people known as '*gunin*' has a huge stock of myriad numbers of *mantra-tantra* even today.

Adivasi Culture

When the Sundarban area was gradually developing, the landlords and Nilkar sahib (indigo merchants European), brought various Adivasi tribes from Santal Parganas, Ranchi, Chotanagpur, Purulia of Bihar as also from Odisha as labourers. Although they belonged to separate social groups, after coming to Sundarban and living side by side with the Hindu and Muslim societies, their sectoral prudence began to fade away to some extent. In his novel, '*Aranyak*' Bibhutivushan Bandyopadhyay, has told us about king Doborupanna Virbarddi, who with great pride declares that his family descends from the Surya Bansa (Sun family). Once upon a time, their kingdom extended over hills, forests and the whole world. Their family does not bear any history of cultivation. It is only hunting that tops all other professions.[23] The tribal people delve into a world of their past glorious days. On festive days, they draw pictures of bow, arrow, axe and lancet around their rooms with the help of a rice provider. Each of the houses is decorated with red flags, either of paper or cloth to remember the past glorious days of their lost kingdom. They cannot accept farming as an occupation from the very core of their heart. Till today, their heart seeks for preys in the forest. The Adivasi festivals start from the month of Vadra (August-September) few of them are as follows:

Karampuja

The Santals, Bedia and Oraons of Sundarban celebrate Karampuja with grandeur. The celebration is either on the *ekadashi* of bright lunar, half of vadra, or the last day of vadra. The main object of this worship is a branch of a karamtra, and various types of grains. Karamandja of the tribals is a cultivation-centred rural festival — The principal performance of Dharam Karam is to glorify its excellence.[24] A detailed discussion has been made in '*Banglar loko devata and Samaj Sanskriti*' by Devabrata Naskar, which is worth mentioning work in this aspect.

Tusu Festival

Tribal people believe that if they worship Tusu Devi, the goddess of food, there will be no shortage of food in the family throughout the year. The main worship is done on the Paush Sankranti day (the last day of Paush month). The idol resembles either that of goddess 'Ganga' or goddess 'Laxmi'. An idol is posited on a small earthen *sara* or plate.

Incense stick, lamp, flower, milk are the objects of offerings and either the male or female member or both can worship the goddess. The worship continues throughout the night accompanied by various devotional songs. These songs hold the real spirit of the tribal society.[25]

Vitarghar Puja

The tribal people dwellings in the Sundarbans of 24 Parganas, celebrate special worship for their ancestors which is known as 'Vitarghar Puja'. Vitarghar means a sanctified room of the house, where the souls of the ancestors are believed to be locked in. This room is usually used as the prayer room of the family. Whenever the dwellers are on a move from their house for an auspicious purpose, they first offer their prayers in this room and then only go out of the house.[26] However, the original tribal people usually observe many other festivals, which are not found in this locality.

The history of the mentality and the way of thinking of a sect is their real history. The high roads of civilization do not keep the records of the true pictures of society. The true picture is recorded in the alleyways of history. The habits, celebrations, festivals pala-parban, songs and lyrics, rituals of the downtrodden peoples of the society need true analyses. And then only the true reflection of the land and its culture will be unveiled. Shibsankar Mitra in his book writes "Unique is this Sundarban . . . but more unique is the people of Sundarban. They face thousand and one disastrous situation like waggling through the brine water and brine silt, they fight inch by inch with ferocious wild animals and reptiles for life and death, they breast cyclones and giant whirlpools and still live on. Not only they live, but they also collect their food regularly from these forested tracts with their robust physique and a strong set and determined mind."[27]

Again, in the story 'Sundarbaner chhata-bari-lathi' he has made their nesa (addiction to liquor) more susceptible to their socio-economic crises, than their occupations — out of 200 households, 175 households have windows from the ravages of the man caters. But not only the tigers are the guiltiest, the young men's eagerness to venturing into the forest and urge for fishing, are also equally responsible for these calamities.[28] It is clear then, that there exists a constant battle between the forest and the human locality. The question of responsibility between man and animal yet goes unanswered. Both are endangered but succumb to their necessities. As such they beget trouble from each other.

In the short stories by Monoj Basu about Bada locality, like 'Bada banergaan', 'Bana marmar', 'Prithibi Kader?', 'Bagh', 'Vatchor' etc. the smell of sweat and blood of the people of Sundarban can be traced. Saktipada Rajguru, the storyteller of Sundarban based issues, travelled through the islands of Sundarban for a long period. He got himself accustomed to the daily living of the people of the land and felt the agony of their struggle in the heart of his heart. According to him — the people of Sundarban live a different life — they have imbibed a rudimentary set-up for living. Their struggle for life is also to some extent reproductive.[29] Their struggle for life has been well reflected in 'Bagda' by Baren Gangopadhya, 'Vaat', 'Behula' by Mahesweta Devi, 'Rijudar songe Sundarbone' by Buddhadev Guha, 'Jal Jongaler Kabya', by Sunil Gongopadhaya. The restrictions, sorrow and grief of these marginal people have been reflected in each of the writings of Sohorab Hossain, Vikas Kanti Middya, Utpalendu Mondal etc.

However, from the very beginning of creation, man has been regulating his surrounding environment in various ways. It is only the man, out of all living beings, who can cope up with all types of anti-climatic environments. His cultural background helps him to imbibe techniques of symbiosis with the surroundings. The ecological set up helps to grow a man-environment relationship which culminates in setting-up various cultural environments. The man is related to the ecological balance with strong inner bondage that regulates his various notions and activities. Culture is the reflection of a harmonious balance between man and nature.

The forest culture is the very age-old cultural expression of human life. The initial hunting and food gathering livelihood, which the primitive people imbibed, was naturally dependent on the forest. The life and livelihood analyses of the people of Sundarbans show that men here, have established an amicable relationship with the trees and forest environment through various festivals, rituals, faith and celebrations, and the same relationship continues its spell without any break. The tribals collect flowers, fruits, roots, tubers, creepers, leaves, wood and fulfil their daily needs from the forest. Their most important occupations are animal hunting and honey collection. Forest Ecology and Forest Culture are closely interlinked. Not only that they have mutually been influenced by each other. Their separation from the forest will culminate in cultural disorganization.

NOTES AND REFERENCES

1. Dr. Promit Roychowdhury, "Dakshin Chobbis Porganar Swadhinatar Songramer Ruprekha", Gokul Chandra Das (ed.): *24 Parganar Ancholik Itihas O Sanskriti*, Progressive Publishers, Kolkata, November 2004, p. 66.
2. *Ibid.*, pp. 66-67.
3. Santosh Kumar Barman, "Oupanibeshik Amole 24 Pargana Jelar Krishi Samporko O Tebhaga Andolon", Chandra Das (ed.): *24 Parganar Ancholik Itihas O Sanskriti*, Progressive Publishers, Kolkata, November 2004, p. 80.
4. Dulal Chowdhury, "Sundarboner Bonodevata O Byaghro Sonskriti", Gokul Chandra Das (ed.): *24 Parganar Ancholik Itihas O Sanskriti*, Progressive Publishers, Kolkata, November 2004, p. 149.
5. Ranjan Chakraborty, *O Indrakumar Mistri, Sundarboner Orthoniti Jan Sanskriti O Poribesh*, Reader Service, Kolkata, January 2007, p. 38.
6. Gokul Chandra Das, "Unish Shotoker Chobbis Pargana: Samaj O Orthonitir Rupantar", Gokul Chandra Das (ed.): *24 Parganar Ancholik Itihas O Sanskriti*, Progressive Publishers, Kolkata, November 2004, p. 31.
7. *Ibid.*, p. 31 & Resely, H.H., *Tribes and Castes of Bengal*, Vol. 1, Kolkata, 1891, p. 183.
8. Ranjan Chakraborty, *O Indrakumar Mistri, Sundarboner Orthoniti Jan Sanskriti O Poribesh*, Reader Service, Kolkata, January 2007, p. 39.
9. Narottom Haldar, "Gangaridi O Ganga Nagar Prosonge", Gokul Chandra Das (ed.): *24 Parganar Ancholik Itihas O Sanskriti*, Progressive Publishers, Kolkata, November 2004, p. 10.
10. Gokul Chandra Das, "Unish Shotoker Chobbis Pargana: Samaj O Orthonitir Rupantar", Gokul Chandra Das (ed.): *24 Parganar Ancholik Itihas O Sanskriti*, Progressive Publishers, Kolkata, November 2004, p. 32.
11. *Ibid.*, pp. 32, 33.
12. Ranjan Chakraborty, *O Indrakumar Mistri, Sundarboner Orthoniti Jan Sanskriti O Poribesh*, 'Ancholik Orthoniti' Reader Service, Kolkata, 2007, p. 39.
13. Sanat Kumar Naskar, "Dakshin Chobbis Parganar Lok Sanskriti Bhugol", Gokul Chandra Das (ed.): *24 Parganar Ancholik Itihas O Sonskriti*, Progressive Publishers, Kolkata, November 2004, p. 238.
14. *Ibid.*, pp. 241-43.
15. Wahed Ali, *Bonbibir Bon* (Commonly Popular).
16. Ranjan Chakraborty, O Indrakumar Mistri, *Sundarboner Orthoniti Jan Sanskriti O Poribesh*, Reader Service, Kolkata, 2007, pp. 109-14.
17. Haridev, Ray, *Mangal Kavya* (Commonly Popular).
18. Debabrata Naskar, *Banglar Lok Devata O Samaj Sonskriti*, Ananda Publishers, Kolkata, October 2018, p. 236.
19. *Ibid.*, pp. 237, 238.
20. Commonly Popular.
21. Ranjan Chakraborty, O Indrakumar Mistri, *Sundarboner Orthoniti Jan Sanskriti O Poribesh*, 'Geeti Pala' Reader Service, Kolkata, 2007, p. 153.
22. *Ibid.*, p. 14.
23. *Ibid.*, p. 125.
24. Debabrata Naskar, *Banglar Lok Devata O Samaj Sonskriti*, Ananda Publishers, Kolkata, October 2018, pp. 239-42.
25. Ranjan Chakraborty, O Indrakumar Mistri, *Sundarboner Orthoniti Jan Sanskriti O Poribesh*, Reader Service, Kolkata, 2007, pp. 129-30.

26. Debabrata Naskar, *Banglar Lok Devata O Samaj Sonskriti*, Ananda Publishers, Kolkata, October 2018, p. 249.
27. Rajiv Ahmed (ed.), *Sundarboner Itihas* (1st Part), Gatidhara, Dacca, 2012, p. 202.
28. Shivsankar Mitra, *Sundarboner Chhata-Bari-Lathi*, Sundarboner Samogra, Ananda Publishers, Kolkata, 2009, p. 423.
29. Subrata Chottopadhya, *Sundarboner Patobhumite Bangla Chhoto Golpo O Uponyas*, Tothyo O Sonskriti Bibhag, West Bengal, 2000, p. 349.

4

Socio-Cultural Changes on Traditional Medical Practice of Santal Community

Mohan Haldar

Before Independence from till today Santal community is including in the ethnic group circle. Their economic development was not healthy and they lived in an inaccessible jungle. They were living an unsafe life devoured by wild animals and birds. They have to face disease, their ideas as to the origin and causation of disease their superstitions and fears, their various attempts to appease and satisfy the malevolent powers supposed to be responsible for disease the professional medicine men, especially the Ojha and his doing his magic and religious endeavours. Here I focused on Socio-Cultural changes in traditional medical practices of the Santal community. Traditional medicine is a complex matter that involves indigenous groups, along with traditional local cultures and based on indigenous knowledge. Western medicine has brought destruction and discredit to traditional medicine. This process can also be understood as a form of competition that was part of colonialism and post-Western colonialism.

Approximately 8.08 per cent of the population of India has been designated as Scheduled Tribe. The term refers to the communities specified by the President of India under Article 342 of the Constitution. It is an administrative term that is area-specific and envisaged to reflect the level of socio-economic development rather than a distinct ethnic status.[1] Here I have discussed on Social and Cultural Life of the Santal community from medical perspectives. Also, I have seen that how to work out traditional medicine in this community? The Santals are one of the oldest ethnic groups and descendants. They lived in inaccessible jungles in a hospitable climate guided by the transparent rhythm of natural bodies like sun, rain and wind in the inaccessible past.[2] The Santals are a jungly people, they have to be classified as agriculturists but they have even now a good deal of the roaming nature of their ancestors in them. They like an open-air life sleep outside and live more in the open than inside their houses. Their villages are much more sanitary than what one generally sees among the neighbouring races. The houses are put up around a courtyard, into which door lead. The Santals' houses are not sanitary. They have only one door and no windows. They are consequently dark.[3] They were living an unsafe life devoured by wild animals and birds. They are people who believe in many superstitions and are very moral. In the glorious life of nature, they rely on the mercy of invisible forces and forces that guide them in every aspect of their lives. Religion and magic were considered sacred and unholy which governed and controlled their lives.

As primitive people, they were afraid of two things, disease and gods and spirits are essential features of primitive people and most likely they extend hand in hand. So many evil spirits were blamed for the disease.[4] The health standard of the Santal is good than that of the other tribes like Mahali, Munda, Kharia, Lodha, Birhor, Saura, Sabara, Juanga etc. They excel other tribes in terms of the environment as well as personal hygiene. As regards the sanitary habits, they are neat and clean yet they suffer from various types of diseases. All the tribes primitive or advanced consider disease as pernicious and detrimental to normal life. Disease means illness, suffering, fear, expenditure, unhappiness foreign and inimical to man.[5]

They have to face disease, their ideas as to the origin and causation of disease their superstitions and fears, their various attempts to appease and satisfy the malevolent powers supposed to be responsible for disease by the professional medicine men, especially the Ojha and his doing magic and religious endeavours. Santal becomes an Ojha a description is given of the annual village course in Ojha Science and of various matters connected with this a number of songs used when this course is finished are recorded; specimens of the Ojha's *mantras* and *jharnis* are also given.[6]

The Santal Ojhas play a very vital role in catering to the health care needs of thousands of their population. They use some methods that have support from religious beliefs to cure people suffering from disease and disabilities. They are capable of demonstrating an amazing range of medical skills and expertise that extends from treating emergencies like poisonous bites and safe delivery to curing asthma and their bronchial

This process can also be understood as a form of competition that was part of colonialism and post-Western colonialism time.[15] There is scarcely a grown-up Santal man who has not some knowledge of the kind of medicine treated here as is only natural considering the lack of real professional help amongst the people, everyone has to some extent on himself. One man knows a remedy for cough, another for diarrhoea, a third for snake bite, and so on. It is reported to have helped some then why not others? Some are regular specialists in the treatment of tuberculosis or venereal disease, charging specialists' fees. Some persons may have established quite a reputation and are sought by patients from far away.

Some know remedies for several diseases and a few have taken up seriously medicine as a profession and are all-round medicine men who try to or profess to cure all diseases and ills not caused by supernatural agencies by bongas or by witches. For most, it is a mode of earning just a little outside the ordinary a means of getting good food and a drink now and then. For some, it may mean a good income in addition to their agricultural earning.[16]

Lack of access to modern health care facilities either because of physical inaccessibility of the Primary Health Centres and hospitals, ill-equipped health centres or not accessing modern health care facilities for several other reasons lead to the incidence of disease. While the latter could include many reasons there is a tendency in the literature to attribute such lack of access to customary and erroneous tribal health beliefs. While poverty, depletion of forest resources are cited as explanations that contribute to ill health, studies of the specificity of these processes involved are lacking. Thus disease and illness among the tribals are not examined in the larger political economy context. The prevalence of malnutrition for instance among the tribal is often attributed to faulty food habits, lack of knowledge on balanced diet etc., thus underplaying its social causes.[17] Modern medicine has not replaced the traditional and spiritual medicine that had been destroyed so there was nothing left to protect them. In practice, drugs and medicine never came, hospitals or nursing facilities were inaccessible for various reasons and geographical or racial separation.[18] The ingredients are mostly what are to be found in the forests of the Santal community. Bodding remembered that only two are of clear European origin that of Cod-liver-oil for night blindness, quite recently received through missionaries and carbolic acid used against syphilis.[19] Some may have originally come from one of the Hindu systems of medicine. Those who have studied these will be able to tell whether this is so or not. Some Santal Ojhas have learned from non-Santal Ojhas, from some belonging to the *kamar* (blacksmith), *dom* and other castes, also from Paharias and even Jolhas.

It may in this connection not be out of the way to mention, that the traditions of the Santals state that their ancestors have learned ojha 'science' from Kamru Guru undoubtedly a non-Santal, very likely a Hindu. The impression that what the Santal ojha has learned from Kamru guru, whoever he may be, is not so much medicine as magic, *mantras*, charms, with which to subdue or drive away from the supposed malevolent. Kamru guru has in any case been a teacher of more than medicine. It might be remarked that his followers the ojhas of the present-day base their reputation as doctors just as much or perhaps even more on their supposed ability to deal with the supernatural powers as on their knowledge of medicine.

Many years ago a dog famed for his exploits as a snake killer. Once during my absence from home this dog was badly bitten by a poisonous snake on his neck, Bodding afterward told swelled up to a large size and all were sure the dog would succumb. Then the dog was seen to a place in the compound and there are some herbs or other, whereupon he recovered.[20] The Tribal medicine men adopt various methods for the diagnosis and treatment of different diseases. Usually, they initiate the diagnosis by feeling the patient's pulse and heartbeat. Apart from that they observe and recognize the symptoms of the diagnosis. In this way out of their own experience and knowledge, they easily define the disease that a patient suffers from sometimes for the sake of diagnosis of ailments of the broken bone or intestinal disorder they touch and feel the aching body part. Urine tests are also done for certain diseases like jaundice, stomach pain, tuberculosis etc. In the patient's urine, mustard oil is put. Depending on how the colour of urine changes in what direction the urine mixes with the oil, how it spreads and whether bubbles are created the medicine men make all the diagnoses of the disease. Here he plays the role of a pathologist without using the microscope. The tribal people have pharmacopeia of their own for their manifold diseases like malaria, smallpox, cholera, leprosy, scabies, venereal disease, bowel complaints, influenza, optima etc.[21]

Among the ingredients used for smallpox are the conical prickles of the simol tree and warts found on the leaves of the Ficus glomerata, Roxb both likely reminding a Santal of the smallpox eruptions. The remedies just mentioned may be classified as belonging to what is called homeopathy magic. They have a fair number of these especially for the many kinds of what is called bai, convulsions, cramps, and an involuntary state or malevolent of the body or any part of the body over which one has no control.[22]

Take tuberculosis of the lungs. As may be expected they do not recognize the nature of the disease in its first stages. It is then called cough of some sort generally getting a name according to the peculiar sound of the coughing or the amount of phlegm expectorated. In its more advanced stages, it is mostly called *dhok*; this name is also used for some form of bronchitis. Hemoptysis sets in all other names are discarded and it is called raj rog, the king disease that is not the disease of kings, but the sovereign disease. The ordinary Santal often thinks that an entirely new disease has taken possession of the patient when the spitting of blood commences. Tuberculosis in other parts of the body than in the lungs is naturally not recognized as such.

Any venereal disease may be called *gurmi*, a name meaning heat and also used for some other quite different ailment. During the later stages when sores break out, these sores have different names according to site and appearance and are generally considered to be due to different diseases.

A disease like cholera has many names. Their regular name for this is hawa duk, lit. air affection, a name that points to the supposed origin or spreading of the disease. The most common name is, however, maran lac odok stomach out coming. Another name is arhaia, lit. two and a half viz. pohor periods of four hours each the ten hours. This name refers to the rapid course of fatal cholera. Murhuc jom leprocy is often called maran rog, the disease. Guti smallpox is frequently referred to as latu kasra large scabies.[23] Tuberculosis is becoming fearfully prevalent among them in spite of their outdoor life. Their lack of understanding of nature and the infectiousness of this disease makes them careless. When the disease has entered a family it generally reaps a fearful harvest. Leprosy was not common among the Santals formerly during the last generation it has become alarmingly.

Bodding's wife who is a qualified doctor tells me that in her experience malaria is prevalent far ahead of all other diseases also among the Santals. Next come skin diseases such as scabies, eczema, ringworm etc. and bowel complaints. Dysentery is very common and often fatal.

Eye disease is very frequent and many have lost their sight through sheer ignorance and want of timely treatment. It might be noted that the

Santal generally has splendid eyesight cataract is very common and often seem to afflict people at an earlier age than is usual in our countries.

Pneumonia and pleurisy are of much more frequent occurrence than one would expect in a hot climate, the same may be said of rheumatic complaints their exposed life and carelessness as to exposure explains this. Some of the horrible diseases caused by Filaria, so commonly met within other parts of India and also fairly frequently seen amongst Hindus living in the same country are very rare among the santals. Among the so-called infectious diseases common in Europe most occur also among the santals with a couple of exceptions.[24]

Among epidemic diseases, the Santals recognize four or five cholera, small-pox, measles, plague and chicken-pox. As regards the plague (with a borrowed name called *mahamari*) they have fortunately not had it among themselves and consequently have only vague ideas regarding it, it has, however, been near enough to them to let them know its deadliness.

As regards chickenpox, it is fairly common among them; this is not, however, classified as disom duk on account of its mild character and medicines are scarcely used. If anyone should become very ill or even die from this, it will be thought to be real smallpox with which this disease is often confused by them and it is then treated accordingly.

Their ideas about cholera have been mentioned elsewhere; they know its dangerous character and are very much afraid to it. It will be found among the 'prescriptions' that some medicine men warn against in any way touching the patient and against taking food or drinking water in their houses and the person who takes the medicine to the house is advised to have a quid of ginger and some other stuff in his mouth as a prophylactic. About smallpox, they know the seriousness of the disease its common course and symptoms and they are very much afraid of it.

In the month of Magh (January-February, the month when the Santals change from the old into the new year), the entire male population of the village at a day fixed and after the usual preparation of the village, at a day fixed and after the usual preparations and abstinence, at the end of the village street sacrifice a black female kid and a black puilet and bury them there. At the same time, they make vows to the spirits of the village boundaries that they will give them certain sacrifices next year if they remain free from disease during the whole year. This precaution refers to all kinds of disease both among the men and beast also against misfortunes and accidents but especially also to smallpox and cholera.

The sacrifices are followed up by giving some pills to every person found in the village. These pills are made by grinding some 46 different kinds of medicinal stuff and mixing them with country liquor. Where the sacrifices are performed they are divided into as many portions as there are households in the village whereupon the ojha prepares some rice water in a leaf cup. With the whole in a winnowing fan, the whole assembly starts for the villages and entering every courtyard beginning from the village street end the ojha sprinkles the waterpots with the rice water whereupon the pills are given.[25]

The roof may permit some ventilation but much is left to be desired here. As a rule, they cook their food outside but always have a fireplace inside. During the cold season cook their food inside the results being that the house especially at night is suffocating full smoke. As regards food they are scrupulously clean both when preparing it and when eating. They wash and scour their plates and cups; if they use leaf cups and leaf plates these are thrown away after use and never used twice. Hence discussed on traditional life of the santal community and how to work out Ojha in this community. Ojha became known as a guru. However, Santals have developed advanced pharmacopeia of their own by incorporating the medicaments from Siddha and Ayurvedic systems of medicine.

NOTES AND REFERENCES

1. C.R. Bijoy, *The Adivasis of India*, 1999, https://www.researchgate.net/publication/295315241
2. Subash Chandra Karua, *Traditional Healing Practices among the Sandals and their Relevance: An Ethno Medicine Study*, Indian History Congress, 2015, p. 555.
3. P.O. Bodding, *Studies in Santal Medicine and Connected Folklore*, Kolkata: The Asiatic Society, 2001, p. 145.
4. Subash Chandra Karua, *Traditional Healing Practices among the Sandals and their Relevance: An Ethno Medicine Study*, Indian History Congress, 2015, p. 555.
5. *Ibid.*
6. P.O. Bodding, *Studies in Santal Medicine and Connected Folklore*, Kolkata: The Asiatic Society, 2001, p. iii.
7. Subash Chandra Karua, *Traditional Healing Practices among the Sandals and their Relevance: An Ethno-medicine Study*, Indian History Congress, 2015, p. 561.
8. P.O. Bodding, *Studies in Santal Medicine and Connected Folklore*, Kolkata: The Asiatic Society, 2001, p. 135.
9. P. Cianconi, C.B. Lesmana, "Health in Tribes: Global Crises and Resilience", Ed. Ranjana Ray, *Tribal Health Care System*, Kolkata: The Asiatic Society, 2019, p. 60.
10. *Ibid.*, p. 61.

11. Subash Chandra Karua, *Traditional Healing Practices among the Sandals and their Relevance: An Ethno Medicine study*, Indian History Congress, 2015, p. 560.
12. P. Cianconi, C.B. Lesmana, "Health in Tribes: Global Crises and Resilience", Ed. Ranjana Ray, *Tribal Health Care System*, Kolkata: The Asiatic Society, 2019, p. 61.
13. *Ibid.*, p. 63.
14. *Ibid.*, p. 64.
15. *Ibid.*, p. 66.
16. P.O. Bodding, *Studies in Santal Medicine and Connected Folklore*, Kolkata: The Asiatic Society, 2001, p. 134.
17. Arima Mishra and Sumita Sarma, *Understanding Health and Illness among Tribal Communities in Orissa*, Indian Anthropological Association, 2011, p. 5, https://www.jstor.org/stable/41921930
18. P. Cianconi and C.B. Lesmana, "Health in Tribes: Global Crises and Resilience", Ed. Ranjana Ray, *Tribal Health Care System*, Kolkata: The Asiatic Society, 2019, p. 67.
19. P.O. Bodding, *Studies in Santal Medicine and Connected Folklore*, Kolkata: The Asiatic Society, 2001, p. 136.
20. *Ibid.*, p. 137.
21. Subash Chandra Karua, *Traditional Healing Practices among the Sandals and their Relevance: An Ethno Medicine Study*, Indian History Congress, 2015, p. 559.
22. P.O. Bodding, *Studies in Santal Medicine and Connected Folklore*, Kolkata: The Asiatic Society, 2001, p. 138.
23. *Ibid.*, p. 141.
24. *Ibid.*, p. 142.
25. P.O. Bodding, *Studies in Santal Medicine and Connected Folklore*, Kolkata: The Asiatic Society, 2001, p. 144.

5

Criminal Tribe to Primitive Tribal Group

Ecological Changes of the 'Lodha' Tribe in West Bengal

Kausar Ali

The Lodha tribe of West Bengal is considered a Particularly Vulnerable Tribal Group (PVTG). The Lodha was mostly known as a hunter-gatherer community. Gradually shifting their profession from hunting to agriculture, for which they have to leave their house early in the morning and return in the evening. British historians have expressed different views about the origin of Lodha Caste. M.A. Sherring has written in his book called '*Hindu Tribes and Caste as Representative in Benaras*' that the people of Lodha caste originally sold the bark of a tree called 'Lodh' which was used for colouring and medicine, hence this person is called Lodha (Sherring, 1878).[1] Jhon C. Nesfield has written in his book '*Brief View of Caste System*' that the word 'Lodha' is derived from the word clod-breaker in English. Here clod means 'lod' and breaker means 'ha', adding this form the word Lodha (Nesfield, 1882).[2] W.W. Hunter identified them as a Hindu caste (Hunter, 1876).[3] This caste is an ancient Hindu caste living in India. In the ancient Verna system, this caste was considered to be Kshatriya Varna and was known as Lodh. Over time, this caste came to be known as Lodha and was identified as a hardworking farmer. During the Colonial period, the Lodha caste has been considered the dominant cultivator. The Lodha tribal in Sundarbans is mainly dependent on natural resources. The present occupation is forest produce collection and agricultural day labourer. The Lodhas, especially the women, go to the forest to collect various items like wood, creepers, different types of forest resources etc. According to their views, '*earning is most essential than education*'. This community people can speak both their traditional language and Bengali language.

In the Indian map, the tribal people are found within or adjacent to the forest areas. Their entire life has been rotating round the forest. So they had made an intimate relationship with the forest ecology for their survival.

In West Bengal, the Lodhas are anthropologically not only more interesting but they had also played the most notable role in the history of forest-dwelling communities of this region. At present, they mainly reside in the Midnapore district in a multi-ethical environment with Santhals, Kheria, Oraon, Bhumij, Mahils, Mundas, Mahtos, Brahmans, and Sadgops. Except for Midnapore, they also lived in the Mayurbhanj district of Odisha and East Singhbhum district of Jharkhand. According to the 1971 Census report, the Lodhas were merged with Savar and Kheria tribe to dilute their independent identity. Now they were termed as Lodha-Savar and Kheria-Savar (Devi, 1997).[4] Meanwhile, since 1956, the Lodhas came to be recognized as a Scheduled Tribe, and later they were categorized as a primitive tribal group in 1982. According to the 1981 Census report, in West Bengal Lodha population was 53,717 (Sharma, 1995).[5] Akin to many forest-dwellers, Lodhas also lived mainly in the jungle of Midnapore district and depended on hunting, and collection of edible minor forest products like root, nuts, tubers etc. For many years, in rural Bengal, the collection and trading of jungle products were mainly existed by Bhumijs, Santhals, and Lodhas (Samadar, 1998).[6]

The Lodhas were involved in few subsidiary occupations and their major professions are directly linked with the economy of their surrounding ecology. From the jungle they catch snakes and sell the skin to merchants. Collection of firewood and mat-making is an important economic pursuit of Lodhas, especially the aged persons of the community (Paty, 2003).[7] Fish catching during the rains or autumn and selling it to their neighbours is another occasional vocation of Lodhas. They used to grow tusser cocoons from the Asan trees and collect mahua flowers or fruits to supplement their income (Bhowmick, 1990).[8] They also used wild fruits, roots, and flesh of small animals as the content of their meal. Thus their food habit and economic activities were very closely associated with their habitat. The large number of clan names of the Lodhas are associated and identified with the forest resources and animals such as *mallik* (kind of fish), *dandpath* (tiger), *pramanik* (a kind of bird) etc. Their God/Goddess, folktales, myths and songs reflect their close relationship with the forest. The *sal* and *Mahua* trees are considered as their village deity. Joychandi or Chandi believed to reside in the jungle, is the deity of Lodhas. Thus Lodha's socio-economic life, culture, and traditions were always interrelated with forest. This was the earlier pattern of their tribal life.

The Lodhas as Criminal Tribe

The British government was facing many administrative difficulties like murder, dacoity etc. It was a feeling of government that these offenses were generally committed by some communities who were hereditarily criminal by profession (Gupta, 1952).[9] This could only be controlled by some strict law. So the British government passed the Criminal Tribes Act in 1871, to control the criminal activities of such groups. An amendment of this Act in 1897 empowered the local administration even to segregate the children of those groups aged between (5-20 years) from their parents. The Act made such offenses non-bailable. In 1911 made it compulsory for the members of these tribes to give their finger prints and to report the change of address to the nearest police station. It authorized the government to restrict their movement within particular areas. On the whole, it placed certain communities under strict supervision. The background of the Lodha's being brought under the purview of the Act was as follows — In 1900 there were many criminal cases like theft, burglary, dacoity etc. committed by Lodhas. It created problems for the administration. So eventually Lodhas were categorized and declared a criminal tribe in 1916 by the colonial government (Bhowmick, 1969).[10]

In the year 1937, the Criminal Tribal Committee headed by V.N. Tiwari observed that the criminal activities of these tribes were the result of the harmful social atmosphere. So it recommended repealing this Act. But only in 1952, the Criminal Tribes' Act was repealed. Hence about 2,71,02,180 people of 153 communities, including the Lodhas were freed from the stigma of criminality (Gupta, 1976).[11] At this time, with the formation of the Backward Commission, the Government of India made suggestions as they should be called De-notified *Vimukta-Janajati* (ex-criminal) and should be included in the category of either Scheduled Tribe/Scheduled Caste or other backword community. At the same time, it also declared that rehabilitation should be provided to them. Immediately after the revocation of the Criminal Tribe Act the initial measures were taken by the Home (Police) Department covering all the Lodha-centred villages in the district of Midnapore. Some administrators and few social workers arranged regular meetings and discussions for creating awareness among the people about the issues of Lodhas socialization and rehabilitation process. It was much appreciated by the Lodhas themselves because after this move the torture and harassment by the police department were immediately stopped. Soon the government started many schemes and projects among the Lodhas. Some voluntary organizations also started welfare schemes by receiving financial assistance from the government. Moreover, a number of multipurpose cooperatives and campuses were formed. Some lands as well as agricultural implements, seeds and bullocks were provided to transform them into a settled agrarian community. At the same time various subsidies like goats, cows were made available to them. To raise these unfortunate people from the abysmal depths of ignorance and backwardness, Dr. P.K. Bhowmick an anthropologist played a significant role. He formed many self-help groups, village committees, vocational and educational schools and hostels (Bhowmick, 1990).[12] The above efforts helped the Lodhas to be changed from hunter-gathering people to agricultural ones. All these efforts intended to provide them a stable economic background as well as to introduce cultivation among them at par with all other progressive communities of the region.

Action and Reaction

The greater society more or less failed to rationalize the changed image of the tribe and continued to suspect them for their past activities. The honest intention and effort made to rehabilitate the Lodhas to the life of dignity and self-respect did not, however, fully succeed (Bhowmick, 1982).[13] It proved the saying that a "lost good name is never retrieved" (De Leo, 2003: 54).[14] Furthermore, the non-Lodha communities become jealous of Lodhas to some extent for the care and assistance that was received from the ongoing schemes. Out of reaction, other communities started to indulge in the killing of the Lodha people. Though Lodha-killing had been a regular feature in West Bengal, but since 1961 a spurt in it was visible. In that years a mass attack was made on the Lodhas by other tribal regional groups. This was repeated in 1968, 1979, 1981, 1982, 1984, 1986 and 1989 (Bhowmick, 1982).[15] The general trend was to impute the blame on the Lodhas for any or every crime committed in the locality and to indulge in their killing. Mahasweta Devi, a well-known human rights activist, who works with the Lodhas in West Bengal has presented a brief analysis of the situation. She has observed that though Lodhas were de-notified in 1950, the rural population still thought of them in the same way. Whenever there is theft or dacoity, it is customary for the police to harass the Lodhas. "*Although it is well known to the police and the administration that the upper-class village worthies are the brain behind these efforts, the Lodhas being only their tools and the receiver of the stolen goods are the real criminals, but on one dares to touch them*" (Devi, 1997: 116).[16]

At present other communities also admit that in comparison to the past their criminal activity is less than 2-3 per cent instead of 90 per cent in the locality. But a deep prejudice prevails among the neighbours, starting from the children up to the educated people, the social workers and even those social scientists who worked directly with the Lodhas. They are still presenting the Lodha first of all as an ex-criminal tribe, instead of a Scheduled Tribe or simply a primitive tribal group. The burning example of Chuni Kotal — a 27-year old graduate girl from the Lodha community. The stigma of the criminal tribe is so deep-rooted that she has always been harassed by society. The harassment forced Chuni to commit suicide on 16 December, 1982 (Devi, 2002).[17] This single incident may be an eye-opener and sufficient for explaining their social negligence and exploitation by the civilized world for centuries. Moreover, the Lodhas still find it very difficult to adapt themselves to an unusual system that was so different from the original one when they lived in the forest. It has been found that they prefer working day labour rather to cultivate their land because cultivation required time and patience which they lacked. So what happens is that they sell their land instead of honey or paddy. Similarly, they failed to maintain the cow, goat and bullock which had been offered to them by the government. Often, they tended to sell their cattle to others. Actually, due to their traditional link with forest ecology, they still find a forest-based economy rather than an agricultural economy. In recent few years, the government is trying to provide and restore their original environment through reforestation programme in some selected areas, but there are very few who are enjoying this ecology because it is also now irrelevant to them because of the rupture that had been already convenient to their livelihood. Over the six decades, a huge amount has been spent in the name of Lodhas but we find that the community has still low literacy, instability and lives a life of acute poverty.

Conclusion

The Lodha tribe of West Bengal faces structural discrimination within the society. Unlike the Scheduled Castes, Scheduled Tribes are a product of marginalization based on ethnicity. In India, the Scheduled tribes' population is around 84.3 million and is considered to be socially and economically disadvantaged. Their percentage in the population and numbers, however, from state to state. They are mainly landless with little control over resources such as land, forest, and water. They constitute a large proportion of agricultural labourers, casual labourers, plantation labourers, industrial labourers etc. This has resulted in poverty among them, low level of education, poor health and reduced access to healthcare services. They belong to the poorest strata of society and severe health problems. Thus becomes clear that a tribe rooted in a lifestyle and culture built around a forest gets distorted when they are evicted from their natural setting. Howsoever honest be the subsequent effort of socialization the tribe, unfortunately, fails to acclimatize itself to the new setting and way of life. The problem is compounded when the greater society fails to dispel the prejudice against the community which creates meanwhile. One may ultimately be forced to conclude that displacement of the forest people from their ecology for earning greater revenue or to privilege the affluent and mighty at the cost of the poor tribes ultimately marginalize the poor and benighted whose rehabilitation turns out to be an uphill and mostly a failed venture. Though traditionally Lodhas are socially discriminated against as criminal tribes by the non-tribal people, they only communicated during the profit-making transaction.

NOTES AND REFERENCES

1. Sherring, M.A. (1878). *Hindu Tribes and Castes as Represented in Benaras*, Calcutta: Trubner and Co., pp. 348-349.
2. Nesfield, John C. (1882). *Brief View on the Caste System of North-Western Provinces and Oudh*, Allahabad: North-Western province and Oudh government press, p. 14.
3. Hunter, W.W. (1876). *A Statistical Account of Bengal*, Vol. 3, London: Trubner & Co., p. 50.
4. Devi, Mahasweta (1997). *The Lodhas of West Bengal*, New Delhi: Seagull Publication Private Limited, p. 114.
5. Sharma, R.C. (1995). *Indian Tribes through the Ages*, Publications Division, Ministry of Information and Broadcasting, New Delhi: Government of India, p. 42.
6. Samadar, Ranbir (1998). *Memory, Identity and Power: Politics in Jungle Mahal-West Bengal, (1899-1950)*, New Delhi: Sangam Publication, p. 37.
7. Paty, Amit Saurabh (2003). *Role and Status of Lodha-aged of West Bengal*, Ranchi: Ranchi University Press, p. 15.
8. Bhowmick, P.K. (1990). *Applied Action Development Anthropology*, Calcutta: Institute of Social Science Research and Applied Anthropology (ISRAA), p. 207.

9. Gupta, R.K. (1952). *The Working of an Act: The Case Studies of the Lodhas and the Karwal Nats since 1952*, vol. 1, Calcutta, New Shakti Press, p. 71.
10. Bhowmick, P.K. (1969). *The Lodhas of West Bengal—A Socio-economic Study*, Calcutta: Punthi Pustak, pp. 10-14.
11. Gupta, R.K., *op. cit.*, p. 72.
12. Bhowmick, P.K. (1990). *Applied Action, op. cit.*, p. 63.
13. Bhowmick, Sarita (1982). *Lodha Odyssey: A Journey between two Worlds, Man and Life*, Vol. 08, Calcutta: Samaj Sevak Sangha Press, pp. 172-74.
14. De Leo, Paulo Francesco (2003). *Bidisa: Role of Voluntary Organization in the Development of Lodha Tribe*, M.A. Dissertation, Ranchi: Department of Anthropology, Ranchi University, p. 54.
15. Bhowmick, Sarita, *op. cit.*, p. 172.
16. Devi, Mahasweta (1997). *op. cit.*, p. 116.
17. Devi, Mahasweta (2002). *Adivasiyo Ke Beech in Jharkhand Persist-2*, Ranchi: Prabhat Khabar, Neutral Publication, p. 4.

6

From Barter to Cash
A Review of Changes in Commercial Activities of the Apatanis of Arunachal Pradesh, 1947-1987

Arindam Ghosh

Arunachal Pradesh is the northeastern state of the Indian Union. This state covers an area of 83,743 sq.km. with a population of almost 14 lakh souls. This state connects three international borders with Bhutan in the west, China in the north and Burma in the east. During colonial rule, it was a part of greater Assam. In independent India, a special agency was formed named North-East Frontier Agency in 1954. The well-known NEFA converted to Union territory and was renamed Arunachal Pradesh in 1972. In 1987, it gained the status of the full-fledged state of the Indian Union.

Trade has always been an important activity in Arunachal Pradesh. The people of Arunachal Pradesh especially those residing in the border areas have been traditionally trading with the neighbouring countries without proper regulatory provisions. This State has always been considered as an isolated territory but people never remained confined to their respective settlement areas. They continuously moved around neighbouring villages, other territories, and even across the border through different trade routes like explorers and travellers. From the very outset, each community of Arunachal took part in these trading activities. Apatanis were one of those who had a well-developed commercial economy. This chapter argues four points:

> Firstly, the well-developed agrarian economy and agricultural surplus provoked the Apatanis to develop their trade and commerce that were local and distant in nature.

Secondly, the traditional unit value system helped the Apatanis to form a decent barter economy.

Thirdly, from 1950 onwards the Apatani valley witnessed drastic changes that led to the transformation of the Apatani economy.

Fourthly, there is a general impression that Arunachal Pradesh was isolated from the rest of India. Since 1950s the coming of outsiders, the growth of the modern economy, and the changes of the commercial route of the Arunachalee people, especially of the Apatanis led to create a cultural link between Arunachalees and the people of the rest of India. The new commercial link turned out to be a major monitoring force for the smooth integration of Arunachal Pradesh with greater India.

Apatanis are the member of the Tibeto-Burma family residing in the Ziro valley in the Lower Subansiri district of Arunachal Pradesh. They have migrated from the Tang-Sangpo valley of Tibet and settled themselves in the areas beyond Khru and Kamla rivers during the Neolithic era. The homeland of the Apatanis has originally consisted of seven large villages, namely *Hang, Hari, Bula, Dutta, Hiza, Mundian-Tage* and *Michi-Bamin*. Later, two towns are emerged, named Old Ziro and Napoli. As per the Census report of 2011, total population of Hopolic is 60,000.

Traditional Trade Relation

Agriculture is the most important economic activity of the Apatanis. The arable land of their valley was full of naturally abundant soil that resulted in yielding crops every year. They evolved deskbound agriculture, chiefly in the form of wet rice cultivation. Besides the cultivation on flooded land, they cultivated a variety of rice called *Timpi Emmo* on the dry land of the valley. As a result, Apatanis were self-sufficient in terms of their requirements and vegetables while their neighbours, Nishyis[1] and Hill Miris[2] were unable to produce sufficient food grains for their consumption. To quote Christoph von Furer-Haimendorf,[3] "while the Apatanis are primary agriculturalists, the Nishyis are indifferent cultivators, mostly without the knowledge of irrigation and terracing, but living in settlement loosely scattered over extensive areas of jungle-covered area."[4] Apatanis' skill as a rice cultivator, therefore, enabled them to supply their neighbours. So, a daily social and economic transaction in the form of barter was developed through the exchange of agricultural surplus. Under the barter system price of an item was usually determined by its immediate necessity instead of value. Rice was usually paid for mithan. In normal years, thirty carrying baskets of rice were equivalent to one full-grown female mithan. In case of scarcity, the value decreased and it became only fifteen baskets. Rice was also obtained on credit and many of the disputes between Apatanis and their Miri neighbours resulted from trade deals that began with the sale of rice on credit.[5]

In the region of eastern Himalayas, Apatanis were very popular for their handmade clothes which were very good in quality. These clothes were well-liked in the villages of the Subansiri region as well as in Tibet. The Nishyis were solely a key factor behind their reputation. Though Nishyis were unable to produce sufficient rice, they used to grow a good amount of cotton in their dry fields. The Apatanis used to buy raw cotton gin, spin, and dye it. Then they weave it into clothes some of which were sold to the original suppliers of the cotton. They used to weave not only to meet their own needs but also with the definite idea of using their products for barter transactions with their tribal neighbours. In this mode of transaction raw cotton was bartered for Apatani swords and knives. Haimendorf informs that Apatani clothes were equivalent to one long sword (*dao*) or a small pig. Through the Nishyi traders, Apatani clothes were distributed to the villages of Upper Kamla valley, Khru valley, and Upper Panior valley of the Upper Subansiri region. From those regions, these clothes were reached even in Tibet. In exchange for these clothes, Apatanis used to buy pigs, fowls, tobacco, cotton etc. Salt was one of the major items imported by the Apatanis.[6]

It is said prior that the traditional Apatani villages were self-sufficient where few families originated with different occupations. Blacksmith and pot makers were notable among them. Few Apatanis were very expert in making of cane and bamboo articles, especially the people of Bula and Dutta villages. The bamboo made articles were considered economically important in inter-tribal trade. The Apatanis used to purchase raw cotton, pigs and mithan from the Nishyis in exchange for bamboo shoots, cane belts, cane hats, and other items made of bamboo. Earthen pots were also an item of trade. Pots were made only in two Apatani villages, namely Hang and Michi Bamin. Interestingly, Nishyis were more skilful than Apatanis. The women of several neighbouring Nyshi villages, especially Jorum and Talo, were experienced potters and often sold their wares to the Apatanis in exchange for rice.[7]

Whether the Apatanis had a direct trade link with the Tibetans or not — this has created an endless debate. Verrier Elwin opines that the people of Apatani valley had an old trade link with Tibet.[8] Noticing the immense popularity of Tibetan goods in Apatani villages, few scholars supported the view. But Haimendorf argues though Apatani had taken part in distant trade, they rarely went to Tibet. Thake Kani, an eminent Apatani scholar, firmly stated Apatanis had no direct trade link with the people of Tibet.[9] However, Apatani goods were well-liked in Tibetan villages. This demand was fulfilled by the Nishyi traders. Their neighbouring traders used to export all the Apatani goods to Tibet and *vice versa*. Recent researches prove that the Nishyis had retained their commercial link with the Tibetan through six trade routes.[10] Nevertheless, all these statements are yet to be proved and confuted due to the lack of written documents.

The introduction of currency was an outcome of distant trade. Haimendorf opined that the Apatanis used to use beads, small bell-metal bells and bell metal dices. These were locally called *maji*. To him, this object had then the character of a currency.[11] The existence of *maji* had also been questioned by the recent scholar. According to them, Apatani had no idea of currency in their traditional and social economy. Every exchange was in the form of barter. They questioned the method of Haimendorf again. To rewrite the history of Apatanis their oral legendaries and folktales should be given due importance. One needs to keep in mind all the aspects of those folktales before reaching a concluding remark. To them, Haimendorf talked with few people and was usually unknown about the contrasting stories prevalent in different villages. To pen down his anthropological knowledge Haimendorf had only emphasized the opinion of his companion.[12]

Barter Trade and Traditional Units of Value

Before the advent of the market economy, money was almost absent in business transactions in Eastern Himalayas. Rice, pigs, and mithans instead of money were generally accepted as a measure of things. Thake Kani firmly stated that before the advent of Haimendorf there was no currency used in a trade transaction. Rather these tribes developed their system of value. Being an experienced scholar and having good relation with the local people, he was able to present a good deal of information on the traditional unit value system.[13]

1. *Pachu he:* This unit is valued for two eggs or one small chicken or one day wage of a man or woman.
2. *Paro he:* This unit is valued for middle-sized chicken or eggs or a small knife.
3. *Sohe:* This unit is valued for one hen or a big knife or is half the *puhe*.
4. *Puhe:* This unit is valued as double of *sohe*, or a cock, one piece of plain cloth, or a medium-sized Apatani *dao*.
5. *Piilyee he:* This unit is valued for middle sizes pigs or the average size of Apatani *dao* or one piece of Apatani cloth with a red and blue border. Locally this is known as *Pyami Pulye*.

The *puhe* unit increases as *punye* (two), *puhin* (three), *pupe* (four), *pungo* (five) and so on are mainly used for round and oval-shaped materials. To measure the grain, mainly rice there were a variety of buskets, such as *pachu yagii, paro yagii*, and *puhe yagii*. Two *puhe yagii* grains were equivalent to one unit of *piilyee yagii*. The smallest measuring unit for cereal grain is *kiiche* and the largest one is *Giidapata Yagii* or *Yakhang*.

The cost of landed properties and ornaments was counted in the unit of *Dore*. The full-grown mithan has known *Subu Anii* is equal to four units that are *Dorpe* means four animals. The full-grown mithan or cow is counted as *Anii* (full grown), *Dorin* (one-third of *Anii*), *Siido* (half of *Anii*) and *Penge* (one 4th of *Anii*), and this is counted based on the length of grown horn mithan. The full-grown cow or ox is counted as two units that are *Dornye* (two).[14]

Another bartering item of those days was the pork or bacon, which was indispensably used in social and religious ceremonies. It was measured in terms of breadth in a unit of *Nange* (size of palm), *Gohe* (size of stretch of middle and thumb fingers) or unit of *Piilyee Anii* (full-grown skin pig) was counted as *Pilyee Anii*. The thickness of the bacon was measured in a unit of *Kuti* (safety pin) that is used for the wrapping of clothes. The long length and breadth of goods and thing, place, distance etc. we are measured in the unit of *Lyenge* (the stretch of hand), *Tuhe* (stick) and *Yare* (a length of bamboo).[15]

In this way, we can perceive that a self-sufficient economy was developed in the traditional Apatani villages. The entire economy was largely dependent on well-developed agriculture and prosperous trading activity. Apart from these, hunting, fishing, knitting, weaving, cane and bamboo article making, woodworks and animal husbandry contributed to the economy of an Apatani individual. Despite their contribution, the

Apatani economy turned out as a social economy with the shared role of every member of this community where the value of solidarity and participative role of each and everyone was given due importance.[16] The growth of individualism was noticed after the development of the modern economy.

The Emergence of Monetized Economy and the Modern Trends of Trade

The reason behind the growth of the social economy of the Apatanis was, of course, isolation. For a long time, the Apatanis were free from the control of any state power. Both the Tibetan power in the North and the Ahom power in the south never conquered the valley. Even the British adopted a policy of non-interference towards the tribal people of Arunachal. But after the Second World War, the situation was drastically changed. The strategic importance of this region was profoundly realized. On the other hand, the newly independent state, India, was unwilling to continue the policy of 'leave them alone'. The North-East Frontier (present Arunachal Pradesh), previously 'Excluded Area', was brought under the regular administration of the Indian Union. To incorporate the isolated region the statesman adopted a policy of cultural integration. The aim was to bring positive changes without harming the tribal value system.[17] The government embraced a tribal-friendly development policy.[18] The initial goal was to introduce road construction projects to reach into the interior villages and make the people self-reliant without contaminating their cultural features. The construction of various government offices, hospitals, and schools in the Apatani valley was an outcome of this initiative. The Apatani inhabited Ziro valley was set up as district headquarters of the Subansiri region in 1965.

As a result of this initiative, Apatani valley witnessed drastic changes. Due to the extension of administration, several people entered the valley from different parts of India as district administrators, road engineers, health officers, medical staff, school teachers, postmen etc. The intrusion of security and the military officer was also seen. The roads and bridges in the valley were constructed by the military department.[19] In all aspects, the entry of the outsiders and their permanent residence led to the transformation of this valley from an enriched village to a well-administered town.

Apatanis never delayed to take the opportunities of this new economic climate. To cater to the immediate needs of the newcomers, they opened few small shops and cooperative stores. A large number of Apatanis, who were accustomed to agriculture or other traditional occupation, also opened shops. Even the Apatani weavers, who used to produce items for traditional inter-tribal trade, started to depend more on the demands of the newcomer.[20] As a result, Old Ziro and Hapoli became the centre of commerce. In the meantime, a noteworthy change was seen in society. The independent Indian government took a venture to abolish the practice of slavery. Some people came out of traditional bondage. They took part in road building and construction projects as labour.[21] Few influential Apatanis get the job of supervisor in government projects. Their mode payment was in cash. The introduction of cash compelled them to go to the market to purchase their daily necessity. From the 1970s the first batch of educated Apatanis established themselves in various government jobs. They also get their salary in cash. Thus, cash became important instead of goods in daily economic transaction.

Ziro valley was always famous for agriculture. But in this new economic atmosphere trade and commerce began to play a pivotal role, especially in Hapoli area. Shopkeeping turned out to be an important occupation of this time. Though Apatanis never realized the necessity of shopkeeping on their own, it was a Bengali who first opened a shop in Ziro.[22] He came to the valley as a medical pun. Noticing the prospect of shopkeeping he resigned from his government job and devoted him entirely to commercial activities. After acquiring huge affluence from Ziro he eventually moved to a town in the plains of Assam and opened there a much larger establishment. Not only this person but also Haimendorf engaged in shopkeeping.[23] He opened a trade depot at Dutta Parpii, near old Ziro where he used to sell Erri or Muga cloths, matchbox, safety pins, beads, and salt. Late Nada Rika was appointed as Chowkidar-*cum*-salesman of his shop. Noticing the engagement of the outsiders, the Apatanis started to take business ventures.

The example of the outsiders was soon emulated and resulted in the rise of the rural business class. Havung Havung was the first Apatani ever who opened a shop in Old Ziro. Soon he became successful in the commercial field but he died at a relatively early age. His successors were unable to retain that level. Kago Bida from Hija village also opened a shop in Ziro besides his agricultural venture. Hage Hale from Hari village was also a good example. Padi Laliyang was the most successful man in the sphere of a new economy. Despite being a resident of Reru, he bought land and constructed his house at Old Ziro and opened few shops both in Old Ziro and Hapolic. He helped one of his sons to establish a bakery. Indeed, Laliyang was one of that agricultural elite who existed in the rural arena before the 1950s. He was the owner of various mithans and numerous slaves. After the emancipation of slaves, he obtained a large amount of compensation and invested that amount in his new business venture. To quote Haimendorf, "His (Padi Laliyang's) business ventures were so successful that in 1970 he offered to invest 2 lakh rupees if I (Haimendorf) could be persuaded to match the sum and go into partnership with him in establishing a large department store.[24] Later, his son became the speaker of the Legislative Assembly of Arunachal Pradesh. Thus, we can see the people who were agricultural elite in previous days, took the opportunity of the new economic environment, accumulated adequate money, and became business elite. Their power and prestige were not decreased at all. In the 1960s and 1970s, we get to see a sort of horizontal social mobility which was visible in the traditional elite class of Apatani society.

The variety of shopkeeping was expanded in Apatani valley with great effort. Haimendorf informed that there was a variety of shopkeeping like radio shop, photoshop, watch shop, book store, cycle shop, and carpentry shop was established in 1978. The only pharmacy shop was maintained by Kuru Hasang, son-in-law of Padi Laliyang, who was a licensed pharmacist. From the late 1970s, Apatanis began to develop a new source of income based upon the coming of outsiders. They had begun to run the lodging of houses where visitors can stay for a night. The natural beauty of this tranquil valley and spectacular view of Eastern Himalaya enabled them to open lodges and hotel businesses which were extended gradually towards nature-based tourism, ecotourism, and adventure tourism.[25] The Apatanis borrowed a culture to drink rice beer by tradition. They popularized rice and millet beer in the business sector and offered the visitors for consumption. Soon, the brewing and selling of beer were turned into a profitable business. Many Apatani girls used to brew beer as an independent income.

Indeed, the Apatani economy was become promising because of the entrance of the outsiders. Haimendorf mentioned there were 26 large shops controlled by non-Apatanis. Eight Bengalis, three Assamese, three Biharis, two Nagas, one Sherpa, and one Madrasi among the outsiders who were working in the various shops at Hapoli in 1978. Initially, the Apatanis were unable to acquire the skill of various works. That is why a Bengali ran a photo studio. But the Apatanis restricted the outsiders to achieve dominant character. This Bazar Committee of Hapoli did not permit established merchants especially Marwaris or other business classes to set up shops on a hill. No doubt, this effort helped the relatively inexperienced Apatanis to be successful in business.[26]

One of the major achievements of this thriving economy is the rise of the bank. The monetization of the local economy had led to the accumulation of money in the hands of the Apatanis. To promote the programme of cultivation government helped poor farmers by providing agricultural loans. A sum of ₹ 7,500 was allotted as an agricultural loan in 1971-72. In the same year, the State Bank of India was opened at Ziro. Another important bank of Ziro was Arunachal Pradesh State College operative Apex Bank Limited that was opened in 1981.[27] The banking facilities encouraged the people for their savings. To quote Haimendorf, "In the branch of the State Bank of India in Hapoli about 1200 tribesmen, most of whom were Apatanis, have current accounts, a good many with balances of over ₹ 1,00,000."[28]

Reorientation of Distant Trade

The most important feature of this new economy is the reorientation of distant trade. In the earlier paragraphs, we have noticed that Apatanis were accustomed to their local commercial activities. In some cases, they were depended on Tibetan goods that were brought by the Nishyis. Though they were interested to begin a trade relationship with the people of Assam, they could not succeed. In the period of our review, we can witness two major changes in this Himalayan region.

Firstly, After the Chinese invasion of 1962, the traditional trade routes with Tibet were closed. As a result, the northern commercial link of the people of the Subansiri region was blocked.[29] Secondly, due to the road-building projects, new roads were constructed to create a link between hills and plain. As a result, Apatanis gradually became habituated to commercial exchange with the people of Assam instead of Tibet.

In the period of our review Apatani trade and commerce has largely been depended on Assam because of few important reasons:

> Firstly, the government officials entered the Ziro valley from various parts of India. They were accustomed to Indian goods which were primarily available in Assam. They always looked for their preferred commodities in Apatani valley.
>
> Secondly, educated Apatanis established themselves in various jobs. They were becoming familiar with modern and luxurious

goods. Gradually they became dependent on Assamese market goods.

Thirdly, by observing both the Apatani and non-Apatani officials, the rural people were more or less influenced. The people, who have become already rich, started to imitate the servicemen. How much the luxurious goods of the outside world impacted the tribal mind, can be known from the lucid narration of Basudeb Basu.[30]

As a result of these aforesaid causes, the demand for Indian goods was largely increased. The traditional Tibetan goods became less valuable. Though the social value of tribal goods gradually decreased, its cultural value remained the same. For instance, Tibetan Earrings, Tibetan beads and silver spoons were not regularly used. Rather it was seen on a ceremonial occasion. However, the value of Rokse (Tibetan *dao*) never decreased. Apatani priests used them with scabbards on ceremonial occasions.[31]

In this new era, a change in the way of life of the Apatanis was visible. They were becoming habituated with some iron cooking pots instead of earthen pots, metal buckets replacing ground vessels, some tin boxes with padlocks in place of storage baskets. Young men in government employment began to wear shorts, shirts, and shoes instead of their traditional dress. The wealthy villagers preferred to wear trousers and well-tailored jackets in Western style to look fit and handsome. To quote Haimendorf, "By 1978 the scene had greatly changed. Among domestic utensils there was a variety of plastic and enamel mugs and vessels, electric torches were common possessions, and some wealthy men even had chairs and tables. The men's dress was a mixture of traditional and modern style.[32] So, in the period of our review, most of the daily necessary goods were imported from Assam. Retail trade (mainly grocery shops, stationery goods, bakery and vegetable shops) was carried on by a considerable number of Apatanis. They usually obtained their goods from wholesalers of North Lakhimpur, Charduar, and Doimara in Assam. They started to send these goods to other tribal zones like Itanagar, Kimin, Kokila, Doimukh, Yazali, Hapoli, Raga. From the plain areas, they import clothes, brass, and bronze plates, bowls, cups, aluminum saucepans, iron frying pans, woollen baskets etc. Besides this Apatanis purchase a good number of fowls and cows which they rear for the future. The cooperative societies have also been playing a very important role in the commercial sector of development and economy in this tribal area.[33] According to the Census of 1971, there was 585 government, quasi-government and private establishments were noticed in the Subansiri district of Arunachal Pradesh.[34] All these became possible with the encouraging endeavours of the Indian government and direct commercial links with the trade centres of Assam.

Conclusion

Arunachal Pradesh was a geopolitically isolated region for a long time. During the 1950s a feeling of Indianness was yet to emerge in this tribal land. Rather the tribes like Adis, Nishyis, Apatanis etc. were culturally closer to China and Tibet. After the 1960s all the commercial links with Tibet were brought to an end. On the other hand, the intimacy of the Apatanis with the government officials and military jawans awakened their feeling that they were part of this country and they had adequate space in it. Through the spread of education, a feeling of Indianness has grown into them that also boosted the process of emotional integration. As a whole, cultural contact was the key factor behind the growth and development of Indianness and their recent trend of commerce turned out to be the main medium. Last but not the least, with these trading activities a relation of interdependence was grown-up among the Apatanis, Arunachalees, and the people of the rest of India. As a result, Arunachal Pradesh became an inseparable part of India.

NOTES AND REFERENCES

1. Nishyis are most populous tribe of Arunachal Pradesh who are found in Subansiri district (both upper and lower). As per Census of 1971, Nishyis' population was 80325, 21.74 per cent of state population. In Ahom and British era they were known as *Dafla*. Today their population is more than 2.5 lakh.
2. Hill Miris are one of major tribes of Arunachal Pradesh. Most of them reside in Upper Subansiri district and few northern part of Apatani villages. The term Hill Miri was given by colonial administrators to create a difference between Plain Miris of Assam and Hill Miris of Arunachal Pradesh.
3. Christoph von Furer-Haimendorf (1909-1995) was an Austrian anthropologist and Professor at the School of Oriental and African Studies in London. In 1944-45 he stepped in the Apatani valley as a Special Officer appointed by colonial government. From 1945-1978, he visited the valley thrice and penned down his knowledge and experience on the people of Subansiri. Arguably, Apatanis became globally popular for his immense contribution.
4. Quoted in, Christoph von Furer-Haimendorf, *A Himalayan Tribe: From Cattle to Cash*, Vikash Publishing House, New Delhi, 1980, p. 59.
5. Christoph von Furer-Haimendorf, *The Apa Tanis and Their Neighbours: The Primitive Civilization of Eastern Himalaya*, London, 1962, p. 49.
6. *Ibid.*, pp. 50-51.
7. *Ibid.*, p. 50.
8. Verrier Elwin, *India's North East Frontier in the Nineteenth Century*, Oxford University Press, Bombay, 1959, p. 202.

9. Thake Kani, "Units of Value in Bartering of the Apatani Society," in *Border Trades in Arunachal Pradesh* (ed.) Dr. Tage Tada, Shri R.N. Koley, Dr. Radhe Yampi, Directorate of Research, Government of Arunachal Pradesh, Itanagar, 2015, p. 76.
10. Y.S. Wunglenton, "The Barter Trade Between Nishyis and Tibetan through the Northern Border of Unidivided Subansiri Area and Its Impact," in *Border Trades in Arunachal Pradesh*, (ed.) Dr. Tage Tada, Shri R.N. Koley, Dr. Radhe Yampi, Directorate of Research, Government of Arunachal Pradesh, Itanagar, 2015, pp. 69-71.
11. Christoph von Furer Haimendorf, *op. cit.*, 1980, p. 63.
12. Dr. Rubu Tani, personal communication, March 16, 2019. Time: 11:00 am. Rubu Tani, age 31, is an Apatani by born from Tajang village of Ziro. He is a promising scholar of Department of History, Rajiv Gandhi University, Doimukh, Arunachal Pradesh. Since his childhood days, he is very keen to know the story of their past from the aged persons of his village. Gradually, it turned out to be the most important intellectual capital of his research. Now, Dr. Tani is an Assistant Professor of Dera Natung Government College, Itanagar.
13. Thake Kani, *op. cit.*, p. 77.
14. *Ibid.*, pp. 77-78.
15. *Ibid.*, p. 78.
16. Sarah Hilaly, "Culture of Friendship among the Apatanis of Arunachal Pradesh," in *Space and Culture, India*, Vol. VI, No. I, ACCB Publishing, England, p. 38.
17. Jawaharlal Nehru, foreword to the 1st edition of Verrier Elwin's, *A Philosophy for NEFA*, Shillong, 1959.
18. For further details, see, Verrier Elwin, *A Philosophy for NEFA*, Shillong, Second Edition, 1959.
19. Thake Kani, *The Advancing Apatanis of Arunachal Pradesh*, Itanagar, 1993, p. 219.
20. Christoph von Furer Haimendorf, *op. cit.*, 1980, p. 66.
21. For further details see, Arindam Ghosh, "From Traditional Bonding to a New Form of Domination: A Historical Analysis of Slave System in Apatani Society of Arunachal Pradesh," in *Pondering the Past: Glimpses of Our Society and Culture*, Vol. III, (Ed.) Sutapa Sengupta, Paiolck, Kolkata, 2019, pp. 23-24.
22. Christoph von Furer Haimendorf, *op. cit.*, 1980, p. 67.
23. Thake Kani, *op. cit*, p. 78.
24. Quoted in, Christoph von Furer Haimendorf, *op. cit.*, 1980, p. 68.
25. Maila Lama and Amitava Mitra, "Tourism Development in North East India: A Study in Arunachal Pradesh," in *Perspective of North East India: Tradition and Modernity in Arunachal Pradesh*, Pulipaka, Sanjay and Others (Ed.), Kolkata, 2013.
26. Christoph von Furer Haimendorf, *op. cit.*, 1980, p. 71.
27. *Arunachal Pradesh District Gazetteers: Subansiri District*, ed. by S. Dutta Choudhury, Government of Arunachal Pradesh, Itanagar, 1981, p. 214.
28. Quoted in, Christoph von Furer Haimendorf, *op. cit.*, 1980, p. 69.
29. For further details see, Dr. Tage Tada, R.N. Koley, and Dr. Radhe Yampi (ed.), *op. cit*, pp. 85-87.
30. Basudeb Basu, *Nefa Sundari Nefa*, Dey's Publishing, Kolkata, 1960, pp. 130-133.
31. *Arunachal Pradesh District Gazetteers: Subansiri District*, Ed. by S. Dutta, Choudhury, Government of Arunachal Pradesh, Itanagar, 1981, p. 216.
32. Quoted in, Christoph von Furer Haimendorf, *op. cit.*, 1980, p. 67.
33. *Arunachal Pradesh District Gazetteers: Subansiri District*, Ed. by S. Dutta Choudhury, Government of Arunachal Pradesh, Itanagar, 1981, p. 228.
34. *Census of India, 1971*, Series 24, Arunachal Pradesh, Part III-A&B, p. 11.

7

Society-Culture-Economy of Santhals in North Bengal
A Historical Analysis

Kalikrishna Sutradhar

The Santhals are one of the largest tribes in India. Santhals are accustomed to live a hard working and simple life. At present Santhals are indigenous people living in the state of West Bengal. Most of the Santhals in West Bengal migrated from the Santhal Parganas and Chotanagpur of Bihar. This chapter highlighted the social, economic and cultural aspects of Santhal people of North Bengal.

The Santhals did not have any written books. Yet this tribe is the most talked about among the primitive peoples of India. Historians and Sociologists have written books on Santhals, usually based on folklore. Mr. E.G. Man has written the first informative book about Santhals. After the Santhal Rebellion of 1855, the British government formed *Santhal Parganas* to settle the Santhals. E.G. Man was the Assistant Commissioner of this *Santhal Pargana*. His name is written in the book — *Santhalia of and the Sonthals*. This book was first printed in 1867.[1] Subsequently, many European Missionaries, British and Indian Historians and Sociologists have written important books on Santhals.

Origin of the Name 'Santhal'

The "*hor*" the name which all Santhals used among themselves. The word "*hor*" means man. According to Suniti Kumar Chattopadhyay, "Santhal" is probably the Sanskrit word "*Samantapala*" complaining about the out. "*Samantapal*" means border security guard. In the Middle Ages, the word "*Samantapal*" became "*Samanta Al*" and later converted to Santhal. According to the Santhal tradition, the Santhals originated from the "*Kharwar*" stream. The Santhals also identify themselves as the "*Kharwar*" clan.[2] Present-day, they have been identifying themselves by that name. In this regard, Dr. Hang said in an article, "*What at present is known commonly as the Santhals, Mundas and the Hos are the same Adivasi tribal group of India. They come from one Connon stock.*"[3] Later "*Kharwar*" clan spread throughout the land was divided into various branches. Earlier, a part of Ancient Medinipur was called "*Saont*" or "*Samana Bhumi.*"[4] Many historians believe that the word "Santhal" originated from this.

Original Homeland of Santhals

According to the primitive identity and linguistic anthropologists, there are various doctrines regarding the original homeland of Santhals. According to some scholars, the Santhal people are the original inhabitants of India. However, Suniti Kumar Chattopadhyay in his book *Kirat-Jana-kriti* says India Santhal primitive inhabitants theory dismissed and he writes, "*So far, it has not yet been proved that any kind of man evolved on the soil of India — although it is not unlikely that man of a type persisting, or, it may be, long-extinct, may have originated from some kind of anthropoid ape and so may have been autochthonous to India, but we have no indication of it as yet.*"[5] Mr. H.H. Risley writes in his book *The Tribes and Castes of Bengal*, Vol. 2, introduces the Santhals, "*Santal, Santhal, Saontar, a large Dravidian tribe, ceased on linguistic grounds a Kolarian, which is found in Western Bengal, Northern Odisha, Bhagalpur and Santal Parganas.* According to Mr. Skresrud, *the Tribe after their sojourn for several generations in the country said to have been called Kharwar, the root of which, Khar, is a variant of 'Hor' man, the names which all Santals use among themselves.*"[6]

Arrival and Settlement of Santhals in North Bengal

In the early nineteenth century, Santhals settled in different parts of Bakura, Birbhum, Manbhum, Chotanagpur, Hazaribagh. In these areas, they cut down the forest, removed the stones and started farming. But coming to *Santhal Pargana* did not bring any benefit. Their lives became unbearable due to the oppression of traders, zamindars and moneylenders. Exploitation and oppression began at the behest of the Britishers. In 1856, about 10,000 Santhals died in retaliation for the above atrocities. After the revolt, unspeakable government repression came down on them. When the resistance of the Santhals broke down under the pressure of government repression, several Santhals fled and saved their lives. A group of Santhals came and settled in different districts of North Bengal to save their lives in this way. Moreover, the situation created by the rebellion made it convenient for them to be brought to the tea garden in an organized manner. In other districts of North Bengal too, it is estimated that the Santhals came mostly after the rebellion. In the first half of the nineteenth century, the masters of the indigo factory brought a large number of Santhals from the Chhotanagpur area of Bihar to work as labourers in indigo factories. The masters imported cheap labour from the impoverished tribal areas to increase their profit margins.

The Santhals are not indigenous to North Bengal. They came here from the Chhotonagpur region of Bihar and other places and settled here. The Santhals in the Terai and Duars areas of Darjeeling and Jalpaiguri districts started coming from the last phase of the nineteenth century. The first arrival and settlement of the Santhals in the Jalpaiguri district was in 1891. The immigration of the Santhals to Jalpaiguri was introduced by the hand of D.H.E. Sunder the then Survey and Settlement Officer of the district. In his report, he wrote that "*While holding charge of Buxa sub-division, I communicated with Mr. Stark, Deputy Magistrate, who was then in charge of the Damini forests, in the Sonthal Parganas, and I also sent my Sonthal servants, at my own cost, to that district to find out whether Sonthals would be willing to come and settle in the wastelands of the Western Duars. The reports which reached me made me very hopeful that they would do so, and I accordingly recommended, in my letter No. 769G of the 4th January, 1890, to the Deputy Commissioner of Jalpaiguri, that a Sonthal colony be started in the Duars. Rev. A.J. Shields of the Church Missionary Society, then came from Godda with a party of Sonthals, who was so pleased with the land which I had selected for them between the Gaddadhar and Rydak rivers, east of Alipur, that a batch of 500 of them — men, women, and children, are settled there in the following year, and will now remain permanently.*"[7]

At present Santhals are living in almost all the districts of North Bengal. In North Bengal, the Santhals first came to Malda and Dinajpur districts. Bhutani, Gazol, Habbipur, Baman Gola, Chanchal, Kharba, Harishchandrapur, Ratua, Manikchak, Kaliaganj, Ingrejbazar, Old Malda are situated in Malda district.[8] At present they are living in Tapan, Balurghat, Gangarampur, Kumarganj, Hili etc. areas in South Dinajpur district and Chakulia, Chopra, Goalpukur, Kanki, Karandighi, Kaliaganj etc. areas in North Dinajpur district. They are living in Kharibari, Batashi, Bidhannagar in the Darjeeling district. In the present Alipurduar district, Santhals have settled in Shamuktala, Rydak, Rahimabad, Kalchini, Shishubari, Madarihat, Birpara, Hamiltonganj, Hasimara, Nagarakata, etc. areas and Banarhat block of Jalpaiguri district.

Population

At present, the Santhals are the largest group of tribals in West Bengal. As of the 2001 India census, 22,60,540 people were living here. In 2011 this number increased to 25,12,331 people. But before and after the Santhal Rebellion, when the Santhals came to different districts of the then Bengal, they were not so numerous.

Physical Appearances

In terms of ethnicity, the Santhals belonged to the Proto-Australoid or Pre-Dravidian group. Their height is short and their body is well-formed. Approximate height from 1596 cm. to 1614 cm. Skin colour is dark brown to black. The Santhals were tall and dark-complexioned. They had curly to straight hair. Their physical appearances were like Negro people. Nose wide, lips thick, long and narrow head, mouth wide, forehead low.

Language

The Santhali language was part of the Austro-Asiatic family, distantly related to Vietnamese. Santhali is the second most spoken language in West Bengal after Bengali. The Santhals speak the Santali language. It is impossible to match Munda and other Austronesian languages with this language. According to Campbell, the language of the Santhal people is richer than that of other indigenous people. Their language has enriched Hindi and Bengali considerably. In the Duars of Jalpaiguri and Terai of Darjeeling district, the Santhals were forced to speak the 'Sadri' language. Sir G.A. Grierson in his book "*Linguistic Survey of India*", mentions the languages of Santhal, Munda, Ho, Bhumij, Kora etc. as Sherwari languages. He wrote that Santhali, Mundari, Bhumij, Kora, Ho, Turi, Asuri and Korwa are different forms of the same language.

Script

The Santhal script was a relatively recent innovation. The Santhals did not have a written language until the twentieth century and used Latin/ Roman, Devanagri and Bengali writing systems. A need for a distinct script to accommodate the Santhali language, combining features of both the Indic and Roman scripts was felt, which resulted in the invention of the new script called *Olchiki* by Pandit Raghunath Murmu in 1925. The Santhali script or *Olchiki* was alphabetic and did not share any other symbolic properties of the other Indic scripts such as Devanagari. After the recognition of the Santhali script by the government of West Bengal in 1983, books have been written in Santhali language for primary schools and the district of Midnapore, Purulia and Bankura in the state of West Bengal. In Jalpaiguri district, there was no arrangement for teaching Santhali language in "*Olchiki*" script.

Education

At present, the Santhal community has taken a leading role in education. Many missionary schools have sprung up in the Duars and Terai regions. There are missionary schools in Birpara, Jalpaiguri, Siliguri More, Pradhan Nagar, Gayaganga, Ghoshpukur, Mozilpur in South Dinajpur district. Santhal boys and girls study here in groups. Advancing in the field of education, many MLAs, Customs Officers, Manager of Hindustan Fertilizer Company, Officer-in-Charge of Siliguri Information Centre, etc. are engaged in various positions. If we look further, we can see that they are holding high positions in income tax offices, post and its departments, air licences, various educational institutions.

Different Sects

The internal structure of the Santhals were singularly complete and elaborate. There were twelve exogamous sects: (1) Hasdak, (2) Murmu, (3) Kisku, (4) Hembrom, (5) Marandi, (6) Soren, (7) Tudu, (8) Baske, (9) Besra, (10) Puria, (11) Chonre, and (12) Bedea.[9] The first seven were said to be descended from the seven sons of *Pilchu Haram* and *Pilchu Burhi*. The five others were added afterward. All these sects were patriarchal. The Santhals call their group '*hor*' and all those outside groups '*Diku*'. They are divided based on Paris or tribe title. The Santhals each follow the rules of their respective tribes and respect the religious symbols of the tribes. The tribes are again subdivided. The sub-tribe is called '*Khut*' in the Santhali language. At present, there is no trace '*Bedea*' sect. Another thing about the tribe is that in the past, the people of different tribes of the Santhals used different symbols. The cow would give it that mark on the buffalo. Cows could recognize buffaloes by looking at the signs. For example, the symbol of *Kisku* tribe was stick, the symbol of *Hembrom* tribe was *Ankashi*, the symbol of *Hasdak* tribe was *Hansuli* etc.

Village Organization

In social, economic and religious life Santhals give much importance to their village organization. No one disobeys the instructions of the village organization. Anyone who behaves anti-socially or breaks social norms is deported. The phenomenon of deportation is called "*bitlaha*". Every Santhal village has its panchayat. The Santhal women enjoyed more freedom than their counterparts in Indian society. Each Santhal village had a *Jagmanjhi* whose most important duty was to look after the morals of the boys and girls. There was also a *Paramanik* whose function was to attend to the farming arrangements. There was also a village priest called *Neua* or *Nayaki*. However, on a village level, the Santhals were governed by a *Panchayat* or council of village elders. On a wider level, the Santhal village Panchayat was subordinate to a *Pargana* of ten or twelve *Panchayats* under the leadership of a single headman. The final authority of the Santhal polity, however, was vested in the *Lo Bir* or hunt council, regarded as the council of people.

Judicial System

There were three types of meetings in the ancient Santhal society for governing the society, namely — (1) *Ato*, (2) *Bahre*, (3) *Sendra*. All meetings were held under the leadership of *Majhi*. Pargana meetings are held under the leadership of *Parganait* and *Senda* or *Desh* meetings are held under the leadership of *Dihri*. The villagers will help the middleman in this meeting. *Khushiyara* of his subordinate village will help *Parganait* in the meeting outside. And in the *Desh* meeting that takes place in the night of *Sendra*, everyone helps *Dihri*. If he is not satisfied with the judgment of the *Majhi*, he can appeal to the *Parganait* and if he is not satisfied with the judgment of the *Parganait*, he can ask for reconsideration from *Dihri*. But after the trial of the *Desh*, there is no appeal. '*Kalhi Dirup*' is the judicial meeting.

Social System

The rules and regulations of their society are still strictly followed.

Santhal society is divided into three parts, namely — 1. *Bindir Hor Samaj*, 2. *Safa Hor Samaj*, and 3. *Isaiyah Hor Samaj*.[10]

(1) ***Bindir Hor Samaj:*** In this society there are five nobles or *Karta*. These are, respectively: (i) *Majhi Haram* (village foreman), (ii) *Paramanik* or *Paranik* (sub-foreman), (iii) *Godayet* or *Godet, Gorait* or *Kylie* (messenger of the festival to everyone in the society), (iv) *Jagh Majhi*, (v) *Jugh Paramanik*. And one of the leaders of the village society is *Nike* or *Pujari*. He worships at festivals. And his assistant *Kudum Nike* has special activities to appease the ghosts of the mountains.

(2) ***Safa Hor Samaj:*** Like the *Bindir somaj*, the customs and principles of their society were prevalent. The number of foremen is also the same. However, their marriage style is a bit different, such as the marriage of *Bindi's Har Samaj* is in *Dala*, but their marriage is to get a seat in the middle of *Marwar*.

(3) ***Isaiyah Hor Samaj:*** *Isaiyah Hor Samaj* is again divided into three parts. They were different from the above two societies. It is pertinent to note that in the beginning, their society was *Bindir Hor Samaj*, but later it was divided into two different customs.[11]

Marriage System

In Santhal society marriage is considered as a very important ceremony. Their marriage is called '*Bapla*'. In Santhal society, marriage was one of the sacred events of life and marriage added up considerable respect in society. There is no child marriage in Santhal society. When the son and daughter grow up, the father and mother nominate the bride and groom. However, there are seven types of marriage in this society, such as 1. *Doar balla*, 2. *Tunki Dipil Bapla*, 3. *Or Bapla*, 4. *Apangir Bapala*, 5. *Gardi Jayar Bapala*, 6. *Shakha Bapla*, 7. *Iptut* or *Bapla*. Again, there are mentions of six types of marriage somewhere. They are: 1. *Bapla* or *Firing Behu*, 2. *Khardi Jayar*, 3. *Iptut*, 4. *Nir Bolak*, 5. *Sanga*, 6. *Firing Jayar*.

Although there is a practice of widow marriage among the Santhals, a widow can never marry her brother-in-law. Incidentally, it should be noted that young people of two different positions cannot get married. For example, no one with the title of *Mardi* and *Kisku* or anyone with the same title can get married. If that is the case then you have to be expelled from society. However, lately, this rule is being violated in many places.

Divorce

Divorce can be according to the wishes of the husband and wife. However, in the event of a divorce without error, the person seeking the divorce will bear the costs. For example, in this case, the husband does not get the money that was previously given to the daughter. Apart from that, he has to pay a fine and the daughter has to pay the customary dues. On the other hand, if the daughter wants a divorce without a valid reason, her father is forced to pay the dowry and fine. The divorce was made in the presence of the assembled villagers and the husband was made to stand facing the sun on one leg. He had a cloth around his neck and held the edges in the hand along with three *Sal* leaves. Then taking the name of *Sin-Bonga* he tore the Sal leaves as a token of separation and upset a brass pot full of water. My wife repeated that too. There was the belief that if the Sal leaves were not fully torn or the *lotta* (brass pot) was not wholly emptied then the couple must again come together.

Birth Ceremony

If a Santhal boy or girl is born, a ceremony is held on the third or fifth day after birth. This ceremony is called '*Napata*'. The first son of the family was named after his grandfather. Grandmother's name is the first daughter of the family. When the naming ceremony is over, everyone is sprinkled with flowers and water. Then the guests present eat rice boiled with neem leaf powder. When the child is five years old, another ceremony is celebrated. The name of this programme is *Sakhi*. There is a practice of drawing on the chest of a girl or in one hand.

Festivals

The Santhals are a festival-loving people. Santhals celebrate different festivals in different seasons. Their cultural life is traditional and colourful. Festivals can be observed centring on the birth, death, marriage and worship of almost every Santhal. Numerous ceremonies centred on the stages of sowing, reaping and harvesting of agricultural Santhals, and the combined dance songs of men and women are noticeable in each festival. The '*Eraksim*' festival is celebrated during the sowing of seeds and the '*Hariyar Sim*' festival is celebrated after sowing the seeds. During the harvest season, they celebrate the '*Jan Thar*' festival and when the crops are harvested, they go to Mete for the '*Sohrai*' festival.

(1) ***Sohrai or Badna Parab:*** The most notable of all these festivals is *Sohrai* or *Badna Parab*. After the main crop of paddy is harvested in the month of *Poush, pachani* (desi paddy wine) is kept in the house. After eating this *pachani*, they started dancing with *madals*, harmoniums etc. from one end of the village road to the other. This festival lasts for seven days.

(2) ***Baha or Dolajatra:*** The greatest festival of the Santhals is the '*Baha*' festival. '*Baha*' is a very sacred religious festival of the Santhals. The '*Baha*' begins on the Twelfth day of the white wing of the month of Falgun. The Santhals do not eat *Mahua* flowers until they observe *Baha*. Girls also do not wear shawls on their heads. In this festival, Santhals get involved in the colour play. Just as food and drink and feasts are made with roosters, pigs, goats etc., *puli* is also made on various backs from house to house.

(3) ***Nabanna:*** Like other communities of the popular agrarian society, this festival is held on the occasion of cooking new rice in the month of *Aghran*.

Apart from this, there are other important festivals like *Erok-Sim (Ashar), Hariar-Sim (Bhadra), Irigundli nanai, Gundli (Bhadra), Janthar Puja (Aghran), Sankranti Puja (Poush Sankranti), Magh-Sim (Magh)* etc.

Cock Fighting

The simple source of joy for the Santhals was to go to the market or fair near the village and enjoy the joy of cockfighting. Many of them used to go to the market with their Cock, accompanied by some villagers. If they won their cock in the fight, everyone would enjoy it together. The owner of the defeated rooster would hand over his defeated Cock to the owner of the winning Cock as a reward for winning. The hats and fairs of the village inhabited by Santhals filled the hats with joy as they watched and participated in the cockfighting competition.

God

The most important deity of the Santals is '*Thakur*'.[12] Of course, they worship him for a long time. Because, he is the past of human good and evil. Some consider '*Thakur*' to be the Sun God. The most popular deities of the Santhals in general are *Marang Buru, Moreko, Jair Era, Gonsai Era, Pargana* (head of the Bengal or gods and witches) and

Majhi. The main deity of the Santals is '*Marao Baru*'. In all the festivals, the Santhals worship '*Marang Buru*'. Another deity of the Santhals is *Sibonga* or Sun God. *Sibonga* does not harm anyone. He protects everyone from all dangers. Besides, Santhals also worship *Morko Turaiko, Jaher Era, Gosai Era, Seema Bonga* etc. Everyone is afraid of the Santhals in *Seema Bonga.* That is why he is worshipped in the village every year. Other deities of Santhals include *Jammin Bonga, Pachgala Bonga, Majhi Haram Bonga, Bura Bonga, Dadi Bonga, Bir Bonga, Sut Bonga, Kisad Bonga, Baghut Bonga, Rangairuji Bonga* etc. Apart from that, each family has two separate deities, namely, *Orak-Banga* or house god and *Abgebanga* or secret god.

Occupation

Most of the Santhals of Malda and North and South Dinajpur districts earn their livelihood by farming. However, most Santhals do not have their land. They share and work on other people's land. However, when the farming season is over, they continue to live by hunting birds. Agriculture is done by Santhal husband and wife both son and daughter. In Santhal society girls are active enough, can work hard enough. According to many, Santhal women are again more industrious than Santhal men. But they do not get the value of this hard work. Because everyone exploits them in various ways, be it in North Bengal or other regions. However, most of the Santhals in Jalpaiguri, Alipurduar and Darjeeling districts are involved in the tea industry. They mainly work as tea workers. However, many Santhals in Malda and North and South Dinajpur districts also make a living by farming. The Santhals also make a living by collecting forest resources and fishing. Again, educated Santhals are employed in various government and non-government jobs. This is not the case here again, as they earn some money by working as temporary labourers in their rest time in the tea gardens of Terai and Duars.

Production of Agricultural Products

Santhals are mainly agricultural communities. Paddy is the main product. Apart from paddy, they produce wheat, maize, cotton, pulses, mustard and others various other vegetables. They divide the cultivated land into three parts. The land adjacent to the ecosystem is called '***Berge***' land, where maize, barley, mustard and various vegetables are cultivated. The high ground is called '***Gadda***'. This land is not far from reality. Barley, cotton and wheat are produced in this land. The third type of land is called '***Khet***'. Paddy is produced in this land. The farmland is further divided into three categories, namely—(1) '***Chaham***' field—very good paddy is not produced in such land. (2) '***Soem***'—this land is relatively low, medium type of paddy is produced here, (3) '***Sol***'—this land is low and wet, this land is the best land for paddy production. Santhals cultivate by planting method. Employs bullocks or buffaloes for plowing. The seeds are first sown in June-July. When the seedlings are 4-6 inches large, they are planted flat on a large land with a ladder after repeated plowing. The land uses dung manure, ash as fertilizer. Dams are built around the land to hold water. Both men and women work equally on agricultural land for agriculture. Only women are forbidden to plow. Because it was their religious barrier. Moreover, men and women equally participate in planting, weeding, harvesting, threshing, and weeding.

Handicrafts

Santhal girls are very skilled in handicrafts. Evidence of this can be found in the walls of their houses. The walls are painted with various colours to enhance the beauty. Both men and women are very good at dancing and singing. Dance and song keep themselves in the limelight all the time. ***Madals*** or ***Mosha*** is their ethnic musical instruments. The instrument of the song is the big flute made of bamboo and also the flute is made from the horns of the buffalo. Santhal men specialize in woodworking. Moreover, *Mahua* can produce oil in the mill from the fruit. So Santhal, whether male or female, both specialize in handicrafts.

Domestic Animals

Cattle, buffaloes, dogs, cats, goats, sheep, pigs, ducks, and chickens are the main domestic animals. They are accustomed to drinking cow's or buffalo's milk. He employs cows or buffaloes for plowing etc. Dogs are extremely helpful during hunting.

Food

The main food of Santhals is rice. They call rice was '***daka***'. They eat rice twice a day. In the morning ***Panta*** eats rice which is soaked in water all night. They go out to work after eating ***panta*** rice. Along with this, he eats fried chilies and vegetables. He comes back from work in the evening and cooks hot rice and eats it. Eats fish, meat and vegetables. Santhals use two types of drugs. Eating rotten rice is a feature of their national life. The second type is to be obtained from ***Mahua*** flower, i.e. to make wine and eat it. ***Chutar*** is smoked when ripe in tobacco leaves. Now-a-days they have become accustomed to smoking *bidi* and cigarettes.

Ojha and Witchcraft

Gunin or *Ojha* devotees who believe in *Tabij, Kabaj, jharphuk, mantras* etc. Most Santhals are uneducated. When they are sick, they look for ways to cure the disease in *Jharfuk*. If the disease is severe, seek the help of *Gunin* or *Ojha*. Do not go to easily Doctor and *Kabiraj*. The origin of the uneducated *Ojha* is from this Santhal community. Santhal Community was believers in ghosts. *Ojha* came to the patient's house and played the role of the chief guest. He was diagnosed with the disease after eating good and bad for a few days. All these sorcerers come at any time and immediately diagnose the disease. Their clear announcement has caught the patient in witchcraft. The witchcraft practice was a bad reform, which was prevalent in Santhal society. *Ojha* usually appoints a Santhal woman, a widow in her fifties, as a witch. Again the old married Santhal women were designated as a witch. The witch resembles a demon. The ghost returned with his companion. At the instigation of all these witches, the villagers beat the innocent people to death by appointing them as witches. The witch perishes. Now-a-days the government has become very vigilant. The police appear at the right time when their misfortune causes any persuasion and when the news is received from the government.

Dresses and Ornaments

Santhal girls love to wear ornaments. They use more silver ornaments. Girls love to dress up after the festival. Tattoos are common in Santhal society. The costumes of the Santhals are also very common. In earlier days, men wore towels or thick cloth woven in five or six handlooms. Present days, boys are wearing full pants and shirts. At present, of course, the identity of modernity is found everywhere. Santhal girls, especially those who are fair-skinned, wear tattoos of various designs on their foreheads and necks to beautify themselves. The Santhal boys take an odd number of three, five, seven or nine '*shikas*' in their left hand. Hunting spots are like ticks.[13]

Houses

So far the Santhal people have built houses in a different style of construction in the original settlement area of their ancestors, but at present, it is safe to say that the construction style is not followed. The houses of the Santhals in this region are built mainly on financial compatibility. Visiting Santhal village, it was seen that the houses of most of the well-to-do families were paved floors, paved houses with tin roofs on paved walls. Most of the poor Santhals have raw bamboo fences on the walls of their houses but corrugated tin has been used for the rice huts. In some places, the walls of the house have been built on the bamboo fence of the house by mixing rice straw with mud. At present only 15-20 inch wide or thick walls have been built with mud. No one is currently building such a thick wall for a dwelling house, given the number of villages and the cost. Moreover, the *Indira Awas Yojana* and the grants given for the construction of houses for the development of the tribes, houses are built in the government model. As a result, although there is no variety in house construction in Santhal Para, their houses are very clean, dung-covered, *Tulsi mancha* in some houses, flower gardens in many houses, earthen walls of some houses or cross marks are painted on the entrance of the house.[14]

Furniture

Almost every family has a bed. It is woven with rectangular wood or bamboo and *sabui* rope. For eating, use *shalpata* or *Kasa*, aluminium dish bowl. Every family must have a *Kaser* '*jambati*'. Earthenware pots are used for transportation and storage. Use bamboo baskets coated with dung to store food. This is called '*gawni*'. It uses bamboo-covered '*pata*' to hold clothes and ornaments. '*Kun*' means tapping to escape the rain.

Funeral System

The Santhals cremated the dead body like Hindus. However, the dead body of pregnant women and children were not cremated who were burned. They carried out the dead body to cremation "*ghat*" by throwing parched rice and seeds of cotton. They also slew a chicken before setting fire to the funeral pyre. After five days of cremating the dead, a programme was arranged called "*telnahan*". In this programme they sacrificed a hen and "*haria*" that was domestically prepared wine to the *Maran Baru* (main god) and the dead's ancestral spirits.[15]

Conclusion

Finally, it can be said that the Santhal society has changed a lot at present. With time, modernity in Santhal society has touched them. Their education is improving a lot. Many educated people are participating in politics. They are also getting government facilities. Among them, the influence of superstition and witchcraft has diminished. All in all, they have slowly entered the light of modernity.

NOTES AND REFERENCES

1. Asitbaran Chowdhury, *Santhal Somaj, Daini O Bartaman Sangkot*, A. Mukharjee and Pvt. Ltd., Kolkata, 1985, p. 9.
2. Susmita Som, *Malda Jelar Itihas Charcha*, Depali Publishers, Malda, 2002, p. 102.
3. Ratan Biswas, *Uttarbangaer Jati O Upajati*, Punarsho, Kolkata, 2001, p. 177.
4. *Mahendra Debnath, Uttarbanger Pranthabhumir Janajattii Itihas O Sanskriti*, Mitram, Kolkata, January 2001, p. 177.
5. Suniti Kumar Chatterjee, *Kirat-Jana — Kriti*, Royal Asiatic Society of Bengal, Kolkata, 1951, p. 4.
7. "DHE Sunder", Edited by D.C. Roy, *Final Survey and Settlement of the Western Duars in the District of Jalpaiguri*, NL Publishers, Siliguri, West Bengal, 2013, p. 213.
6. *Op. cit.*, p. 179.
8. Ashok Gangopadhyay, *Uttarbenga Parichay*, Grantha Tirtha, Kolkata, p. 103.
9. Siddharta Guha Roy, *Malda: Subarna Rekha*, Kolkata, 1988, p. 12.
10. Pradyut Ghosh, *Malda Jelar Itihas*, Pustak Bipani, Kolkata, 2000, pp. 136-37.
11. Ratan Ghosh, *op. cit.*, p. 185.
12. Prodyut Ghosh, *op. cit.*, p. 140.
13. Mahendra Debnath, *op. cit.*, p. 194.
14. *Ibid.*, p. 193.
15. *Ibid.*, p. 193, Ratan Biswas, *op. cit.*, p. 190a.

8

The Rabha and Their Cultural Life

A Case Study of Tufanganj

Prasenjit Sarkar and *Sahel Bepari*

The Rabhas are a branch of the Kirat or Sino-Tibetan people of North-East India. They are commonly known as Koch or Rabha. They live in North-East India, especially in Kamrup and Goalpara districts of Assam and Jalpaiguri, Dinajpur, Cooch Behar, Darjeeling districts of West Bengal. Ordinary people refer to them as Rabha, but the Rabhas are more eager to introduce themselves as Nang-Kocha (we are Koch). Among the Mongoloid groups, in ethnographic judgment, the Rabhas are a prominent indigenous people. They bear a striking resemblance to the people of the Mech and Garo. Sri Arvind Kar, the editor of *Kiratbhumi*, wrote in his article that, the Rabhas gradually migrated from Tibet to the Bengal plains.[1] The Rabhas were non-Aryan and the aboriginal community originated from Indo-Mongoloid race. Reboti Mohan Saha wrote that it is known from various elements that, their predecessors came to the North-Eastern part of India from Siberia through Mongolia, China, Tibet and Brahmadesh before circa 3000 B.C.[2] According to linguists and anthropologists, Rabhas belong to the Koch group of the Indo-Mongolian Brahmanical branch of Mongolian descent. They entered India through the northern frontier pass and settled in Tripura, Manipur, Garo hills of the Brahmaputra valley, in the plains of Assam and some parts of West Bengal. In the past, the Rabhas was known as 'Koch'. Even now the term 'Koch' is used to refer to the identity of their community, language and culture. The Rabhas consider themselves the sons of the Hindu God Shiva who brought them into this world. According to Rabha folktales and beliefs, Lord Shiva brought Rabhas from heaven (*Rangkrang*) to earth (*Hasong*). M. Martin, an earliest British scholar and explorer writes, "The Rabhas constitute a tribe of Kamrup which is chiefly confined to the parts of this district that lie towards its eastern extremity. They are akin to a branch of the Kuch tribe known as Pani Kuch who are thinly scattered over all parts of Assam and the lower parts of Bhutan."[3] E. Dalton argues that the Rabhas and the Hajongs are the branches of the Kachari race and are connected with the Garo.[4] Many scholars believe that the Rabha people originated from a combination of Garo and Kachari. Their language is defined as the Boro branch of the *Bhot Brahma* family. Orally music, rhymes and folklore etc. are prevalent among them. There is no script in this language.

In the Rabha language, the *Gotra* is called '*Hosuk*'. The *Gotra* occupies a special place in the Rabha society. Like other tribes in North-East India, the Rabha society was matriarchal. In other words, females took the responsibility of the whole family. They were governed by their own culture and they governed their lives by their own rules and customs. They even had their own *Gotra* or clans. But this *Gotra* or clans does not indicate any caste system, because *Varna* or caste system was not prevalent in the Rabha society. This division was formed based on their occupation. Like the rest of the society, the Rabhas were bound by kinship within their group. We know from the various accounts that the Rabhas living in the Cooch Behar district belong to the Koch group. The Rabhas are also in the process of Sanskritization. Like other tribal communities, they are also changing their style of living and thinking. Tufanganj is the only sub-division of the Cooch Behar district having Rabha people. There are two types of Rabhas in this region — one practicing Hinduism and another practicing animism. The village Rabhas of Tufanganj generally speak the local Bengali dialects, but the Rabhas who live in the forest villages have retained their original Rabha dialect.

Although Hinduism and Christianity influenced the Rabha community, in some sections of Tufanganj, the Rabhas are still trying to preserve their traditional ways of life. It is an attempt to preserve its heritage, which has been around for a long time. There are considerable differences in ritual practices among forest Rabhas and village Rabhas. The Rabha tribe can be divided into two distinct sections — One is forest Rabhas and the other is village Rabhas. The forest Rabhas usually resides in Rasikbil, Paglirkuthi, Takomari, Chengtimari etc. forest vicinity areas of the Tufanganj subdivision. On the other hand, village Rabhas usually reside in Rampur, Singimari, Barokodali, Baroshalbari, Haripur, Mugabhog etc. areas of the Tufanganj sub-division. Rabhas living in forested areas depended on the forest for their livelihood and was employed as a labourer in various departments of forest department. Yet that trend can be noticed. Exceptional examples can be found in a few cases. Besides they are also dependent on agriculture for their livelihood.

The forest Rabhas considered themselves much better and holier than the village Rabhas. The main reasons behind this, as the village Rabhas have long lived in places with mixed cultures; many new cultures have entered among them. They adopted many new cultural beliefs and traits which were prevailing among the non-Rabhas of the locality. Ethnically, there are ten divisions in Rabhas. They are — *Koch, Dahuria, Bitlia, Rangdania, Maitoria, Hena, Shonga, Pati, Adahi* and *Totla*. However, most of the Rabhas of North Bengal belong to Koch community and for that, they are called *Koch Rabha*. The *Rangdania* Rabhas in the above divisions are comparatively much more conservative. They are reluctant to adopt any new culture from their neighbouring Bengalis and Assamese. Compared to that, the most liberal Rabhas are the *patis*. Because they adopted multi-cultural features including language from Bengalis and Assamese. To improve themselves, they adopted a plough cultivation system from the Bengalis and Assamese. Among the above divisions of the Rabhas *Pati, Rangdania* and *Maitoria* enjoyed superior social status.

Rangdanias are such a group of Rabhas who try to temporarily forget people's sorrow by playing dance — songs and musical instruments in the funeral festival. *Maitorias* group of Rabhas used to arrange meals at the funeral festival. *Mai* (cooked rice), *Tou* (fowl), pork etc. were usually used as food in this ceremony. '*Chungas*' (a kind of undivided bamboo piece) were used as water pots. The *Patis* used to arrange dishes at the funeral festival and plantain leaves were used as a dish. This means that each group had different responsibilities which they used to perform in different social events. These groups also played the almost same role in *Baykho* or *Khokhchi* which was considered as a national festival of the Rabhas. In this context, it can be said that *Runtuk* was the oldest deity worshipped by the Rabhas.

Clans or *Gotras*

No clear information is available about the origin of the Rabhas. But according to the Rabha legend, they are the descendants of the God *Rabha Rishi*. However, most of the Rabhas of North Bengal belong to the Koch group and that is why they are called *Koch-Rabha*.

According to the matriarchal rules, the mother's *Hosuk* (*Gotra*) is the identity of the child. *Hosuk* or *Hadam* (*Gotra*) is very important in terms of identity. When a relative comes home, he or she is asked about the *Hosuk* (*Gotra*). If there is a similarity between the *Hosuk* (*Gotra*) of both the families then it is assumed that he is a close relative.[5] They also think that they may even have blood ties to their ancestors. Establishing marital relations within the same *Gotra* is strictly forbidden. If a man or a woman of the same *Hosuk* (*Gotra*) unknowingly entered into a marital relationship, they would have to be punished and atone according to social norms. According to the law of atonement, the man or woman had to take a *Gotra* loan from someone from another *Hosuk* (*Gotra*). In most cases, the woman did that. The woman who lent to her *Gotra* must have been childless. In return for the *Gotra* loan, the woman was given various items including food and clothes etc. On the other hand, the breeding of her *Gotra* was also done very fast. If a woman marries a man from another group, her children are identified as the mother's *Gotra*. Similarly, if a man marries a woman from another *Gotra*, his children get the title of father. For example, here is a list of several *Gotras —Mauji, Maujidong, Bandha, Bandhadhay, Haundoum, Kattang, Uchichitak, Nakman, Labak, Dwarhat, Champet, Banag, Bantao* etc.[6]

Different types of strict provisions have been given for consuming different food items according to the *Gotra* or clans. The importance of the *Gotra* or clans is immense during funeral activities. In this programme wine or water is offered for the peace of the soul of the deceased, which is called *Chikabouroi* (to offer water). Not everyone can do this. A person belonging to the same *Gotra* or clan as the deceased belongs to is eligible to donate water. Each *Gotra* or clan has its own separate water donation rules. These rules are secrets that are not shared with anyone else. The only maternal elderly woman kept it secret for the rest of her life. On the eve of her death, she passed on the reserved word to a suitable daughter. If she does not have any daughters, then she gives the word to someone suitable in the same *Gotra* or clan. This ritual is called *Hosuk houdum* or *Chikabouroi* ritual. This tradition has been going on since time immemorial.[7] Even this trend still exists in Rabha society today.

Language

The Rabhas have their cultural heritage which they have been following since ancient times. They have their language. The Rabhas usually use colloquial language which can also be called their mother tongue. Its name is *Kochakru* language. According to Sir George Abraham Grierson, an Irish administrator and linguist in British India, the Rabha dialect belongs to the Bodo group of languages of the Assam-Burmese branch.[8] They have been using many poems, songs, folktales etc. orally in their region since ancient times. They are also proficient in speaking and understanding their neighbour's languages such as Bengali, Rajbanshi and Hindi equally.

House

The place where the Rabhas used to build their own houses was called *Kocha Hadam*. Their house was called *Nogou Ju*. However, the Rabhas of North Bengal usually refer to it as a *Ghar*. The houses of the Rabhas in the forest areas are called *Haprang Nogou*. The roof is thatched with *shan* grass. These are the parts that are usually noticed in Rabha houses — *Chasang* (the granary), *Thakan* (ceiling), *Darban* (wall), *Akhni Hoqa* (bedroom), *Fangkar* (fire place for cooking), *Har Tar Kang* (courtyard) etc. The verandah (*Bouchl*), Kitchen room etc. are also observed in the residence made by them. They usually build their houses with materials like wood, bamboo, sand, mud, thatching grass, reed pipe etc. The walls of the village Rabha huts are made of bamboo sticks, jute sticks and wooden splits. Doors and windows are usually made of wood or bamboo. The only entrance to each hut is called *Nugdur*. Each part of the house is divided by walls which are usually made of bamboo or wood. The *mejia* (floor) is usually coated with mud and cowdung. Financially backward Rabhas used thatched *shan* grass for *Haprang* (roof) construction. The tin roof was connected to the pillars by jute rope. By the interaction with other communities, the Rabhas have changed the model of their usual houses. However, with the advent of the modern age, they have mastered the ever-new technique of building houses from the neighbouring Bengalis. Recently the use of cement, stone and even tin in their construction has been observed. They used to perform certain rituals to protect themselves from evil eye or negative forces after choosing a place to live. They believed that if these rituals are not observed, the family will be affected by the influences of ghosts or some divine power. They have been following different types of folk beliefs from generation to generation. However, some changes have been noticed in these rituals now, because now Rabha society is much more advanced in the education system than in the past.

Furniture and Domestic Utensils

The Rabhas usually use wood and bamboo-made furniture. They use wood and bamboo-made chairs, tables, beds etc. as furniture. However, with the advent of the modern age, they have been able to modernize themselves. So they have been using modern furniture lately. They beautify the furniture by covering it with colourful fabrics made at home. Wealthy families in Rabha society can be seen using sophisticated furniture lately. They use chairs, tables, sofas, dining tables, almirah made of wood and iron.

In addition to using furniture, they use a lot of utensils which is very vital in daily work. In earlier times, most of their utensils were made of wood, bamboos, leaf and earthenware. Earthen pitchers which are known as '*tangi* or *mukh*' in Rabha language are very much used in their daily domestic life. The bamboo-made container they use to store food grains is called 'dully' in Rabha language. They use bamboo-made *Ba-chung* as water containers. The wooden spoon they use is called *Chaplaq*. The wooden cooking spud they use is called '*Maykan*'. Also, these are the utensils that they use in their daily life — *Hariha-kambai* (earthen cauldron), *Kattai* (bill-hook), *Shelu* (stick), *Bhusuri* (knife), *Dabor* (big earthen pitcher) etc.[9] They also used the leaf of plantain tree and skin of plantain tree as utensils. They also use different types of choppers (like *Pantam, Kangka*), *Kodal* (spud), *Bakeng* (axe), *Kinchi* (scissors), *Bhusuri* (knife) etc. in their daily life. Along with the use of these traditional utensils, they are also seen using metal utensils these days.

Food

In previous times, they used to collect various fruits and vegetables from the forest. In addition to this, they relied heavily on hunting and fishing for their livelihood. All of these practices are now limited to the folk story because they now follow many modern customs for food collection. Rice is the main food like Bengalis and it is called '*May*' in the Rabha language.

In the present era, the Rabhas, like other Bengali and Assamese people, consume all kinds of food. Huge changes in their eating habits can be noticed compared to the past. However, one of their traditional foods is *Haria* (one kind of local wine). In addition, the most popular foods are dry fish, chicken and pork. They take them as food in any social festival. They even use this type of food for entertaining guests.

One type of dry fish known as *Nakhem* (pulverized dry fish which is preserved in bamboo tubes for a long time) is very popular in Rabha society. They also had other food items — *Panchak* (various vegetables), *Na* (fish), *Kan* (meat), *phap* (cake), seeds of pulse, milk, ghee etc. According to the Rabha language, breakfast is called '*Main fani sarni*', lunch is called '*Rasan dupar ni*', dinner is called '*Gasam sani*'. Gradually when Rabhas came into contact with the neighbouring Bengalis, their eating habits changed a lot. They also mastered many aspects of eating habits from the Rajbansis. They also made their own homemade *Chakat* (rice beer) which is a very popular drink among the Rabhas. Everyone, men and women, was accustomed to smoking. They also smoke *Biri* and cigarettes. In addition to this, all men and women chew *Gay-Pan* (betel leaves).

Dress and Ornaments

Clothing varies among different people in Rabha society based on economic status, social, political status and enlightenedness. Rabha women used to wear clothes divided into three parts for their body covering. Women use *Kambang* dresses to cover up to the waist. On the other hand, they wear *Kyalet* to cover from the waist to the knees. They wear a garment called *Faakcheek* which they use as a scarf around their necks. They wear *Khodabang* to cover their hair. In previous times, Rabha women used bamboo-made handlooms to prepare garments. Women usually wear different colored clothes. They also wear *Sari*. Traditional male dress is known as *Pazal*. It covers the lower part of the body. It is the most popular cloth among the Rabhas. Another type of dress is the *Pachar*. In Rabha society, both men and women wear this dress as a wrapper in winter. Men wear *dhoti*, shirts and *Chadar* (shawl). In addition, men wear the turban. Design is abundant in women's clothing compared to men's clothing. The type of clothing commonly worn by the Rabhas is the *muffler* (scarf), *Gamcha* (towel), *Chadar* (shawl). Seasonal changes in their attire can also be noticed. Now-a-days, both men and women of Rabha wear modern attire like the Rajbangshi and the Bengalis. In winter they wear thick woollen clothes and a sweater. Earlier times, financially affluent Rabhas used one type of wooden or bamboo-made sandal, which was '*Kharam*'. But now everyone in society, rich and poor alike wears different types of shoes.

In Rabha society, there is an abundance of different types of ornaments or jewellery among women. From this, it is understood that jewellery was very popular among women. They use silver garlands like *Chandrahar* and other silver ornaments like *Labak, Suki mala, Bingta* etc. Rabha women usually use many types of ornaments. Financially affluent Rabhas use ornaments made of gold and silver. The ornament that is worn on the ear is called *Nambri*. The ornament that is worn on the nose is called *Nakpati*. The necklace worn around the neck is called *Hingchil*. In addition to this, they also wear finger rings, namely *Chhoushitan*.

Diseases and Medicine

Diseases such as fever, dengue, dysentery, smallpox etc. are common among the Rabhas of Tufanganj. They are more convinced of the traditional method than the modern medical methods for curing diseases. The Rabhas did not give much importance to modern medicine earlier. The patient is taken to *Huji* (priest) who usually prescribes herbal medicine for recovery. Apart from this *Tantra Mantra* and worshipping (*Puja-parvana*) are also famous in the Rabha society for their healing of the sick. Besides, worship of many goddesses exists in Rabha society to deter the patient from insane behaviour. Even in recent times, if a person has a physical illness; it is assumed that he or she is affected by evil goddesses.

The Rabhas worship maleficent gods and goddesses for the health and well-being of their family members. They worshipped a deity named *Longu* when their child was suffering from fever or any other disease. They also worshipped the soul of their predecessors like *Dekal, Jourakal* etc. to satisfy them. The Rabhas thought that the three maleficent deities are responsible for the cause of children's illness. They were Michicbai, Nurbai and Joka-Jukini. They think that Michicbai deity enters the newborn baby and as a result, the newborn baby starts getting sick. They immediately called the *Huji* (priest) and follow his advice and dedicated a duck to the goddess to cure the baby. The Rabhas worshipped another evil deity called Joka-Jukini. Babies between the ages of five months and ten years old are mainly attacked by this deity. As a result, children suffered from various diseases. Then they worship the deity to please her. In addition to this, when children are influenced by another evil deity Nurbai, similar worship methods are prevalent in their society. In addition to this, they also worship many evil deities such as Tukini, Bulua-bai, Paniya-bai etc. to save people from madness behaviour.[10]

The Rabhas are quite aware of the medicinal plants. They use wild honey, lime, saltwater, *Tulsi, neem, methi* etc. as medicine. In addition to these, they have some traditional believes in daily life, which they follow. If they see a person carrying a log of wood or someone carrying an axe or spud, they consider it an ominous sign. They usually stop their good work if they see this awful signal. On the other hand, if they see a basket of fish on the road or pitcher full of water, they consider this a good signal for their object. Then they try to perform the proposed work.[11] However, after getting the touch of modernity from the neighbouring Bengalis and Rajbansis, many in the Rabha society have become believers in modern medicine.

Education, Singing and Dancing

The Rabhas did not have the opportunity to be educated in formal education in ancient times. They did not even have a script to read or write. They received as much education as they needed to make a living and to survive by struggling in the environment. They gradually began to learn the techniques of weaving, hunting and farming. But later when the princely state of Cooch Behar was influenced by British rule, the door of education was opened to all. Then they started participating in the formal education system. Since taking part in the formal education system, a large number of Rabhas have had the opportunity to work in various departments of the administrative structure of the state and Central Government on their own merits which continues.

The Rabhas have been practicing their folk literature since ancient times. Folk literature was developed by some prominent personalities and talented people of the Rabha community and enlightened the people of the society. The main subjects of folk literature are many ancient historical stories, events related to birth, death and marriage, events related to worshipping and social festivals, social rules and laws etc. Along with this, various subjects of nature have found a place in folk literature. They use different folk songs for different social occasions. Various folksongs have been performed based on some festivals and cultural programmes of the religious, social and personal life of the Rabhas. Most of these folk songs are directly related to folkdance. The *Sathargeet* song of the *Baikhu* festival, marriage related *Tutakami* song, death and funeral ceremony related *Tarangkaji* song, *Maroi* or *Maare* song of Bikhhori worshipping, *Huyomaru* song of *Runtuk* worshipping etc. are some of the examples of their folksongs. Song and dance are the most important part of Rabha's entertainment. Maximum Rabha women can both dance and sing. They organize dances and songs in every religious and cultural event, marriage ceremony and every occasion of joy and sorrow. In their language dance is called *Basini*. Rabha women participate in dance and song collectively. The dance that is performed at the funeral ceremony is called *Marbar changi*. The dance that is performed in the holy festival is called *Basar Pidan*. The war dance is called *Handa Baru*. Apart from these, there are many other such dance styles in Rabha society. In addition to dance and songs, they use a variety of musical instruments mainly made of wood, animal skin, bamboo etc. They have a unique dance form named '*Nakchung Reni*' to celebrate fishing in the forest rivulets.

The Rabha has its tradition in the world of music. The musical instruments they use at various festivals are mainly made of bamboo, wood and brass metal. The flute they use is made of bamboo. One such flute is '*Karha brangsi*' which is much longer in size. They use a stringed instrument known as 'badungduppa', which is also made of a big bamboo tube. Another instrument 'gugumel' is made of bamboo and the 'buburenga' is made of reed. The large size drum is known as 'Kham' is a popular musical instrument among the Rabhas. Other musical instruments famous in Rabha society are Singa (traditional wind instrument), Nolkara (wind instrument) etc.

Hunting and Fishing

Hunting and fishing have been very popular in Rabha society since time immemorial. In the past, they relied on hunting and fishing for their livelihood. In the past, they hunted boar, deer, rabbits and different kinds of birds. However, hunting is not common in Rabha society now. But fishing activities are very popular in Rabha society. For fishing, they use various types of nets, spears, bamboo equipment etc. In fishing, Rabhas use indigenous technology. '*Burung*' is a fish trap that is made of split bamboo strips. They use it for small fishing in the river. '*Doksa*' is another type of fish trap whose shape is large conical. It is also made by split bamboo strips. '*Tapai*' is rectangular shaped trap that is also made of bamboo. In Rabha society, there is a fish poisoning method of fishing which is called '*Bishkutul*'. This plant is usually easily found in the wetlands of Duars. In this process, the whole plant paste is spread over a part of the river. Due to the toxic effect of this plant, the fish move to the upper surface of the water. Then it is very convenient to fishing. In addition to the above methods, there are many other methods of fishing in Rabha society.

Marriage and Divorce

Marriage is an important part of Rabha society because through this system the spiritual relationship of one family with another is formed. Among the Rabha, community marriage is known as *Biye*. According to Friend-Peneira, the Rabha society sanctions three types of marriage — by purchase, by gift and by servitude.[12] In Rabha society, marriage usually takes place through conversation between two families. Usually, communication is established through a match-maker in most cases. In Rabha society, the groom is called *Tarao* and the bride is called *Namsa*. The Rabha social system is very different from other social systems. In this society, girls are the owners of all property. The male has no right over the property. So the males had to stay as *Ghar Jamai* (a man who lives in his Father-in-law's family at the latter's cost). *Ghar Jamai* is called *Kilang Dapangi* in Rabha society. The prospective bridegroom had to marry for labour and live as a *Ghar Jamai*. In some cases, the opposite is also seen. In that case, the prospective bride would work hard for a year or more at the prospective bridegroom's house and then get married.[13] This type of marriage is called *Namsa Cheiyei*. Examples of such marriages are usually found in poor families. Another type of marriage method is *Falemoni-sani*. It was a marriage in exchange for a dowry. In this method, the bride was brought and married in exchange for a dowry. In this case, the bridegroom party used to pay dowry. However, the marriage system has changed a bit compared to the past. Another type of marriage system in Rabha society is *Raybouloung* or the method of marriage by sacrificing hen in front of the deity. This marriage system was usually practiced in financially weak and poor families. This marriage was performed at a very low cost and through family discussions. There was another type of marriage which is called *Gundugar*. This marriage was to be done in case of widowhood or the death of the wife. Another type of marriage system was prevalent which was illegal or stigmatized in the eyes of society. If a man or a woman gave birth to a child due to an illicit relationship, they would be given in marriage on behalf of society. This method of marriage was called *Badamal* marriage. On the day before the marriage of the Rabha society of *Tufanganj*, worship of the Thansiri is organized. The word *Thansiri* means the beauty of a homestead.

Everyone follows the rules of monogamy. In some special cases, polygamy is allowed. Widow marriage is recognized in their society. If there is a disagreement between the couple, they choose the path of divorce. The custom by which couples choose the path of divorce is called *Pan-Chenra*.

Previously the Rabhas believed in animism, but now they are intermix with Hinduism. The structure of the Rabha society was matriarchal in the past, but in modern times the structure of Rabha society in Tufanganj has become patrilineal. Recently, some rituals of Hinduism have also been observed in the Rabha community. The Rabhas of Tufanganj do not usually follow their *Gotra* very strictly. There are considerable differences in ritual practices between the forest Rabhas who still live in the forest villages and village Rabhas.

In the Tufanganj subdivision of Cooch Behar district, the Rabhas are minor in numbers. But their traditions, customs and beliefs are rich enough. Each area of daily life has its cultural characteristics. Living in a multi-cultural environment they often come under the influence of neighbouring communities like Bengalis and Rajbangsis. They have lost many of their language, traditional beliefs, arts, customs and rituals etc. as a result of multi-culturalism infiltrating them from neighbouring Bengalis and Rajbangsis. Changes can be noticed in their lifestyle and livelihood. Nevertheless, some sections of the Rabha community are still struggling to preserve their past heritage. Influenced by the surrounding cultural influences, the Rabhas are not observing their traditional ceremonial rites. Significant changes can be noticed in the various social rituals of the Rabhas. In most cases, they now follow the local Hindu method in performing various rituals. At the same time, the village Rabhas worship different Hindu deities.

NOTES AND REFERENCES

1. Dilip Kumar De, "Rabha Upojati O Loukik Devdevi", in *Uttar Prasanga-17*, Debabrata Chaki (ed.), number-3, Cooch Behar, 2011, p. 15.
2. Reboti Mohan Saha, "Rabhader Sangit O Badyo Jontro", in *Kiratbhumi*, 125 celebration, Vol. 1869-1994, Jalpaiguri, 1994, p. 312.
3. Anil Kumar Sarkar, *Tribes of Sub-Himalayan Region*, New Delhi, Mittal Publication, 2021, p. 19.
4. *Ibid.*, p. 36.
5. Dhananjay Rabha, "Koch Biharer Janajati Rabha O Tader Jibon Dhara", in *Koch Bihar Zila Sankhya, Paschimbanga*, ed. Sukhendu Das, *Tathya O Sanskriti Bibhag*, Paschimbanga Sarkar, Kolkata, 2006, p. 98.

6. *Ibid.*
7. *Ibid.*, p. 99.
8. Anil Kumar Sarkar, *op. cit.*, p. 20.
9. *Ibid.*, p. 98.
10. *Ibid.*, p. 125.
11. *Ibid.*, p. 129.
12. Amal Kumar Das and Manis Kumar Raha, *The Rabhas of West Bengal*, Calcutta, Scheduled Castes and Tribes Welfare Department, Government of West Bengal, 1967, p. 50.
13. Pramod Nath, "Uttar banger Adivasi Bibaha Paddhati", in *Uttarer Lok Sanskritir Dhara-I*, Sukhbilas Barma and Others (ed.), Cooch Behar, 2019, p. 137.

PART – II

Women: Religion, Emancipation and Partition Sufferings

9

Traditional Views of Women in Vaishnava Religion in Bengal

Akhil Sarkar

It is very difficult to say exactly when the origin and the spread of Vaishnavism took place in Bengal. However, Vaishnavism was certainly prevalent in Bengal in ancient times and there is ample evidence of it. Between the 4th and 15th centuries, various archaeological inscriptions and statues of various incarnations of Vishnu were discovered in different parts of Bengal and the process is still very much in existence today. In other words, Vaishnavism had been quite popular in Bengal, as a part of the great tradition of Hinduism. This religion flourished widely under the patronage of the Sena rulers and its name reached far and wide owing to Jayadeva's *Gitagovinda*. Apart from that Chandidas's *Sri Krishna Kirtan* was a testimony to the popularity of Vaishnavism. But, since the end of the fifteenth and sixteenth centuries, under the influence of Chaitanya Deva, a new equation was introduced within Hinduism and Vaishnavism. On one hand, the fame of Nabadwip as a mythological learning centre in Nadia district of Bengal touched the horizon. Attracted by the influence of the *Nabya Nyaya* or New justice of this region, knowledge-thirsty students and *pundits* of our scriptures or the *Shastra* used to get united at Nabadwip for different corners of India. As a result, Nabadwip's scriptural verdict became the social law of the whole of Bengal. The imposition of various scriptural provisions on the social system, especially on women and the lower classes, made their lives extremely cursed and miserable. Sri Chaitanya Dev himself was endowed with a lot of knowledge, so after finishing his education, he set up a tole at Mukunda Sanjay's house and arranged for the distribution of knowledge. However, Sri Chaitanya Dev, along with innumerable

Brahmins and non-Brahmins, arranged for the introduction of an innovative basic principle for resolving social, spiritual and cultural crises, which is devotion (*Bhakti*).[1] Sri Chaitanya Dev bestowed the women with the responsibility of distributing the path of devotion to all. He also kept that promise in his performance in Nabadwip which became renowned as his *Nabadwip Leela*. But the crisis was exacerbated when he absolved women of the obligation to distribute devotion after taking *sannyasa*.[2] They started getting more and more predominant as dutiful women, housewives and mothers of children in society. As a result, women began to be incurred closely with social barriers by various provisions of the Vedic scriptures. But in the post-Chaitanya period, based on his ideals, many wise and learned women hit the social system and paved the way for women's liberation and they bore witness to the glory of their knowledge in building a dynamic social system.

Chaitanya Dev propagated Vaishnavism by forming a separate and unique community separated from the Brahminical-based religion. A closer look at his life philosophy bears the testimony to that because it was with his permission, his disciples and the Goswamis like Gopal Bhatta and Sanatan Goswami who wrote a book for conducting social and religious regulations called *Haribhaktibilas* to guide the Vaishnava society in the right direction. This community was called the Mimanandi community.[3] After taking *sannyasa*, Chaitanya Dev did not meet his wife Vishnupriya or even did not address her for once. Chaitanya Dev used to refrain from associating with women in the life of a monk. That was the reason why Krishnadas Kabiraj says:

Paṇḍita haiya mon bichar na kar.
Rāṇḍi brahmanir baloke priti kene kar.
Jodyapi brahmani sei tapaswani Sati
Tothapi tahar dosh sundari jubati.
Tumio parom yubo parom sundar.
Lok kanakani bate deho abasar.[4]

To translate it into English:

Being a great scholar, why don't you judge your mind?
Why do you love the son of that Brahman woman?
Although the woman is caste and spends time in pursuit of God
But her only mistake is that she is young and gorgeous.
You are young and extremely grateful too
Refrain from the boy and stop people talking ill about you.

According to the explanation of the events mentioned by *Chaitanya-charitamrita*, Chaitanya Dev has the strictest attitude towards women. Perhaps he wanted to give folk education by his way of life. Prabhu demonstrated his behaviour in this way so that the monks must not possess the slightest weakness towards women.

Prabhu kohe Gobinda aji rakhile jibon.
Stri parosh hoile amar haito maron.[5]

In English:

Prabhu says Govinda keeps me alive until today.
If I mingled with women, I would have succumbed to death.

On his way from South India to Dwarka, Mahaprabhu rescued a prostitute named Barmukhi in the village of Gogha and inspired her with the Krishna *mantra*. Chaitanya Dev's main objective was to overthrow the conservative society which is strictly tied with tough regulations and build a developed and egalitarian society. During his travels in South India, he noticed that the differences between Brahmins and non-Brahmins were very strong in the Vaishnava community. In the South, doctrines like those mentioned above found little practical support and never led to the levelling of the castes or the adoption of questionable habits. The grip was too strong to be shaken by the Brahmin Vaishnavite and the Shudra followers were generally inferior in importance and never asserted themselves.[6] Ramanuja, the famous saint of South India, never deviated from the strict scriptural rules. He did not agree to provide women and the Shudras the right to recite the Vedas. Sri Chaitanya Dev could not accept this strict regulation of the scripture and so he showed the common people the path of the easy, straightforward, and devotional path of *Bhakti*. Chaitanya Dev baptized socially abandoned women at a place called Jizuri on the way to Khandbar in the Deccan and gave them a chance to return to the mainstream of society. At this time, the daughters of the poor fathers were married to a stone idol called Khandbar and like this way the helpless fathers freed themselves from the bondage of daughters. After this marriage, the girls were transformed into the property of the religious institution of that area and faced extreme social negligence and exploitation. That was the reason why Chaitanya Dev gave them the *Diksha* in the name of Lord Krishna and lamented:

Kemon nithur bolite na pari
Kemone Murari kore apon kumari.[7]

To translate in English:

How cruel is the father, I cannot imagine,
How could they push their daughters to be the slaves of God!

After getting back to Nabadwip, Sri Chaitanya Dev gave his consent to Vishnupriya Devi to worship his idol. It is not true that Chaitanya Dev did not touch women or talk to them after taking *sannyasa*. It is mentioned in *Chaitanyacharitamrita:*

Shatar matar nam Bhattacharjer grihini.
Prabhubhakta teho sneher janani.[8]

To make it in English:

Bhattacharya's wife is the mother of Sata
She is a pious woman and an affectionate mother too.

However, in *Chaitanyacharitamrita* and *Chaitanyabhagavata*, the two best books of Vaishnava literature, Bishnupriya Devi has been completely neglected. The name of Vishnupriya Devi is mentioned only once in *Chaitanyacharitamrita*, while in *Chaitanyabhagavata* the name of Vishnu Priya is mentioned but with no implication. As a result, it is very difficult to reconcile the duality that was found in Chaitanya Deva about women. Apostate men should give up all their material possessions. It can be said that Chaitanya Dev took strict restraint to impart his philosophy of life, sense of duty and folk education from that sense of duty. Chaitanya Dev loved to eat sweets from Parameshwar Modak's wife during *Navadwip Leela*, but Chaitanya Dev became annoyed when Parameshwar Modak's wife came to his place to meet him at Nilachal after Chaitanya's taking *Sannyas.*[9]

Sannash Panditganer korite garbonash.
Nich Sudra Dwara kore dharmer prokash.[10]

To translate it into English:

The lowly Shudras show their devotion
To stoop the Brahmin scholars from their pride.

Chaitanya Dev taught the anchorites the principle of abstinence, but he did not advise them to be anchored by neglecting, ignoring, or disregarding their wife within the household. In this respect, Chaitanya Dev may have perceived the shortcomings of his own life and so he repeatedly tried to speak about protecting the dignity of women. However, in the case of all the men and women of the Gaudiya Vaishnava society, the name Krishna was the principal and only virtue. In this case, women were not allowed to enter during the *bhajan kirtan* of men at the same time men were not allowed to enter during the *bhajan* of women. It was stated that to obtain the divine Lord Krishna, one has to renounce body, mind, offspring, property, desire and seek refuge in Him. Dr. R.G. Bhandarkar argued that the worship of Radha more prominently even than that of Krishna, has given rise to a sect, the members of which assume the garb of women with all their ordinary manners.[11] Chaitanya's main object was to establish and create a unique and reformed community, free from the trammels of the old and medieval Hindu society, particularly the bondage of Brahminical laws and customs. He attempted to revolutionize the current Brahminical law of marriage, which was dominated by the old and medieval laws of the Hindu caste. According to the new Vaishnava, of course outside the circle of consanguinity recognized by the old Hindu law, but without offense marry a Brahmin woman or man. Not only Vaishnava might intermarry with one another but they were also far from the medieval interdiction against adult marriage and widow remarriage. So the marriage system was very much simplified. The exchange of garlands or chains specifically of beads made of the stalks of the sacred *tulsi* plant, which was the denominational emblem or uniform of the Vaishnava sect, was considered enough to legalize these marriages.[12] Many women were deeply influenced by Chaitanya Dev's monastic life philosophy. Even many progressive women wrote many books and devoted their lives to revivify and immortalize the Vaishnava movement. The women of the ancient epoch of *Rigveda* enjoyed the same freedoms and opportunities as men in education and social life, but that right gradually began to be diminished by various scriptural rules. Standing there, the spread of women's freedom, rights and women's education in medieval Bengal was severely hampered. Despite so many obstacles, the door to women's education has not been closed completely. There are references to girls' education in various medieval literatures, for example, women's education is mentioned in famous literature like Ramprasad's *Vidyasundara* and Bharat Chandra's *Annadamangala*.[13] Besides, Rani Bhabani, Anandamoyee Devi of Bikrampur, Vaijayanti Devi of Kotalipara and others possessed scholarly knowledge in Sanskrit scriptures.[14]

In medieval society, women were not given much prominence in their marriages, but according to the theories of *Adityaprakash* and

Chaitanyamangal, women were given special privileges in Vaishnava society, especially in marriage. Sita Devi, the wife of the famous Pandit Adwaityo Prabhu of Shantipur, chose the husband of her choice. Chaitanya Dev also chose his first wife Laxmipriya Devi and married her despite her mother's consent. After the death of Chaitanya Dev in 1533, his wife Vishnupriya Devi did not have to become a *sati*, observing the stricture of the then society. Ramakanta Chakrabarty in his book *Vaishnavism in Bengal* argued that "The real shortcomings of the Vaishnava movement in Bengal consisted in its lack of definite economic motivation. It failed to effect any change in the existing economic organization of the villages. The Vaishnava Brahmana equation made the orthodox Gaudiya Vaishnavas who worked mainly in high society, totally incapable of curing the high caste Vaishnava of their vices and superstitions. The Vaishnava did not participate as a distinct religious group in any movement against widow burning, polygamy, child marriage and baby killing. They grew self-centred and ultimately became extremely conservative."

In the life philosophy of Chaitanya Dev, women, shudras, vile, ignorant, miserable, downtrodden all were initiated in the *mantra* of Krishna name and their social position was elevated under the shelter of Vaishnavism. He established human dignity by associating the neglected men and women in society with Vaishnavism. Probably Chaitanya Dev sent Nityananda Mahaprabhu from Nilachal (Odisha) to Bengal to fulfil this great purpose. As a result, the leaders of Vaishnavism continued to propagate the ideology and Sahajiya religion introduced by Chaitanya Dev among the so-called lower castes and women. That is why the orthodoxy of the traditional plaintiffs suffered a severe blow. Like other provinces of India, a new religious movement started in Bengal and communism spread here through the introduction of Bhakti Marg. According to the interpretation of historians, revolution first emerged in the field of thought. Later it came down to practical work. In ancient and medieval times, the trend of revolution was manifested in the name of religion. The movement introduced by Chaitanya in Bengal adopted that approach and he was the first social monk of Bengal.[15] As a result of various forms of exploitation of the helpless society in Hindu society, countless people started adopting foreign religions. Chaitanya Dev and Vaishnava religious leaders were able to inspire them (Hindus) with their ideals by upholding the ideals and importance of defending Hinduism, and to a large extent, they were successful.[16]

The second phase of Vaishnavism started in Bengal after Chaitanya Dev adopted Sannyasa, and Nityananda Mahaprabhu, Adwaitya Mahaprabhu, Srinivas Acharya, Narottam Das Thakur, Jahnavidevi, Birbhadra and others played important roles in it. During this period, the predominance of women under the auspices of Vaishnavism increased to some extent, especially in the field of education and culture. Besides, they also took organizational responsibility for the movement and management of the Vaishnava religion at this time. In this case, various Sanskrit scholars like Jahnavi Devi, Sita Devi, Hemlata Thakurani led Vaishnavism in a new stream. Nityananda Das, a disciple of Jahnavi Devi, gives a detailed account commending the conduct of the devout Vaisnavas in his book *Prembilas*.[17] Jahnavi Devi's daughter-in-law Subhadra Devi was a well-educated scholarly woman. The name of the book written by her is *Anangakadambabali*. Srinivas' son wrote a valuable book called *Jahnavatattvamarmarth*. In other words, their dominance as female gurus was very significant in the Gaudiya Vaishnava society. Many of them also took the leadership of Vaishnav Mandal as well.[18] Nityananda's wife Jahnavi Devi and Basudhadevi had a well-known *patbari* or hermitage in Chaduria (Malopara) village under Chakdaha police station in Nadia district. The founder of this ashram or hermitage was Purushattam Das Thakur and his son Kanu Thakur. The idols of Gauranga, Nityananda and Jahnavi Devi have a foothold in this temple and also the idols of Jagannath, Subhadra and Balarama are established in this temple.[19]

Kheturi Mahatutsab, the biggest event in the history of the Vaishnava religious movement was organized in Kheturi, North Bengal with the efforts and patronage of Jahnavi Devi. The Kheturi festival was organized from years between 1610 and 1620. Twenty-nine chief gurus of Vaishnavism participated under the leadership of Jahnavi Devi. Basically, after the Kheturi festival, the Gaudiya Vaishnava society had moved in a new direction. Jahnavi Devi played a major role in the promotion and propagation of Vaishnavism in different parts of Bengal and even in Vrindavan. She wanted to unite with the ideology of Vrindavan by resolving many issues and controversies of Vaishnava society and religion. Jahnavi Devi was well versed in Bengali and Sanskrit and was awarded the title of '*Acharyani*' at the Kheturi festival. As a result, she became a Goswami in the Gaudiya Vaishnava society and was accorded the same respect as the Goswami of Vrindavan. The ritual of worshipping Gauranga and Bishnupriya was officially introduced with the twin idols of Radha Krishna with her single initiative. As a result, it was her impeccable and outstanding talent that greatly increased the rights and dominance of women in the Vaishnava devotional movement. She showed the way to free women from various social barriers.

Sita Devi was deeply involved in the Gaudiya Vaishnava movement of Chaitanya Dev from the very beginning. With his great satisfaction, she fed Chaitanya Dev during the festival of Rath Yatra.[20] Like Sachidevi, she also did not become a *sati* after the death of her husband. She even strongly protested against this heinous practice against women. Sita Devi's extraordinary organizational skills set an example of uniting not only the Advaityo sect but also the larger Vaishnava society. Her role as an important social leader in a chauvinist society at that time was outstanding. Vishnudas Acharya wrote *Mitagunakadamba* based on her life philosophy and Loknathdas also wrote an outstanding biographical book called *Sitacharitra*. Sita Devi was incarnated as an inductor or initiator in Vaishnava society. She initiated her son Krishna Mishra and her daughter-in-law Vijaya into Krishnamantra, to make it clear, all these dynamic women did not allow the *kaulinya* ritual to enter their lives as exceptional characters. As a result, their propagated ideology was free from social evils like *satidaha* and child marriage. Even in the Vaishnava society, there are some books written by women which prove that in the Vaishnava society women had the right to education at least to some extent. All these books written by them are proof of that. We got to know that the Vaishnav women used to write letters from the book *Prembilas* written by Nityananda Das.[21] With the passing of time, the Gaudiya Vaisnava society abandoned the path of Chaitanya Dev's ideology and largely followed the path of Vrindavan Goswami. As a result, the Vaishnava social system began to take on a more complex form. That is why Gaudiya Vaishnavism continues to be formed in different branches and sub-branches. However, the main branch of Gaudiya Vaishnavism continued to be governed by the discipline of *Haribhaktibilas* written by Gopal Bhatt. Despite the indulgence of racism, there was some relaxation in women's rights, such as the right to practices religion, scripture and conduct religious ceremonies. Even women were given the right to worship *Salgram Shila*. The worship of one stone *Salgram* is said to be more efficacious than that of thousands of *Siva-lingas*. So the smaller the stone in size, the more auspicious it is. The purchase and sale of *Salgrama* are strictly forbidden. *Salgrama* worship is compulsory (*Nitya*), and even women and Sudras are entitled to worship, the prohibition applying only to those who are non-Vaishnavas.[22] Until the middle of the nineteenth century, Vaishnava women played a leading role in educating the girls of the aristocratic families of Bengal. The enthusiasm of Vaishnava women for education was also quite promising. Digambari Devi, the wife of Dwarkanath Tagore, was visited daily by a Vaishnava woman to impart knowledge of the scriptures of *Bhagavata* and *Respanchadhya*. All these Vaishnava women were well versed in Bengali and Sanskrit. Mr. Adam in his second report on the state of education in Bengal argued that it has been stated that zamindars, for the most part, instruct their daughters in the elements of knowledge and for the reasons there assigned, instances sometimes occur of young Hindu females who have received no instruction of their parents, roof taking lessons, at the instruction of their parents and brothers, after they have become widows with a view to the adequate protection of their interests in the families of which they have become members. The number of principal zamindars in the whole district is about fifty or sixty, of whom more than in a half are females and widows of these two, viz. Rani Suryamani and Kamala Mani Dasi are alleged to possess a competent knowledge of Bengal writing an account which some of the rest are more imperfectly instructed and others are wholly ignorant. Other excepting to the general ignorance are found amongst the medicant Vaishnavas or followers of Chaitanya, amounting in Nattore probably to fourteen or fifteen hundred individuals, who are generally able to write and read and who are also alleged to instruct their daughters in these accomplishments. They are the only religious body of whom as a sect the practice is characteristic.[23]

We came across many dynamic Vaishnava women who were all possessors of profound knowledge, in the nineteenth century, such as Girindra Mohini Dasi, who wrote a play called *Mirabai*. She also published a magazine called 'Janhabi'. She was the editor of this magazine. Kishori Baishnab imparted knowledge to Harsundari Dasi, daughter of Shivchandra Raybahadur. A dynamic woman named Haripriya was in charge of overseeing a Vaishnava arena in Motijheel near Murshidabad. She was recognized as Haripriya Goswami for the glory of her knowledge. Sri Chaitanya Dev created the sweet equation of Radha Krishna's love affair among all Bengalis. As a result, a new religion was created irrespective of race, gender, rich and poor. As a result, their view was that the nature of society would be better only if an unbroken human race could be built in the place of division. His religious movement gradually reached the lower strata of society. Deep changes began to take place in the old society. Vaishnava society, especially women, had the right to unite, to practice religion instead of religious bigotry, and Vaishnava society gave women the right to education. That is why it is said that Vaishnavism in Bengal tried to form the first universally educated society irrespective of men and women. From time immemorial, women have been striving for their own and distinct dignity, but ignoring the patriarchal solid wall of Hindu society, their pro-democracy and pro-democracy movement has never manifested itself. However, they did not lose the language of protest. The fight for that dignity was waged in retaliation for various blows and is still being fought. In the tide of Chaitanya Dev's devotional movement, women got the mental courage and strength to establish their individuality. That is why women's society gained the courage to enter the field of mass protests against the injustice of neglect.

NOTES AND REFERENCES

1. Ramakanta Chakrabarty, *Bange Baishnab Dharma*, Ananda Publishers, Calcutta, 2013, p. 30.
2. Dr. Sutapa Mukhopadhyay, *Vaishnav Jibani Sahitye Nareesamaj*, Progressive Publishers, Calcutta, 1996, p. 52.
3. Dr. Bhupendranath Dutta, *Vaishnav Sahitye Samajtattwa*, Chirayata Prokashini, Calcutta, 2007, pp. 27-28.
4. Krishnadas Kabiraj, *Chaitanyacharitamrita*, Antalila, Third chapter, Gita Press, Gorakhpur, 2009, p. 524.
5. *Ibid.*, p. 605.
6. T. Rajagopalachariya, *The Vaishnavite Reforms of India Critical Sketches of their Lives and Writing*, G.A. Natesan and Company, Madras, 1909, p. 143.
7. *Gobindadas Karcha*, Dwej Publication, Calcutta, 1404, p. 53.
8. *Chaitanyacharitamrita*, Madhyalila, 15/74.
9. Dr. Sutapa Mukhopadhyay, *op. cit.*, p. 63.
10. Krishnadas Kabiraj, *op. cit.*, p. 548.
11. Dr. R.G. Bhandarkar, *Vaishnavism, Saivism and Minor Religious System*, Hindustan Offset Press, Delhi, 1965, p. 86.
12. Bipan Chandra Pal, *Bengal Vaishnavism*, Modern Book Agency, Calcutta, 1933, pp. 120, 121.
13. Ramesh Chandra Majumdar, *Bangla Desher Itihas*, Vol. II, Madhyajug, Calcutta, 1373, p. 315.
14. *Ibid.*, pp. 314, 315.
15. Dr. Bhupendranath Dutta, *op. cit.*, pp. 91, 92, 93.
16. *Ibid.*, p. 61.
17. Ramakanta Chakrabarty, *op. cit.*, p. 89.
18. Dr. Tapas Basu, *Sri Chaitanya: Ekaler Bhabna*, Bangiya Sahitya Parishad, Calcutta, 2014, pp. 294, 295.
19. Dr. Pabitra Chakraborty, *Chakdehar Itihash O Sanskriti*, Nabapatra Prokashona, Calcutta, 1994, p. 240.
20. Hangsha Narayan Bhattacharya, *Jugabatar Chaitanya*, Farma K.L.M. Private Limited, Calcutta, 1984, p. 367.

21. Dr. Sutapa Mukhopadhyay, *op. cit.*, p. 228.
22. Sushil Kumar Dey, *Early History of the Vaishnava Faith and Movement in Bengal*, Farma K.L. Mukhopadhyay, Calcutta, 1961, p. 468.
23. William Adam, *Report on the State of Education in Bengal (1835 and 1836)*, University of Calcutta, 1941, p. 189.

10

Women's Emancipation in the Nineteenth Century Bengali Periodicals
A Research

Md. Mainul Islam

The importance of periodicals and newspapers as elements in composing social history is immense. The role of the media as a tool of mass awakening in Bengal in India in the nineteenth century has been elaborated by Brajendranath Bandyopadhyay in his book *Sakaler Kotha in Sangbadpatre* and Binoy Ghosh in his book *Samajchitra of Bengal in Samayikpatre*. Recently, researchers like Anisuzzaman, Muntashir Mamun and Swapan Basu have worked hard to compile old newspapers and periodicals, highlighting various aspects of the history of Bengal and India in the nineteenth and twentieth centuries. In the nineteenth century, the social value of Bengali newspapers was very high for the creation of the Bengali language and Bengali public opinion. In the early days of the Company's rule in Bengal, if a Bengali boy did not know Persian, he would not be able to work anywhere. At Fort William College, there was a lot of official attention to the Arabic-Persian Department, because Bengali parents taught Persian to Bengali boys without bothering. The Persian department received two-thirds of the money allocated to the college sector.[1] Government assistance in publishing Sanskrit and Arabic books was generous. In the early nineteenth century, Sanskrit scholars also looked down on the Bengali language.[2] Neglect of the Bengali language can be noticed in the pre-nineteenth century. During the Nawabi period, if they wrote in Bengali instead of Persian, the staff of the revenue department would not accept any application.[3] In the nineteenth century, it became full of English words, just as Bengali was Persian-tainted during the Nawabi period.

The neglect of the Bengali language shocked *Tattvabodhini*.[4] '*Sangbad Prabhakar*' expresses its pain over the neglect of mother tongue.[5] Bhabanicharan Bandyopadhyay's 'Babu Upakhyan' in '*Samachar Darpan*' is the first prose story in Bengali.[6] 'Samachar Chandrika', expresses the opinion that his writings were corrected by society. Akshay Kumar Dutt's socially conscious article 'Vidyadarshan' has been published more than once on the page of '*Tattvabodhini*'. Ishwar Gupta, the editor of '*Sangbad Prabhakar*', has given news of the consciousness of the Bengali society in the nineteenth century. Parichand Mitra's 'Monthly Magazine' exemplified social consciousness by making Bengali women useful to the nation.[7] Bengali newspapers played a helpful role in the balanced outcome of the Bengali reform movement through debate. The publication of *Samachar Darpan* (1818), the first Bengali language media, brought word art to the doorsteps of the common educated people. The printed form of language is not only in the library or on the table of the scholar — it is reaching the hands of the less educated people. As a result of the publication of Ishwar Gupta's '*Sangbad Prabhakar*' (1831), the literary movement of this public meeting became more rapid and wider towards public life. Ishwar Gupta is the proof of how the hand of the writer became from public meeting to public meeting, from public meeting to greater public life. Parallel to the events of the social, cultural and political life of Bengal, the discovery of endangered literary works, the discovery and publication of folklore and the publication of works by new writers have proved the unique historical role of this magazine. His incomparable fame is the collection and publication of works of various poets and panchalikars. He published three more journals, '*Sangbad Ratnabali*', '*Sangbad Sadhuranjan*' and '*Poshandpeeran*', to speed up the literary practice, making it controversial and popular. The *Tattvabodhini*, a periodical published in 1842 under the editorship of Akshay Kumar Dutt, published only articles on theology, literature, philosophy, history, archaeology, science and geography, as well as high-quality articles on women's education and support for widow marriage and anti-child marriage. One hundred years after the publication of *Samachar Darpan* (1818), in 1918, the monthly *Sahitya Patra* was published under the editorship of Mohammad Nasiruddin. Liberal and progressive outlook, a believer in the practice of free will, a supporter of the women's liberation movement in Muslim society.

Newspapers in India were started in 1780 AD by James Augustus Hickey through the Bengal Gazette. In 1818, the Christian missionaries of Srirampur published the first periodical in Bengal. John Marshman published *Dig Darshan* in 1818. Marshman later published a weekly called *Samachar Darpan*. In 1821, in opposition to the missionary initiative, Raja Rammohun Roy published the magazine '*Brahman Sebdhi*' and later '*Sambad Kaumudi*'. In this paper, Rammohun used to write against the Sahamar system and in favour of other social movements. Opposing this, Bhavanicharan Bandyopadhyay published '*Samachar Chandrika*'. Parichand Mitra created a new trend in the world of Bengali periodicals by editing the women's magazines '*Hitkari*' and '*Masik Patrika*' (1854). One of Derozio's disciples, Parichand Mitra, a mainstream devotee of the Bengal Renaissance, edited literary works and journals intending to eliminate multiple inconsistencies in women's education, women's rights and socio-cultural life. Brajendranath Bandopadhyay's book '*Bangla Samayikpatra*' (1818-1868) contains the names of 138 periodicals published in Bengali. The 17 major journals of this episode are: '*Samachar Darpan*' (1818), '*Sambad Kaumudi*' (1821), '*Samachar Chandrika*' (1822), '*Bangadoot*' (1829), '*Sambad Timirnashak*' (1831) of the Srirampur missionaries. *Sangbad Prabhakar* (1831), *Young Bengal's Jnananbeshan* (1831), *Sangbad Puranchandrodaya* (1835), *Sangbad Bhaskar* (1839), *Sangbad Rasraj* (1839), *Bengal Spectator* (1842), *Vidyadarshan* (1842), '*Tattvabodhini*' (1843), '*Sarvasubhakari*' (1850), '*Bibidhartha Sangraha*' (1851), '*Masik Patrika*' (1854), '*Saptahik Bartabah*' (1856).[8]

The pages of these magazines contain pictures of various social reaction movements of the time. Some of these magazines were associated with a particular group and some with religious ideologies. But they aimed to propagate the social movement in Bengal. In the nineteenth century, the '*Tattvabodhini Patrika*' was revered by educated intellectuals. It was originally a periodical based on religion, but under the editorship of Akshay Kumar Dutt, it went beyond religious boundaries and became a full-fledged journal. '*Bibidhartha-Sangraha*' is the first illustrated magazine in Bengal. Dwarokanath Vidyabhushan was the editor of '*Somprakash*' which was launched as a weekly in 1857. In the second half of the nineteenth century, there were many periodicals for girls such as '*Abalabandhab Patrika*', '*Bangamahila*', '*Binodini*', '*Hindullana*' etc. But the most popular and important was '*Bamabodhini Patrika*'. Inhuman practices in Bengali social life in the nineteenth century were an affront to women's emancipation. The main goal behind the social change at this time was women's welfare, which was manifested in the abolition of '*Satidah* practice', in the introduction of 'widow marriage' law, in the movement against 'nobility practice'(*Kauln'ya prath*). Social reform was the focal point of the social consciousness of the novice Bengalis of the nineteenth century.

In the first part of the nineteenth century, a big social movement was the 'Prevention of Satidah'. In 1818, a magistrate of Burdwan reported that 99 out of 100 Satidahs were forced. Between 1815-1820, 3613 people became *sati*. In 1828, 639 *sati* were performed in Bengal.[9] News of the co-existence was in almost every issue of *Samachar Darpan*. In most reports, *Samachar Darpan* covered some of his comments.[10] The social significance of the reaction that the constant reports of the periodicals and the demonic and cruelty of some of the news created in the minds of the people were not less. From the very beginning of the nineteenth century, there was a controversy in Bengali society over the practice of *Satidahs*. From 1823 onwards, Bengali newspapers were divided on the issue of *Satidahs*. *Samachar Darpan*, *Samachar Chandrika*, *Sangbad Kaumudi* could not agree on this. In March 1828, in a report on the practice of *satidah*, *Samachar Chandrika* reportedly interfered with the scriptural practice and opposed religious practices.[11] *Sambad Kaumudi* was vocal against *Satidahs*.[12] *Samachar Darpan* expressed the view that banning this inhuman practice would not harm Hinduism.[13] The next day *Samachar Chandrika* wrote that Manu, a Hindu ethicist, did not ban this practice. Even *Samachar Chandrika* was not willing to call this practice inhumane. In opposition to inhumane practices like *Satidahs*, *Samachar Darpan*, *Samabad Kaumudi* started publishing articles and *Samachar Chandrika* used to satisfy the conservatives.[14]

The passage of 'Regulation XVIII' in the Bentinck Council on 4th December, 1829 marked the great victory of the Bengali press. This is a landmark event in the history of social movements in Bengal. After the enactment of this law, the social movement became even stronger. But the *Samachar Chandrika* said that the English had misunderstood.[15] When some people died in a boat sinking at a ferry in Calcutta in 1831, *Samachar Chandrika* reported that it was due to iniquity.[16] This law has been enacted as a result of a misunderstanding by some missionaries and some Hindus. Therefore, on behalf of *Sati*, Belated hopes that this law will be repealed in the appeal to the Privy Council.[17] The social movement in which the newspaper was involved in abolishing the practice of *Satidahs* became more and more entrenched. Discussions about widow marriage began in the 1830s. To the editor of *Samachar Darpan*, some of the noble daughters of unmarried adults in Shantipur prayed for a law on the practice of widow marriage.[18] In support of this demand, some ladies of Chuchara demanded the introduction of widow marriage with the prevention of child marriage and polygamy.[19] This proposal is sharply ridiculed in *Samachar Chandrika.*[20] Motilal Shil, Haldhar Basu and some other widows decided to convene a meeting to encourage marriage.[21] *Samachar Chandrika*, on the other hand, continues to oppose the proposal.

In the third decade of the nineteenth century, discussions on widow marriage began to appear in the magazines '*Gyananbeshan*' and '*Samachar Darpan*'. In the next decade, the controversy over widow marriage reached its climax in newspapers like '*Sangbad Prabhakar*' and '*Bengal Spectator*'. The question of widow marriage has been a topic of discussion in Bengali society since the fourth decade of the nineteenth century. The conservative and moderate debate centred on the educated Bengali society centred on the *Sati* movement turned into a feud between extremists and religious people over widow marriage. It was the Bengali newspaper that prepared the social movement for widow marriage. The revolutionary idea of widow marriage was first published in Bengali newspapers. Progressive public opinion under the leadership of Debendranath, Akshay Kumar and Vidyasagar began to consolidate in the debate on the issue of widow marriage in the society.[22] The *Bengal Spectator* published a long letter with scriptural arguments in favour of widow marriage.[23] Gaurishankar, editor of *Sambad Bhaskar*, wrote "prācīna hindu mahāśaẏarā ē'i samaẏē śāstrīẏa prathānusārē niamabad'dha kariẏā yadi bidhabādēra bibāha pracalita karēna tabē tāṁhāradigēra banśābalīkē uttarakālīna āpada ha'itē mukta rākhiẏā yā'ibēna.[24] *Sangbad Rasraj* wrote, "Śāstrē āchē bidhabārā bibāha karitē pārēna, tathāpi ēkaguẏā hindurā śāstrēra abhiprāẏa grahaṇa karibēna nā, yubatī bidhabādigakē amani rākhiẏā dibēna, bidhabādigēra śarīra ki śarīra naẏa, tāhārā ki mahābala indriẏadalakē hāta buli'iẏā śānta rākhibē.[25] Vidyasagar's classical argument in support of widow marriage awakens the nation's conscience in social evaluation in the editorial of *Tattvabodhini* magazine.

Widow marriage became the main topic of discussion in all the newspapers of that time. In the fifth decade, Akshay Kumar in *Tattvabodhini*, Derozio's disciple Parichand in the monthly magazine, Ishwar Gupta and Deenbandhu Mitra in *Sangbad Prabhakar* wrote in support of widow marriage.[26] Numerous works on widows have been found in Bengali periodicals. Parichand Mitra's writings started appearing in monthly magazines.[27] Sangbad sculptor Sakautu wrote to the opponents of widow marriage, "Bhaṭṭacāryya mahāśaẏarā ēkhana gēlēna kōthāẏa? Cartuddika nīraba, āra yē kichu'i śunatē pā'i nā, tabē ki bidhabā bibāhē sam'mata ha'ilēna 'maunaṁ sam'mati lakṣaṇaṁ'.[28] The Widow Marriage Act was passed on July 26, 1857. Dwarkanath Adhikari, a college student from Krishnanagar, wrote in support of the Hindu widow marriage in *Sangbad Sadhuranjan*,

> *"kichu nā thākibē bāki, śunitēchi habē nāki,*
> *bidhabāra biẏē ē'i dēśē.*
> *Manē manē chila āśā, bṛd'dhāra bhabanē bāsā,*
> *kari āra kichukāla raba.*
> *Sakala ha'ila sārā, bara khuṁjitēchē tārā,*
> *kānē śunē bibāhēra raba."*[29]

The widow marriage law failed to eradicate long-standing reforms. Kaliprasanna Singh announced in *Sangbad Bhaskar* that he would give a reward of three thousand rupees to each widow. Bhaskar, a widow named Hari Chakraborty, lamented in the newspaper that he did not get the promised money.[30]

In the thirties of the nineteenth century, the question of polygamy caused a special stir in Bengali society. In 1831, there was a controversy over *Samachar Darpan* and *Samachar Chandrika*, the remnants of which were published in other newspapers. *Sambad Kaumudi* hopes that this discussion will raise public awareness. *Samachar Darpan:* The letter to the aristocratic daughter states that the efforts being made in Calcutta to be able to marry by undermining the dignity of the aristocracy will alleviate the suffering of Bengali women.[31] The news that the modern aristocracy is not scriptural in the news mirror is the cause of the misfortune of the female nation and the intervention of the government to ban the sale of daughters is sought.[32] Praying to the Governor-General that no one can have more than one marriage, the local newspapers try to arouse the right attitude of the people through regular discussions. From the very beginning of the search for knowledge in 1831, he wrote against this social evil practice. A list of 27 aristocrats and the number of marriages is mentioned in a list. Ramchandra Chattopadhyay of Mayapadar scored 72, Nimai Mukherjee of Jayrampur 60, Aduar Ramakanta Bandyopadhyay 60, Khudiram Mukherjee of Nagar 54, Digambar Chattopadhyay of Malgram 53 and Darpanarayan Mukherjee of Baluti 52.[33] According to the news published in Samachar Darpan, an aristocratic Brahmin named Gobind Chandra, a resident of Bali, has passed away after widowing one hundred concubines.[34]

Mentioning a few articles in the newspapers (*Gyananbeshan, Vidyadarshan, Sambad Bhaskar, Sangbad Rasraj, Sangbad Purnachandrodaya, Samachar Darpan, Sangbad Prabhakar, Samachar Sudhavarshana, Tattvabodhini*) reveals their opposition to the practice of nobility (Kaulīn'yaprathā).[35] He was interested in curbing the evils of this practice in the articles published in Bengali periodicals. Ishwar Gupta, a staunch opponent of the nobility system, worked tirelessly to mobilize public opinion through Sangbad Prabhakar and Sangbad Sadhu Ranjan. In his anti-polygamy article published in Vidyadarshan, Akshay Kumar Dutt did not hesitate to seek legal help to stop this unscriptural practice. Scholars are urged to pay attention to the prevention of this evil practice in theology. An editorial in *Sambad Bhaskar* hopes that "there is no doubt that there will be a monarchy to prevent polygamy." Although the practice of nobility (Kaulīn'ya prathā) was not stopped by law, newspapers gradually created public opinion against it.

The main objectives of the periodicals and newspapers were the social reform movement, women's education, the establishment of democratic values, creating awareness in the public life about Western literature and culture. It cannot be said that the magazine did not have a conservative outlook. But the character of the social movement was progress and enlightenment. Bengali periodicals served as a complement to the events that brought about social change in Bengal in the nineteenth century. These magazines attracted the attention of the public, making them acceptable in society and giving them appropriate explanations. In the nineteenth century, Bengali society trusted the newspaper and valued its views. The value of Bengali periodicals in the nineteenth century in researching the social history and culture of Bengalis is immense. Social reform was the focal point of the social consciousness of the novice Bengalis of the nineteenth century.

NOTES AND REFERENCES

1. *British Orientalism & Bengal Renaissance*, David Koft, p. 86.
2. *Bānlā Bhāṣā Ō Bānlā Sāhitya Biṣaẏaka Prastāba*, Ramgati Nyaratna, 3rd ed., 1317, p. 207.
3. "Early Bengali Literature and News Papers", *The Calcutta Review*, Vol. 13, 1850, p. 131.
4. *Sbadēśīẏa Bhāṣāẏa Bidyābhāsa*, Tattabōdhīni, 69 Saṅkhyā, Baiśākha, 1771 Śaka.
5. *Young Bengal*, Sangbad Prabhakar, 3090 issue, 12.04.1848, p. 19.
6. *Samācāra Darpaṇa*, 14.02.1821-09.06.1821.
7. *Bānlāẏa Nabacētanāra Itihāsa*, Sbapana Basu, Pustaka Bipani, Prathama Sanskaraṇa, 1975, Dbitīa Sanskaraṇa, 1985, pp. 230-31.

8. *Ibid.*, p. 228.
9. *Ibid.*, pp. 109-110.
10. *Samācāra Darpaṇa*, July 1818.
11. *Samācāra Candrikā*, 20.08.1827.
12. *Bānlā Sambādapatra Ō Bāṅālīra Nabajāgaraṇa*, Pārtha Chatterjee, Dej Publishing, Second Edition 2011, pp. 118-20.
13. *Samācāra Darpaṇa*, 29.11.1829.
14. *Bānlā Sambādapatra Ō Bāṅālīra Nabajāgaraṇa*, Pārtha Chatterjee, Dej Publishing, pp. 266-67.
15. *Samācāra Candrikā*, 08.08.1829.
16. *Samācāra Candrikā*, 05.05.1831.
17. *Samācāra Candrikā*, 22.05.1871.
18. *Samācāra Darpaṇa*, 14.03.1835, p. 88.
19. *Samācāra Darpaṇa*, 21.03.1835.
20. *Samācāra Candrikā*, 18.04.1835.
21. *Sambādapatrē Sēkālēra Kathā*, Brajēndranātha Bandyōpādhyā, pp. 98-108.
22. *Gñānānnēṣaṇa*, 21.10.1837.
23. *Bēṅgala Spēkṭēṭara*, 01.04.1842.
24. *Sambāda Bhāskara*, 28.04.1849.
25. *Sambāda Rasarāja*, 08.05.1849.
26. *Widows' Marriage*, (printed in full from *Samachar Darpan*) Sangbad Purnachandroday, 16.07.1849).
27. *Ibid.*
28. *Māsika Patrikā*, (14.05.1655, pp. 113-17), (14.07.1655, pp. 125-29), (13.08.1655, pp. 101-06), (12.02.1658, pp. 74-75).
29. *Sambāda Bhāskara*, 23.02.1856.
30. *Bānlāya Nabacētanāra Itihāsa*, Sbapana Basu, Pustaka Bipani, Prathama Sanskaraṇa, 1975, Dbitīẏa Sanskaraṇa, 1985, p. 287.
31. *Sāmaẏikapatrē Bānlāra Samājacitra*, Binaẏa Ghōṣa, 3ẏa Khanḍa, 1964, p. 377.
32. *Sambādapatrē Sēkālēra Kathā*, (2ẏa), Brajēndranātha Bandyōpādhyāẏ, pp. 246-47.
33. *Samācāra Darpaṇa*, 04.07.1835.
34. *Sambādapatrē Sēkālēra Kathā*, (2ẏa), Brajēndranātha Bandyōpādhyāẏ, pp. 253-63.
35. *Samācāra Darpaṇa*, 07.12.1839.

11

Women Empowerment as Viewed by Mohendranath Dutt

Mrinal Chandra Das

The theme of the renowned Bi-Annual journal '*Journal of People's History and Culture*' is 'Marginal People'. Considering the present theme of the journal it is a tiny honest effort to discuss to some extent the condition, contribution and means of the betterment of women — a marginal group of Indian society in the light of thinker Mohendranath Dutt's views. Mohendranath Dutt thought elaborately about the conditions of women and their upliftment. Here this chapter is intended to focus on some of his relevant ideas on women.

The term 'Marginalized People' and 'Marginalized Group' are used in sociology and other social sciences to identify some segments of the populace as per their act of participation in different socio-economic activities. The words 'Marginal Man' are first used by an American sociologist Ezra Park (1864-1944) in his book '*Marginal Man*' published in 1928. But the term is replaced later on by another word 'Exclusion', especially in Europe. The term 'Marginalized Groups' or 'Marginalized People' is used to describe a certain tendency of society or social relation where some specific section of the population of human society is considered as less-useful or less-desirable by the other and excluded from mainstream society. They live on the edge of society far from the kernel. Because of their unequal power emulation throughout socio-economic and cultural spheres, these marginalized groups face discrimination and exploitation.

People from marginalized communities can be found throughout the world. However, groups of marginal people differ from society to society and country to nation. But in the Indian context, Marginal people or groups are Scheduled Castes, Scheduled Tribes, Women,

PWDs (person with disabilities), sexual minorities, children, elderly etc. Here this research article is intended to highlight the women's condition, contribution, some issues regarding women's problems and means of solutions in the views of Mohendranath Dutt.

Mohendranath Dutt (1869-1956) a scholar, thinker, philosopher, educationist, well-wisher of women, and profound writer of Bengal. He was the younger brother of Swami Vivekananda by birth, yet he was well-known in the intellectual circles of Bengal at the time for his extensive knowledge and expertise on a variety of subjects. He gave a lot of lectures and produced a few books on philosophy, society, art-architecture, painting, and other topics, all of which exhibit his vast knowledge and opinions on various subjects such as science and social science, and which demonstrate his genius. Many noted Bengali intellectuals of that period like Nandalal Bose got influenced by his ideas and philosophy.[1] He was not an ordinary man and it could be realized by the words which are told by famous artist Nandalal Bose. Nandalal Bose used to say sometimes regarding him I didn't just listen to him; it seemed to be in my mind. Whatever I do today, according to his words, whatever goes wrong, it seems to me. There is no doubt that I have found new life in his words. Such was the profound influence of Mohendranath Dutt in his artistic life.[2]

Outlook of Mohendranath Dutt on Women

In India we find wise women like *Gargi* who contributed to Indian philosophy and women are worshipped as Devi (goddess) and on the other hand women have been the subject of exploitation of religious and social prejudice, customs like *Sati*, girl child infanticide were prevailed. In viewing women Mohendranath Dutt had differentiated the outlook of Indian and Western mindset and keenly demarcated exquisite norms that are followed to Indian women. He says where the other nations imagined Divinity in the form of father or master, in India the idea of motherhood of Divinity has been developed. The idea of Motherhood of Divinity is only to be found in Indian culture. We ideated Nature as a mother with tenderness. Therefore, "Nature" or the creative genius of Divinity is identified with the female. The idea of motherhood of women is a unique feature of Indian society.[3]

Women and National Wealth

Women's contributions to nation-building and the development of national wealth are undervalued, yet they are just as important as men's.

Mohendranath Dutt firmly criticized thinking women 'An object of luxury and dalliance' and advocated equal participation in producing national wealth. He suggested women should utilize leisure time in some productive works.

Women's toil and intellect should equally be utilized for the production of national wealth. No woman weather from a humble or aristocratic backgrounds should be kept idle. He enunciates the women of the village should utilize plenty of leisure time in some profitable works for benefit of the society. On the other hand, the learned women of the urban or semi-urban area must call in the less educated or illiterate women and infused in then national ideas, noble ideas and also listen to the grievances and wants. Every available means should be adopted by the women of the upper class to look after the women of the toiling populace.[4]

In gross domestic production, women's potentiality must be utilized so that nation can prosper. To utilize the women's genius and labour he advocated that "The women of the nation are to be a helping hand or be in a parallel line, marching *pari passu* with the male folk." Exploiting the women's potency national wealth might be increased.[5]

Independent Earning of Women

Independent earning is the most significant factor in empowering women for the sake of society and national prosperity and well-being. In empowering women, along with education economic freedom is urgent. It is seen that women got victim of domestic violence due to the want of economic prosperity. In our society, we find that women are kept as mere appendages to the male members of society. Now it is time that women must be educated in some applied sciences, crafts and equipped with some sort of professional and vocational skills so that they might earn an independent living. The women instead of being an appendage, a burden to society and of men, must be self-sufficient in terms of both their lives and their earnings, Mohendranath Dutt remarked.[6] But they should have an independent way of earning respectably without wounding their social dignity, such was his view.[7]

If the women get the right of self-assertive independent spirit, and the men will respect the women in a better sense as equal, he opined. If the status of the women be recognized the national intellect will develop, and family wealth and the national wealth will be increased.[8] The sullen, sad, and dismal aspect of the female psyche will be removed if she earns her living. Young women's hearts will be cheered by their earnings; they will be bright and cheerful.[9]

Education for Women

Without education women empowerment, upliftment and ensuring their economic freedom is not deselection. Therefore, education has a very conclusive and pivotal role in it. Women's education can stimulate social growth and fuel national prosperity. In empowering women, the role of education is very critical. In making better parents, workers, educating females is essential, educated and skilled women can help the nation and society by different means. Therefore, he professed female education and remarks "Girls should have a free scope in school and colleges. Free flight of intellect should be the motto of educational institutions. For, if women are debarred from educational institutions, the national intellect is diminished by half."[10]

Therefore, thinker Mohendranath Dutt extended his opinion for almost all kinds of education should be accessible for girls. In this regard, he laid much strength on 'Art of Teaching' and 'Pedagogy' so that women can efficiently train the tender mind of children. He states that "In thc curriculum of girls' education the art of teaching of children should be incorporated."[11] Girls will be permitted to pursue careers as teachers; experience has shown that female teachers are more appropriate and efficient in dealing with young minds. They have a nice tact of putting the ideas into young minds through a sweet and affable tone.[12] He also advocated "Medical Education for girls". Subjects on health, hygiene, medicine and sanitary laws ought to be taught so that women can cure common illnesses at home without consulting a doctor.[13] In the case of female diseases and children's diseases, female doctors and medical advisers are in higher demand.[14]

Now-a-days girls are allowed to access primary or secondary education, but it is often found that they are debarred from higher education or university education. Mohendranath Dutt is far ahead of this idea. He not only suggested higher education for women but also goes one step forward and said "The female students of all universities will, for a fixed term, go to other universities to study; and not only the boys but also the girls of one university should be invited by the other universities so that female education is promoted, female requirements and advancement might improve and proceed in the same line with common basis and tendencies."[15]

And in the research field, women should have the opportunity. In his words, "Educated women should get an opportunity of making researches in scientific laboratories. In chemistry, physics and electricity female researchers are sometimes more successful and productive than male researchers. The reason is that in researches patience and perseverance is an important factor. Women are by nature patient and perseverant."[16]

Mohendranath Dutt also recognized the importance of music, painting, dance and craft not only as an aesthetic value but also means of earning for women. Music and dance lessons are to be given to the girls because it is an intrinsic part of their nature. His view on music and dance is "It is an expression of divinity through vocal and muscular movement."[17]

Women's nerves are so created and developed, according to Mohendranath Dutt, that they are the best adepts in many forms of art such as painting and photography, sculpture and clay-modelling. Natural gifts of arts are found in girls to a greater degree.[18]

Therefore, women should have opportunities in painting, photography, and statue-making because these are their natural lines and they have an inborn passion for these things. As a consequence, painting and statue-making should be included in university curricula so that young ladies can master these skills.[19] And along with the general or professional education spiritual and moral ideas should also be instructed to them. They ought to be taught the ideas of divinity.[20]

Professions for Women

It is a fact that women are enjoying social rights and but on the other hand, it is also seen that they get exploited and face discrimination in family and society. In a few areas in India, the husband leaves his wife having one or more children without recognizing his responsibilities towards his children and the woman face severe financial and social difficulties, although incidents are rare, it often happens. Women are also exploited in the guise of culture, religion, and tradition. They are also victims of domestic and social crime. It is because of the want of legal information and knowledge. It is because of this that Mohendranath Dutt was in favour of legal education and the legal profession for women. He asserts that "Young women should get the facility of trying their merit in law courts." Because he believes that in criminal law, women lawyers are the most skilled at identifying criminality, even when it is hidden or veiled, using lengthy arguments and plausible reasoning. As a result, young women should have access to the legal profession.[21]

He also counsels, intelligent women should be employed as judges in courts, they will, by their quick discerning intelligence, soon find the real truth in controversy. The fuming and frothing of lawyers will not confound them. Thus, women will not be inferior to male judges. Therefore, in the judicial line women should get a chance to prove their ability.[22]

Mohendranath Dutt wanted women to participate in the legislature. Male-made laws are not always acceptable for women because they do not grasp women's difficulties. As a consequence, women must participate in the legislative process. Women will fill in for the flaws that male politicians ignore. So that women should have seats in legislatures. Likewise in administrative functions, women might be given a chance, he believed.[23]

As it is mentioned that Mohendranath Dutt wanted women's equal participation in all sorts of work including toiling, for the production of national wealth, and he also well aware of their problems and rights. Hence remarks that "In a case where the female labour is employed for the production of wealth, the women can demand to leave with full pay during the period of confinement, say for three months, computing from before and after the delivery."[24] For the less educated women he suggested some clerking-oriented education and training. For the stenographic job in different offices, typing and short-hand typing lessons should be given to women, he made the suggestion.[25]

Marriage, Remarriage and Unmarried Women

Marriage is considered an important social institution in which sensual pleasure is acknowledged. In India, it has a philosophical and spiritual aspect. Before marriage, some cautions should be taken into consideration about girls so that problems may not arise. He was against the girls' marriage before entering puberty.[26] Marriage in Indian society is not just considered to fulfil a biological need but to exchange their soul and heart each other and the couple will be an equal participant of misery and happiness in the family life and worldly life. From these ideas in Indian culture to be specific in Hindu culture divorce system usually does not exist in Hindu law books. The theory is undoubtedly good, but the situation has changed. But, it is an astonishing fact that the remarriage of women is not seen with good eyes yet. Considering the changing situation Mohendranath advocated the idea of remarriage and he says that "The Indian societies have now passed through many changes and other circumstances have come in which must modify the former state of the society. As in the present state of Hindu society, it is found in experience, that the girl-widows are unable to follow exactly the highest ideal and so there is every likelihood of their being led astray, hence it is for the sake of social necessity that they should be married a second time."[27]

But those who want to remain unmarried he made specific provisions for them. In this aspect, he suggests that unmarried women be adequately educated so that they do not go down the erroneous path. They should get such education and training as to enable them to support themselves *via* honest means without relying on others, with special emphasis on moral and religious instruction.[28]

Issue of Fallen Women in the Views of Mohendranath Dutt

From ancient times prostitution is a major social issue not only in India but all over the world. In India, it is found as the '*Devdasi System*' or temple dancer or in the other forms. In India, these groups of women are termed as '*Patita*' (fallen from mainstream society). Some factors cause prostitution, a few of them are bad company, family prostitution, social customs,and lack of sex education, economic causes, poverty and sexual error in teenagers and most important is women trafficking. In most cases, it is seen that women are forced to involve in these spheres. The legalization of prostitution is a solution but yet it is not enough. An effort should be made to get back these fallen women in our mainstream society. He advocated the rights of the fallen women and remarks "The slight female error according to some social code of the locality cannot debar a person for whole life from advancement. Female error is not a heinous thing." For the betterment, he states "They (sex workers) should be given a chance to uplift their status." Here Mohendranath Dutt made a suggestion how to uplift their social condition and improve the dignity which they have lost for some reasons; hence he suggested "Train them up as nurses in hospitals so that they might get a decent earning by their healing professions. But trained matrons of mature age should supervise their work so that they might regain a status of decent living through their new professions. They should also be hired for some commercial work in factories and other labouring workplaces, as well as in village home factories in separate female compartments. Here Mohendranath Dutt strongly advocated that by decent earning social dignity of fallen women should be achieved. And society and government should look after the matter with special care and provide some decent earning so that they can improve their condition and can get rid of this social and mental slander. Thus he thought "It (prostitution) might be minimized by employing fallen women in some national work."[29]

Along with these some mental and psychological treatment is to be given to provide them mental support and that will help in rebuilding their mental health. Ergo he stated that "Mentally the fallen women have the same instinct, have the same love for religions as has in anybody else, but they are deficient in morality. Teach morality to these poor creatures, rouse up the burning zeal for God."[30]

Women's Organization and Female Thinker

He believed that women's problems should be resolved solely by them. As a corollary, he proposed women's organizations at all levels, from the village or town to the worldwide. Such types of organizations will address women's problems and will look for the means to overcome these problems. Such organizations would enable women to exchange their thoughts and express their grievances and possible remedies might be suggested. Problems regarding labour, employment, sanitation, health, hygiene, education and other problems will be discussed and means will be looked for. Thus such organizations from the bottom to national and international levels are to be formed. Thus, the whole of the Asiatic countries will be organized on a female basis.[31] It is through female organizations that women will be able to solve the problems.[32] He does not stop here; he also suggested an annual conference of Asian women should be called in. These conferences of women will bring friendly feelings and stabilize racial affinity in the whole Asian family.[33] In this way he wanted to internationalize women's issues.

Male thinkers are less aware of women's difficulties. Consequently, he believed that unless women's thinkers are involved, women's issues will not be effectively addressed. He suggested that thinkers for women should come from the female line. He says that "For the male thinkers try to solve the problem in their line and scarcely can think out the difficulties of women. In most cases in their thoughts, the women problem is ignored." Therefore, he says that "Women thinkers and women workers must come out from all the Asian countries and shall try to solve the problem of women in their line."[34]

The prosperity of a nation is determined by the place of women in that community and nation. The social growth of women will be greatly slowed unless their stature is enhanced, recognized, and provided a global optimum. All amenities should be made available to the women to expend their energy and mental state. As a result of the additional energy flowing from the women's quarter, the national vitality will indeed be twofold. The women are the lifeblood of the country; they are the pivots upon which the entire country revolves. Every social theorist should appreciate the significance of women and dedicate more attention to their progress to develop national wealth, mind, economy and earning. Women should never be thought of as a burden to society. They are, in fact, indirectly controlling the entire national movement.

NOTES AND REFERENCES

1. Mukhopadhyaya, Devkumar, "Monishi Mohendranath Dutt — Jiban, Tapashya O Karma" in Raghunath Basu and Ajit Kumar Ghosh, eds., *Vivekananda Mohendra — Bhupendra Sanskriti Charcha*, (Bengali) Kolkata: The Mohendar Publishing Committee, 2010, pp. 88-93.
2. Talukdar, Rupa, "Shilpi Nandalal Bosur Shilpojibone Purnyadarshan Mohendranath Dutter Probhab" in Raghunath Basu and Ajit Kumar Ghosh, eds., *op. cit.*, p. 70.
3. Dutt, Mohendranath, *Reflections on Woman*, Calcutta: Seva Series Publishing House, 1923, pp. 5-7.
4. Dutt, Mohendranath, *National Wealth*, Calcutta: The Mohendra Publishing Committee, 1952, pp. 129-132.
5. *Ibid.*, p. 134.
6. Dutt, Mohendranath, *Status of Women*, Calcutta: The Mohendra Publishing Committee, pp. 18-20.
7. *National Wealth*, *op. cit.*, pp. 129-132.
8. *Status of Women*, *op. cit.*, pp. 23-25.
9. Dutt, Mohendranath, *Nation*, Calcutta: The Mohendra Publishing Committee, 1954, p. 14.
10. Dutt, Mohendranath, *New Asia*, Calcutta: The Mohendra Publishing Committee, 1954, p. 20.
11. Dutt, Mohendranath, *Lectures on Education*, Calcutta: The Mohendra Publishing Committee, 2006, p. 119.
12. *Status of Women*, *op. cit.*, pp. 30-35.
13. *Lectures on Education*, *op. cit.*, p. 121.
14. *Status of Women*, *op. cit.*, pp. 30-35.
15. *New Asia*, *op. cit.*, p. 21.
16. *Status of Women*, *op. cit.*, pp. 30-35.
17. *Lectures on Education*, *op. cit.*, p. 123.
18. *Ibid.*, pp. 122-123.
19. *Status of Women*, *op. cit.*, pp. 30-35.
20. *Lectures on Education*, *op. cit.*, pp. 123-124.

21. *Status of Women*, *op. cit.*, p. 31.
22. *Ibid.*, p. 37.
23. *Ibid.*, pp. 30-35.
24. *National Wealth*, *op. cit.*, p. 31.
25. *Lectures on Education*, *op. cit.*, pp. 121-122.
26. Dutt, Mohendranath, *Society and Education: Society and Woman*, Calcutta: The Mohendra Publishing Committee, 1982, pp. 53-54.
27. *Ibid.*, pp. 52-53.
28. *Ibid.*, pp. 51-52.
29. *Nation*, *op. cit.*, p. 36.
30. *Society and Education: Society and Woman*, *op. cit.*, p. 40.
31. *Status of Women*, *op. cit.*, pp. 38-41.
32. *Ibid.*, pp. 38-45.
33. *Nation*, *op. cit.*, p. 89.
34. *Status of Women*, *op. cit.*, p. 21.

12

Pranab Kanya Sangha
An Inimitable Organization of the Twentieth Century Bengal

Bablu Mallick

In the realm of social reform movements, the activities led by Pranab Kanya Sangha (1971), an organization formed by Swami Advaitananda, the disciple of Swami Pranabananda, founder father of Bharat Sevasram Sangha, was the most atypical event in twentieth-century Bengal. Pranab Kanya Sangha is primarily known as an organization dedicated to the amelioration of deprived women. It would be pertinent to mention that though in the said century a number of social service organizations had made their presence felt through their contribution towards material and spiritual upliftment of the society in general, there was hardly any enterprise exclusively dedicated towards the betterment of women. Herein lies the significance of Pranab Kanya Sangha. Though being an ascetic, Swami Advaitananada's activities were not confined within the religious domain; he made his foray into the sphere of society and politics of Bengal. He strived to create a women's society where the inmates would remain safe and free from facing discrimination of any kind. His Guru Swami Pranabananda had envisioned such a dream long before and had nurtured the idea but did not see it being materialized within his lifetime. Pranab Kanya Sangha ultimately saw the light of the day much later in 1970.

Swami Advaitananda was born on the twelfth moonnight in the month of Magh in 1901 (1307 B.S.) at Bharaichi village, Jessore district, located in present-day Bangladesh. His father was Dwarikanath and his mother Barada Sundari Devi. Swami Advaitananda's childhood name was Rajendra. Advaitananda founded the 'Pranab Kanya Sangha' named after his Guru to pave the way for women-welfare and emancipation. To carry out such a mammoth task, he organized both men and women volunteers. With female volunteers, he arranged meetings at several places and formed various groups like 'Mahila Mandir', 'Mahila Mandal' etc. Advaitananda's hard exterior guarded his tender-hearted emotions. Worship of God and mankind were his only objectives in life. Pranab Kanya Sangha is a religious social service organization administered by a group of devout Sannyasins and Brahmacharinis having firm faith in ancient religious tenets of Hinduism. Volunteers dedicated to social service assist the functioning of the Sangha, which is bereft of political or communal flavour.

Founder father of Bharat Sevasram Sangha, Swami Pranabananda used to lament, "Are women inferior to beasts? Should the right to worship, meditation, making offerings to deities always rest on men? Men and women must have equal privileges so far as the religious realm is concerned. If women can enjoy their rights in the fields of nationalistic ideals, education, politics then why should they be barred from participating in religious movement?" Pranabananda always nurtured the idea of forming an organization comprising a group of brave, self-sacrificing women. However, the dream never materialized during his lifetime. As an effort to fulfil the wishes of his Guru, Swami Advaitananda, a vagrant disciple of Pranabananda, came forward. It was with his enormous effort, enthusiasm and blessing that 'Pranab Kanya Sangha' was formed at Hridaypur, Barasat, North 24 Parganas district with five courageous women who renounced their all for the sheer attraction of attaining spiritual freedom. In building the Sangha there was the copious contribution from inhabitants of Hridaypur, and the sacrifice, honesty and struggle of women volunteers. "Religion is Work" — the essence of Bharat Sevasram Sangha still echoes from every centre of Pranab Kanya Sangha. The primary goal of the women volunteers is to implement the preaching of Swami Pranabananda through social service and literacy programmes. Swami Advaitananda longed for the resurgence of women in India. He received encouragement from his Guru for fulfilling the dream. Once at an annual function held at Madaripur Pranabananda told him, "Where half of the society comprises women, how can social reforms or religious reforms be possible without them? While our brothers served the British rulers by aping their lifestyle, it was our women folk who stuck to ancient Hindu customs and preserved the age-old rituals. How can we improve their position in society?" Once two sannyasinis from Jamtara Ashram visited Pranabananda. After they left, Swami Pranabananda told Advaitananda, "The two girls are bright and devout. They have built an ashram at Jamtara where they have opened a school for girls and are also providing them moral education. Had I been able to gather a group of girls like these, I would have trained them. They could have preached ideologies of women in the society." The words of his Guru remained seeded within Advaitananda which propelled him to lay the foundation of Pranab Kanya Sangha at a later time. The prime objectives of the Sangha were: (a) to spread the ideals of Hinduism within and outside India irrespective of caste and creed; (b) laying stress on ethics and moral education and character-building; (c) to provide relief to the poor, impoverished and natural disaster victims; (d) rural development work; (e) to initiate moral and spiritual awakening amongst the masses by reading excerpts from epics like *Ramayana*, *Mahabharata*, *Gita* and *Upanishads*; (f) ushering economic progress by developing small-scale cottage industries; (g) arranging games and yoga sessions for children to help them lead a healthy life and build their moral character; (h) spreading literacy through cultural and religious programmes; (i) to establish communal harmony amongst people; and (j) to establish more branches of the Sangha in India and abroad, and most importantly to eradicate untouchability and ameliorating the condition of backward classes.

Pranab Kanya Sangha has dedicated themselves to ameliorating the condition of women in society. During the outbreak of famine or natural calamities, Pranab Kanya Sangha has exerted themselves in rescuing distressed victims and providing them relief items. It always stood by the poor, impoverished people, especially for the women in dire straits. Pranab Kanya Sangha strived to play the role of a Samaritan by doing philanthropic service to others, whereby their altruistic approach could be interpreted as service to the society. In the year 1999 when a super cyclone had ravaged the coastal areas of Odisha, it was the women volunteers of Pranab Kanya Sangha who came forward in rescue and relief work for the cyclone-stricken victims. Again, during the Tsunami destruction in 2004 and during the total devastation made by a severe-cyclonic storm "Ayela" in many districts of Gangetic West Bengal in May 2009 the sannyasins of Pranab Kanya Sangha distributed aid in the form of drinking water, food items, clothing etc. to the homeless, hungry and the needy. Their relief work was most prevalent in the vast strip of land spread over Sahebkhali, Madhabkati, Bhandarkhali of South 24 Parganas. They stayed by the side of the helpless people even in impregnable areas and have fed the poor. Statistics reveal that during the said period, nearly 2,500 families were benefited who did not receive any help from relief camps or other organizations. Even in later times, female volunteers have carried on with their relief work at other places to serve the destitute. It should be mentioned in this context that comparing with other woman-centric organizations in India, Pranab Kanya Sangha have been more efficient in real-life situations mainly because they undergo an extensive training programme. Because of this, they are usually more adept at handling crisis on the field. Their activities make it noticeable that Pranab Kanya Sangha not only aims at providing one-time relief to victims of calamity but they were dedicated to social reforms. They did not discriminate between religion or sect. The Sangha founded by Advaitananda has been free of communal overtures.

Besides relief work, the Sangha has been equally concerned about eradicating illiteracy. Advaitananda refuted the idea that women can be the source of all evils. Rather than considering women as an object of desire, according to Advaitananda, they must be imparted with education to awaken their conscience which could make them aware of their duties. He believed that the next generation must be kept prepared to take over the mantle. As it is the mother who gives the primary education to her child, the society needs ideal women like Gandhari, Droupadi of the past who could guide her child or even her spouse with the verve of womanhood for upholding the virtues of honesty and uprightness. She would always inspire her male counterpart to fight for justice, woman being the source of primordial divine energy — the reason why ancient sages have said, "kanya pebyang palańiya atijatnātah" (meaning a girl child needs to be raised and educated with utmost care and compassion). Advaitananda had the insight to comprehend the energy that remains latent in a woman and realized that the role of women in building a disciplined society is indispensable. It was the ideals of his Guru which propelled him to take up the momentous task. For assuming a leading role in organizing society, it was imperative that a woman must follow the advice of ancient sages of mastering the routine household chores. According to Advaitananda, to build a nation conforming to the idiosyncrasy of an ideal Hindu society, the women must lead the way, and to make that possible the social education must commence from domestic confines. He further believed that since India as a nation was established on the principles of such sacrifice as could be made by women only, hence it was important for women to be properly groomed so that they do not become outgoing or attention-seeking in their manners.

Pranab Kanya Sangha undertook a number of educational schemes for developing literacy among women. Balowari Primary Vidyalaya was founded in 1971 which received its accreditation of West Bengal Samaj Kalyan Parishad in 1972. In 1973, a library was opened. In 1975, a secondary school was inaugurated which acquired government recognition in 1982. In 1976, education up to the secondary level was initiated for women who were either destitute, or had been abandoned by their husbands, or were widows. In 1981 Pranabananda Shishu Bhavan was established. Madhyamgram Branch of Non-Formal Education was founded in 1984, a school for ashramites was built in 1993. Needless to say, the educational institutions of the Sangha catered education mainly to underprivileged girls. Hostel facilities are also available in the said institutes for girl students up to the higher secondary level. Various public welfare organizations like the authorities of Anandaloke Nursing Home (Salt Lake) or individuals like Indumati Parekh or other women organizations have come forward to help the cause of deprived students. This is a unique aspect of the Pranab Kanya Sangha. Other than providing conventional education, the Sangha had arranged for vocational training especially for underprivileged women to help them become self-reliant. The vocational training centre, computer training centre, as well as centres to learn cutting, dress-making, knitting wools, sewing, embroidery etc. were set up. In addition, West Bengal Khadi Board has donated 20 charkhas which are run by ladies older than sixty years of age, and whose expenses are maintained by the government. Most importantly, in the year 2016, the headquarters of Pranab Kanya Sangha at Hridaypur in collaboration with Netaji Open University has introduced low-priced Diploma Courses on Work Education, enabling women to procure government jobs. The Sangha seeks to develop spiritual awareness in women so that they might be instrumental in helping the nation prosper. Besides spreading literacy amongst the masses the Sangha has been trying to build hostels for girl students in each branch. In the Sangha schools and girl hostels, scores of students are studying at present. Pranab Kanya Sangha has not remained content only by providing education to women but has sought for broadening the faculty of imagination in them and it was with this aim in mind that in 1977 Swami Advaitananda started publishing Sangha's magazine named "Gayatri Mata" which is continuing its successful and uninterrupted run even today. Initially a yearly souvenir, it later became a quarterly and at present a monthly magazine which is published by the Sannyasinis of the Sangha. Both men and women writers contribute to the magazine *Gayatri Mata* which can undoubtedly be termed as a big stride towards the emancipation of women.

Besides spreading literacy in women's society, Pranab Kanya Sangha has been carrying on various kinds of beneficial activities like the free medical centre "Pranabananda Databya Chikitsalaya O Chokkhu Sebakendra" which has been set up to provide homoeopathy and allopathic treatment at a lower cost. To spread treatment facilities to remote villages, a mobile medical unit has been launched. The medical unit travels through villages to provide medical help to the poor. A handful of physicians reach out to visit the remote areas in the mobile medical unit and provide treatment and medicines to patients. The Sangha distributes blankets, clothing and food to the needy from time to time, thereby helping the poor, the helpless, the elderly women, the ill-fated abandoned women, the homeless maidens to the best of their abilities. In this context, it is noteworthy that during annual functions every year clothing, blankets are distributed to nearly 300 impoverished people, both men and women. To enable the local poverty-stricken women to become self-sufficient, all branches of Pranab Kanya Sangha have made arrangements to engage these women in making cottage-industry products like incense-sticks, papad, pickles etc. To care for the aged, abandoned women who have nobody to turn to, the Sangha has established an 'old age home' for elderly ladies at Madhyamgram Kora Chandigarh. Pranab Kanya Sangha has not remained confined within the affluent upper class of the urban society like many other contemporary social service organizations, but had reached out to rural India, and had been able to cater to the needs of the illiterate, hungry people living on the lower strata of the society. It has been able to connect with the Bengali psyche by preaching Indian values and thus have been able to mingle with the ordinary village folk. Advaitananda wanted a coterie of Brahmacharinis to preach the ideals of Hindu religion and unify all the Hindu women together to form a society singularly for women. With this aim in mind, he founded 'Mahila Milan Mandir' and 'Hindu Dharma Sebika Sangha' which are dedicated to ameliorating the condition of women belonging to backward classes and for destitute women using education.

In conclusion, it can be said that the contribution made by Pranab Kanya Sangha founded by Swami Advaitananda in the history of the social reform movement is undeniable. Advaitananda sought to build a society free from discrimination, prejudice, inequity and to materialize his dream he founded 'Mahila Milan Mandir' and 'Hindu Dharma

Sebika Dal'. However, some real life problems prove to be hindrances to the path of progress of the Sangha-centric movement. One major problem is that of getting suitable women candidates who would be eager to lead an austere life. In modern times large families have been divided into nuclear families, a direct result of which is that each girl-child is getting more attention from her parents and thus most of them grow up with a narrow-mentality. They do not get enough exposure to the outside world and thus they get hardly any scope to develop a liberal mindset, so essential to nurturing the qualities of an ascetic. Also, the fact remains that though the Sangha speaks of secular ideals, in practice it is more inclined to assert Hindu nationalism. However, in spite of these limitations, it would be not an exaggeration to say that like other socio-religious reform movements Pranab Kanya Sangha has been proving their worth as a major contributor to the field of rebuilding the society.

NOTES AND REFERENCES

1. Sannyasini Shuddhanandamayee, *Swami Advaitananda Puspanjali*, Pranab Kanya Sangha, Hridaypur, 2002, p. 6.
2. *Ibid.*, p. 6.
3. *Ibid.*, p. 9.
4. Sannyasini Shuddhanandamayee, *Shataborsher Shraddhanjali*, Pranab Kanya Sangha, Hridaypur, 2000, p. 59.
5. *Ibid.*, p. 60.
6. *Ibid.*, p. 44.
7. Sannyasini Shuddhanandamayee, *op. cit.*, pp. 15-16.
8. *Ibid.*, p. 10.
9. Sannyasini Bishwarupanandamoyee, "Sangher Trankarjo O Ailar Obijnata", *Gayatri Mata Patrika*, Sannyasini Shuddhanandamoyee, Pranab Kanya Sangha, Hridaypur, 1416, pp. 37-38.
10. Sakkhatkar, *Sannyasini Atmasthanandamoyee*, Pranab Kanya Sangha, 26/09/2015.
11. *Ibid.*, Sannyasini Shuddhanandamoyee, p. 43.
12. *Ibid.*, Sannyasini Shuddhanandamoyee, p. 35.
13. *Ibid.*, Sannyasini Shuddhanandamoyee, p. 44.
14. Sakkhatkar, *Sannyasini Atmasthanandamoyee*, Pranab Kanya Sangha, 25/09/2015.
15. *Ibid.*, Sannyasini Shuddhanandamoyee, pp. 17-21.
16. *Ibid.*, Sannyasini Shuddhanandamoyee, 17/12/16.
17. *Ibid.*
18. Agomoni Lahiri, "Tyager Pratik Pranab Kanya Sangha", *Gayatri Mata*, Sannyasini Shuddhanandamoyee, Pranab Kanya Sangha, Hridaypur, 1414, p. 14.
19. *Gayatri Mata*, Sannyasini Shuddhanandamoyee, Pranab Kanya Sangha, Hridaypur, 1407, p. XI.
20. Pranab Kanya Sangha Barta, Sannyasini Shuddhanandamoyee, Pranab Kanya Sangha, Hridaypur, 1417, pp. 71-72.
21. Sakkhatkar, Brahmacharini Soma, Pranab Kanya Sangha, 20/10/2016.

13

Partition and Women Sufferings

A Case Study of Jalpaiguri District, 1947-1962

Agnita Pal

Women in Indian history were always being treated as a dependent class on their male counterparts. Though she is the half of human race, her role lacked in historical writings. Early historical writings are almost silent in depicting women's history. It was only after the 19th century, that society seemed to become concerned about the heroism of the avoiding class, who played an equal role in society from ancient times. And gradually it seized a greater interest among the scholars. The history of partition from a gender-sensitive standpoint is also a recent craze. In the rudimentary stage, women were neglected in the chapters of partition historiography. But with time, the old conception regarding lenient sex changed in a phased manner. In the initial stage of the gender-based history of partition, the refugee women were projected from the point of view of victimization due to partition, but in the later phase, scholars stressed more upon the constructive role of the refugee women for the cause of their settlement, survival and above all the empowerment. *Urvasi Bhutalia* played a guiding role in depicting the untold sorrows and sufferings of women who were the worst victims of partition. Her path-breaking book "*The Other Side of Silence*" unearthed the bitter experiences of those refugee women that we are plunged into the profound darkness of oblivion. In the subsequent years,Ritu Menon and Kamala Bhasin produced an epoch-making composition on the greatest human tragedy of partition from women's perspective in their book "*Borders and Boundaries: The women*".

The glorious history of 'India got freedom' is also embodied with the repulsive story of partition. A history of a lifeless line, that seized the lives of many people, and threw their families in a phase of uncertainty.

Many scholars and historians blamed the British policy of "Divide and Rule" and the religious agitation between the Hindu and Muslim communities as a supreme reason behind this misery. After the end of the Second World War, the British government finally decided to quit India and finally end up their almost 200 year's rule in India. To speed up this process Mountbatten came to India as the new Governor-General on 22nd June, 1947. After several meetings with both the leaders of Congress and the Muslim League, he passed the 'Indian Independence Act' on 4th July, 1947. Sir Cyril John Radcliff, a British lawyer was called to draw the boundary line. Accordingly, the Radcliffe Commission drew up a boundary line across undivided Bengal, which had a total area of 78,389 square miles, to create two separate entities — East Bengal, which formed the eastern wing of Pakistan and West Bengal, which became a province of independent India.[1] This resulting 2,736 kilometres long boundary line cut across Jessor, Malda, Nadia, Dinajpur and Jalpaiguri district of Bengal and Sylhet district of neighbouring Assam.[2] Neither two Bengals have left a strong unit after partition. West Bengal was left with a ramp of about 34,000 square miles. As far as East Bengal was concerned, the Radcliffe Award gave it an area of 54,501 square miles.[3]

The history of partition is embodied with the story of migration. In 1947, after the bifurcation of the Indian subcontinent, two independent nations emerged: Hindu majority India and Muslim majority Pakistan. It was followed by the forced uprooting of an estimated eighteen million people belonging to minorities who sought shelter across the newly created boundaries.[4] The massive influx of refugees into West Bengal attracted the attention of a number of researchers. The causes and effects of partition, its impact on common mass, the pathos and trauma of displaced persons have been widely discussed by the researchers. But the memory of violence, bloodsheds, disturbing realities that accompanied partition in North Bengal, particularly in Jalpaiguri district remained blanketed in silence. A bulk of women with their male counterparts in the Jalpaiguri district, have suffered a lot and came out with new flying wings. But their stories are remained almost untouched. Most of the accounts of partition have concentrated more upon the southern part of Bengal and North Bengal has not received the scholarly attention that it deserves. The present study is an attempt towards redressing this historiographical imbalance by bringing those hidden facts into the limelight and fill up the vacuum of previous incomplete researches for the expedition and cultivation of further micro-level studies.

West Bengal is a state coherent to East Pakistan. The borders of the state are bounded by nine districts of West Bengal, viz. *Darjeeling, Jalpaiguri, Cooch Behar, Malda, West Dinajpur* (now divided into North and South), *Murshidabad, Nadia, 24 Parganas* (North and South) and Calcutta (now Kolkata). Due to geographical vicinity and also for linguistic, religious and cultural resemblance, the East Bengal refugees particularly preferred to shift to West Bengal districts. The procession of people from East Pakistan flocked to different regions of India. One wing crossed the Brahmaputra and Barak valleys due to its proximity to East Bengal, another group moved towards Tripura, Mizoram and Manipur.[5] The fact was, the uprooted people wanted to settle in adjacent districts where the geographical features were more or less identical with them. The refugees from Jessor mostly went to be settled in Nadia, while those who came from *Dinajpur* went to *Jalpaiguri* and *West Dinajpur*.

This process of '*Bhita Bodol*' was started before 1947 when the news 'India going to be parted' was floated in the air. Actually, after the Noakhali problem in 1946, Bengali Hindu people started to move.[6] The problem started on 10th October, and within a week the number of refugees in Calcutta was 4000 and 5000 in Agartala.[7] Those days Gandhiji requested them to go back, but they denied because they believed that, where 80 out of 100 people does not want them, then the rest 20 people will stay there for the sake of what. From 1947 onwards and till the 1950s, Calcutta was the recipient of the bulk of migrants from East Pakistan. "In 1947, at the time of partition, only 3,44,000 Hindu refugees came into West Bengal and the year 1948 saw an influx of 7,86,000 people and in 1949 over 2,13,000 Bengali refugees crossed into India."[8]

Table 13.1: Month-wise Break-up of Refugee Influx to West Bengal up to 1956

Month	*Year–1953*	*Year–1954*	*Year–1955*	*Year–1956*
January	5,248	4,077	15,674	17,011
February	5,961	5,710	22,848	42,360
March	7,507	5,821	26,503	15,167
April	6,900	6,002	15,070	18,039
May	6,032	6,656	18,190	34,657
June	4,798	6,354	21,146	24,734
July	5,026	6,208	22,957	27,442
August	4,147	8,127	13,813	—
September	3,223	10,644	9,371	—
October	4,379	10,352	13,757	—
November	3,212	11,073	11,535	—
December	4,214	22,776	18,709	—
Total	**60,647**	**10,3800**	**20,9573**	**1,79,410**

Source: Relief and Rehabilitation of Displaced Persons in West Bengal Department, Calcutta, Home Publishers, Government of West Bengal, 1956, p. 17.

Actually, at the end of 1949, the number of emigrants from West Pakistan gradually decreased, but from East Pakistan, it continued till 1970 at a great level.[9] The average arrival of refugees in West Bengal after 1950 was 4,000 everyday.[10] They presumed to be a catastrophic proportion in April. As the figure showed that refugees trekked to West Bengal on 1st April 4,000, 3rd April 2,350, 4th April 3,600, 5th April 4,480, 7th April 4,500 and so on.[11] The number of people, who came from East Bengal and the number of refugees who registered themselves at the check posts were 41.17 lakh up to 1956.[12] Besides many East Bengal refugees entered without any registration. "*The Story of Rehabilitation*", published by the Refugee Rehabilitation Department, described that the number of illegal emigrants was huge in the count.

Table 13.2: Percentage of Refugee Population on the Total Population of West Bengal

Year	*Total population*	*The number of refugees came from East Pakistan*	*Percentage of refugees on total population*
1951	2,62,99,980	21,04,241	8.00
1961	3,49,26,279	30,68,750	8.78

Source: Shivajipratim Basu, "Chinnomul Rajnitir Uthso Sandhane" in *Desh Bhag: Smriti Ar Stabdhata*, Semanti Ghosh (ed.), Kolkata, Gangchil, March 2008, p. 79.

The flow of migration not only flooded the southern part of Bengal, but North Bengal also witnessed its outrageous outcome. People from the other side of the border flocked to five (now seven) northern districts of West Bengal, viz. Cooch Behar, Jalpaiguri, Darjeeling, West Dinajpur and Malda, crossing the Brahmaputra and Bark valley. Among the five districts, Jalpaiguri remarks a unique history under the period review. Jalpaiguri started its journey as a district in the year 1869. The geographical boundary of Jalpaiguri was like this: Darjeeling and Bhutan on the northern side, Cooch Behar and Rangpur were on the southern side, on the western side was the Purnia district of Bihar and Darjeeling, East Pakistan and Goalpara of Assam were on the eastern side. Due to the partition, the area of the district was reduced to 2,378 sq.mile from 3,050 sq.mile. In the pre-partition period Jalpaiguri was a part of the Rajshahi division, so a large amount of the population of the district was Muslim. That is why the Muslim League demanded the district to be included in East Pakistan.[13] But if viewed from a different point, Hindus were in majority in Jalpaiguri. So, they wanted it within the Indian boundary. As a result, the district was divided.

Table 13.3: Police Station-wise Muslim and Non-Muslim Population in Jalpaiguri Sadar Sub-Division According to 1941 Census

Police Station	*Area (sq.miles)*	*Total population*	*Muslim population*	*Non-Muslim population*
Tetulia	220	27,472	17,282	10,190
Pochagarh	—	33,614	17,807	15,807
Boda	352	74,596	37,844	36,752
Debiganj	—	56,511	14,927	41,684
Panchagram	100	51,618	20,568	31,050
Total	**672**	**2,43,811**	**1,08,428**	**1,35,383**

Source: Kartik Saha, "Desh Bibhag Er Nirikhe Bhoumik Binnyas O' Jalpaiguri" in *Paribartaner Dharai Tistabanger Jalpaiguri Jela*, A.G. Ghosh and Supam Biswas (ed.), Kolkata, Progotishil Prokashak, 2016, p. 395.

The Hindu community of East Bengal maintained a steady inflow towards Jalpaiguri. It became a continuous process. Two categories of Hindu migrants came over to Jalpaiguri: one belonged to the opulent community, whereas the other section belonged to the middle class. The existence of other communities was also available that were known as the lower middle class. They were comparatively a weaker economic group. There was a sub-division named Alipurduar, which was situated in the eastern part of the Jalpaiguri district, most of the elite migrants were eager to settle there. They were mostly from East Pakistan.[14]

Table 13.4: District-wise Statistics of Migration Hailing from East Pakistan to Jalpaiguri District (1946-1951)

Sl.No.	*Name of the districts (East Pakistan)*	*Male*	*Female*
1.	Kustia	426	383
2.	Jessore	784	653
3.	Khulna	451	379
4.	Rajshahi	676	546
5.	Dinajpur	9,662	7,829
6.	Rongpur	13,584	11,759
7.	Bogura	671	553
8.	Pabna	2,185	1,910
9.	Dacca	9,005	7,147
10.	Mymensingh	9,296	7,741
11.	Faridpur	2,540	1,953
12.	Bakharganj	1,056	902
13.	Tripura	985	729
14.	Noakhali	974	648
15.	Chittagong	689	467
16.	Sylhet	280	248
	Total	**53,264**	**43,847**

Source: Asoke Mitra (ed.), *Census 1951, West Bengal District Handbooks*, Jalpaiguri, New Delhi, 1954, pp. 93-94.

This refugee exodus has increased the population of Jalpaiguri on a big scale. In 1941, it was populated with 8,47,841 people, wherein 1951 it became 916,747, in 1961 increased to 13,59,292.[15] The 1951 census reported that almost 99,000 refugees trekked to Jalpaiguri district and after ten years (1961), the number reached 4,20,598.[16] This increasing population was a great threat to the northern district of West Bengal during that time. Radcliff line created many problems for both countries, particularly in the matter of enclaves. In the matter of Jalpaiguri, Berubari was a major problem. Debobrata Chaki in his "*Bratyajaner Brittanta*" has properly described this matter.

The process of migration to West Bengal continued unremittingly over the next couple of decades, while the migration in Punjab was almost completed by the year 1949. Now the vital question arises, whether the border crossers were refugees, migrants, or *bona fide* citizens of India and whether the refugees would be accommodated with temporary relief or permanent rehabilitation. These were the most vital issues on the part of the Indian policymakers. In the early phase, both governments were apathetic to refugee resettlement. But later on, they took several initiatives to give shelter to the refugees. Various camps were arranged. The elite persons, who were able to manage land, constructed their own homes in the suburban areas. Many of them occupied houses unpopulated by the Muslims, who shifted to East Pakistan for their convenience. They also occupied the military camps that were abandoned for a long time. In the cases, where the land was acquired through legal means and procedures, the government termed those areas as private colonies. But in other cases, vacant lands that were owned by the native landholders or legally by the government, which were forcefully occupied by the refugees were termed as 'Jabar Dakhal'.[17] They used to undertake those forcible occupations of land and began to establish squatter colonies.

The elite migrants began to construct dwelling houses after obtaining *khas* lands from the government. Problems were faced by the economically weaker section, who could not afford it. The eroded and empty houses left behind by the Muslims in Jalpaiguri were occupied by the newcomers for habitation. On the side of the river Teesta a vast land of Jalpaiguri was allotted to the scolded families and for their temporary settlement tents were supplied free of cost by the Government.[18] A committee was instituted to supervise the relief works to ameliorate the condition of the migrants. A noticeable thing observed that some able-bodied displaced persons, both men and women, despite their physical fitness depended upon the charity of the Government purposely, which needed to be resolved. A committee was set up to accommodate suitable jobs to those able-bodied persons both men and women. The first refugee colony in Jalpaiguri was established at Fatapukur, a place near Jalpaiguri town. Total 250 farmers from East Pakistan initially settled here and each agriculturist was allotted one *bigha* of land for his family.[19] In post-1950, there were 13 colonies in Jalpaiguri, populated with 1,065 families, which had a total area of 485.75 bighas (1 bigha = 14,400 sq.ft.).[20]

The impact of the partition had a tremendous influence on the lives of Jalpaiguri inhabitants. The new coinage Refugee culture or Udvastu Sangskriti shaped the lifestyle of the Jalpaiguri people to a large extent. In 1950 forceful occupation colonies (*jobar dakhal*) got affiliation of the Government. There were nine colonies in Jalpaiguri till the year 1958. Those were Rajganj, Fakir Para, Mandal Ghat, Alipurduar, Panda Para, Fatapukur etc.[21] In Jalpaiguri, till 1958 1,50,156 refugees migrated but only 5850 people got shelter in government colonies. There were a huge number of colonies in Jalpaiguri district, both Government and private. Few names of the colonies in Jalpaiguri district are being appended below:

Raja Rammohan Pally, Bhakti Nagar Colony (1 & 2), Pranta Pally, Sarat Pally Colony, Bankim Nagar Colony, Shital Para Colony, Purba Phool Bagan Colony, Thakur Nagar Colony, Ananda Nagar Colony, Dacca Udvastu Colony, Dhumdhangi Colony, Bijoy Nagar Colony, Surya Sen Colony, Shri Shri Ma Sarada Pally, Subhas Pally, Niranjan Sen Pally, Ranjan Pally, Sarat Pally, Dinesh Pally, Congress Pally (1 & 2), Hiren Sarkar farm Refugee and so on.[22]

Women Sufferings during Partition and Rehabilitation

Women in early history were always being a part of ignorance. Most of the historical stories of the early days were popularly based on male perspectives. All the discussions were based on glorifying the heroes. But from the 19th century, this concept has been changed due to the initiatives of some feminist writers and scholars. Even some women started to write their biography and in Bengal, Rassundari Devi set the first stone. If we turn out the pages of early Indian history, women would be seen always as the victim of harassment, tease, molestation, violence etc. in the name of tradition and culture in a male dominating society and the terrible condition like partition, made it more worst for them to survive. In Ritu Menon and Kamala Bhasin's language, "*Women who were destitute in one way or another by the event, as forced mass migration led to an extreme disruption of life at all levels and exposed them to a kind of upheaval that could only proclaim the dark side of freedom.*"[23]

The womenfolk faced an extreme level of violence as an impact of partition. They had to pay the highest cost of independence by giving up their chastity and also by sacrificing their lives silently. During the period of turmoil, the women became the common target of all inhuman activities. Sexual assault, abduction, forced marriages, intimidation became regular events in their life. The women who came over from East Pakistan to West Bengal as well as in North Bengal were humiliated and tortured in every possible way in their ancestral place, during their journey and also in their new abode. The decision of crossing the border was not in the hands of the female members of the families. They were even not allowed to speak in some orthodox-minded families in names of social norms. They were allowed to cross the borders either by the order of the male members of the families or in absence of the male members. They were forced by their family members to leave their motherland with the concern to protect their chastity and upholding their dignity. Coming in contact with many victimized women it is highly noticed that every woman left the country following the communal violence.[24] It cannot be ascertained with certitude that all of them were the victims of direct violence or physical violence, but psychological fear also played a vital role in their migration.[25]

The event of partition was not alone, it amalgamated with sorrow, widowhood, hunger, violence and nefarious rape cases. Forced marriage became a daily event. Certain incidents narrated by them, highlighted their condition in more clear terms. For example one of them told Hiranmoy Bandopadhyay, the DM (24-Parganas) and also Rehabilitation Commissioner of West Bengal, that often when the women went to take a bath in the pond, some Muslim men would remark, '*Pak Pak Pakistan, Hindur Bhatar Mussolman*' (This is Pakistan, the husband of a Hindu will be a Mussalman). In yet another incident narrated by another refugee, it was said that one of the Muslims called out to the ladies in the pond '*E bibi, bela je bede chollo, Aar deri keno? Ebar ghore cholo*'. (Oh Bibi, it's evening now, why delay any further, let's go home.)[26] They had to see the murder of their husbands, vermilion marks were forcibly erased and bangles were broken. *The Hindustan Standard* reported on November 5, 1946, that 300 women were raped at Noakhali.[27]

Ritu Menon and Kamala Bhasin are of the view that *"all of them treat women's bodies as territory to be conquered, claimed or marked by the assailant."*[28]

The refugee women were even humiliated and inhumanly tortured on their way to West Bengal during the process of search at the border by the Pakistani customs officers and staff.[29] Some contemporary newspapers recorded the strenuous journey of the women across the borders. Streams of women clutching their babies on one arm and their small belongings on the other were seen walking down the railway tracks. Many died on the way.[30] *Chobi Sarkar*, a resident of Alipurduar who is also a refugee from Dacca, has reminisced her memory of border crossing with tears, "*Those days were very scary. We were scared to go to school. Muslim boys used to tease. My elder sister was very beautiful and they threatened my family to kidnap her. With the thought of safeguarding us, my widow mother has decided to cross the border with my two brothers, one elder sister and me. Although all of us crossed the border they stopped my elder brother with our belongings. So, we had to go back to the border and after facing huge inquiry they let all of us cross the border. From there first, we stayed few days at Maynaguri and then we came to Alipurduar. I was 12 years old that time.*"[31] This kind of the story of women's suffering is also evident in Sandip Bondyopadhyay's writing, where he wrote about two girls named Mira and Dhira and a married woman named Bokul Rani Mitra, who was abducted at the Benapol border after the Noakhali riots.[32]

It was not that, the only border crossing was difficult for them and after that, it was a friendly situation was waiting for them. After crossing the border they faced a more difficult situation. They had no shelter. Many of them took shelter in railway stations and those who could not find any place to stay in Calcutta and its suburban areas marched towards North Bengal. There they took shelter in the houses of their near and dear ones, relatives. In some cases, merciful natives made necessary arrangements for their survival. Some of them even got land for cultivation. But those who could not manage anything for them, had to depend on the relief camps. But there was also a lack of necessary facilities in the relief camps. Ranjit Bhoumik, who has come to Alipurduar in Jalpaiguri, in the year 1951 with his family, described the situation in an interview like this: "*We could not find any shelter and decided to stay in the boats. Forty-eight days we spent on the boats having no relief, no particular arrangement to reside. I lost my younger brother to Enteric disease without any treatment. We were helpless.*"[33] This statement described their condition of that particular time. Due to the intolerable condition, some refugees choose the way of violence. They captured the land of the villagers by aggression. In Sunil Gangopadhyay's novel *Purbo Paschim*, Pratap's sister Supriti is shown as a victim of refugee activities. Her husband was killed in the process of trying to free his land from the refugees who have forcibly occupied it.

It was not that one family got shelter in one place. The refugee families had to adjust with other families at the same place, which was difficult for both men and women and particularly female members. There were no separate toilet for the women. Pregnant women had no facilities. Hironmoy Bandyopadhyay in his "*Uthvastu*" described his visit to Alipurduar district that when he went to Alipurduar the sub-division was already overcrowded with refugees. There were so many one-storied houses with a small balcony. Many families took shelter in each different room.[34] So it was very difficult to survive in this situation for the women whose upbringing was based on an orthodox mind.

The life of the people who entered a new atmospheric situation was not easy and especially for the women. Women, who were always been a part of social harassment, faced more difficult situations in society. Such instances of violence can be observed in many of the later-day narratives and memoirs of the refugees who came from East Bengal. But in a later period, the women succeeded to overcome the traumas to some extent and a good number of women were seen engaging themselves in various activities to face their economic needs and for the well-being and betterment of their family and family members. In East Pakistan, the female inmates of the family could not even think of going outside for outer activities but under the pressure of circumstances, their old conception and attitude changed abruptly. In the mean time to fulfil their requirements some women made them socially and politically aware in meeting the challenges ahead. They set exemplary proof before the inhabitants of the North geographic region of West Bengal to manoeuvre forward to establish their social dignity and to ameliorate the condition, especially of the womenfolk.

Partition in one single stroke brought many women into active public life. The trauma and agony faced by the refugee women indirectly bestowed positive energy to them for their overall development in the later period. Despite numerous obstacles blocking their way, they have dared to face the adverse situation with courage, bravery, flexibility, conservancy and bluffly ambition. Economic independence was a new responsibility which the middle-class and elite women had no experience of. Dipesh Chakrabarty mentioned, "*. . . incidents of sexual harassment and degradation of women, of forced eviction, of physical violence and humiliation, marked their experience.*"[35] It gave a completely new aspect to people's life. Not only the refugee or migrated families experienced its terrible effects, but the rooted persons were also suffered from it. Ranabir Samaddar has concluded the whole event of partition in this manner, "*Partition is linked to a transition — a transition from colonialism to post-colonialism, from nationalist secularism to communalism and separatism and also from united entity to vivisection.*"[36]

NOTES AND REFERENCES

1. Gyanesh Kudaisya, "Divided Landscapes, Fragmented Identities: East Bengal Refugees and their Rehabilitation in India, 1947-79", in *Freedom, Trauma, Continuities: North India and Independence*, D.A. Low and Howard Brasted (ed.), New Delhi, Sage Publications Ltd., 1998, p. 107.
2. *Ibid.*
3. *Ibid*, pp. 107-108.
4. *Ibid.*, p. 105.
5. Debjani Sengupta (ed.), *Map Making: Partition Stories from Two Bengals*, New Delhi, Srishti Publishers and Distributors, 2003, p. 188.
6. Ranjit Roy, "Paschimbanger Udvastu: Kendra Rajya Danda-Rajniti" in *Desh Bhagh: Smriti Ar Stabdhata*, Semanti Ghosh (ed.), Kolkata, Gangchil, First Published March 2008, p. 52.
7. *Amritbazar Patrika*, 19th October, 1946.
8. Gyanesh Kudaisya, *op. cit.*, p. 109.
9. Ranjit Roy, *op. cit.*, p. 52.
10. Prafulla Kumar Chakraborti, *The Marginal Men*, Calcutta, Naya Udyog, 1999, p. 3.
11. *An Alternative Proposal for Rehabilitation of Camp Refugees in West Bengal*, Memorandum, Submitted By U.C.R.C. to Dr. B.C. Roy on 11/8/1958, United Central Refugee Council, p. 17.
12. Ranjit Roy, *op. cit.*, p. 52.
13. Ranjit Dasgupta, *Economy, Society in Bengal: Jalpaiguri 1869-1947*, Delhi, Oxford University Press, 1992, p. 237.
14. Hironmoy Bondopadhay, *Udvastu*, Calcutta, Sahitya Samsad, 1970, p. 29.
15. Gouranga Chandra Roy, "The Changing Demographic Profile in Jalpaiguri Duars (1867-2001)" in *Reflections on The History of North Bengal*, Anil Kumar Sarkar (ed.), Kolkata, Abhijeet Publications, 2018, p. 36.
16. A. Mitra (ed.), *Census 1951, West Bengal District Handbook, Jalpaiguri*, Calcutta, Thacker's Press and Directories, p. 94.
17. Racel Waber, "Re (Creating) The Home: Women's Role in The Development of Refugee Colonies in South Calcutta", in *Trauma and the Triumph Gender and Partition in Eastern India*, Joshodhara Bagchi and Subhoranjan Dasgupta (ed.), Kolkata, Stree, 2003, p. 67.

18. Interview on 24th February, 2021, with Dipak Bhattacharya, Ex-Kanungo Officer-1 (2011-2017), Refugee Relief and Rehabilitation Directorate, Government of West Bengal, Jalpaiguri and also present Organization Secretary of U.C.R.C. State Committee, West Bengal.
19. *Report of the Working Group on the Residual Problem of Rehabilitation in West Bengal*, Published by Ministry of Supply and Rehabilitation, Department of Rehabilitation, Government of West Bengal, March 1976, p. 42.
20. *R.R. Committee's Report*, submitted under the Chairmanship of Samar Mukherjee, Government of West Bengal, August 1981, p. 43.
21. *Manual of Refugee Relief and Rehabilitation*, Vol. 1, Government of West Bengal, Kolkata, Basumati Corporation Limited, 2001, p. 59.
22. Krishnendu Roy (ed.), *Uttar Banger Simanta*, Kolkata, The Shee Book Agency, 2013, p. 218.
23. Ritu Menon and Kamala Bhasin, "Recovery, Rupture, Resistance: The Indian State and the Abduction of Women During Partition" in *Inventing Boundaries: Gender, Politics and the Partition of India*, Mushirul Hasan (ed.), New Delhi, Oxford University Press, 2000, p. 209.
24. Jasodhara Bagchi and Shubhoranjan Dasgupta (ed.), *Trauma and The Triumph: Gender and Partition In Eastern India*, Kolkata, Stree, 1st February, 2003, pp. 4, 5.
25. Nisid Hajari, *Mid Night's Furies: The Deadly Legacy of India's Partition*, Gloucestershire, U.K., Amberley Publishing, 1st August, 2015, p. 10.
26. Hiranmoy Bandopadhyay, *op. cit.*, p. 16.
27. Gargi Chakravartty, *Coming Out of Partition: Refugee Women of Bengal*, New Delhi, Bluejay Books, 2005, p. 7.
28. Ritu Menon and Kamala Bhasin, *Borders & Boundaries: Women in India's Partition*, New Delhi, Women Unlimited, 1998, p. 43.
29. Kirankumar Nitali, "The Partition of India, Through the Experience of Bengali Refugee Women" in *The Criterion*, June 2013, Vol. 4, Issue 111, p. 65.
30. *Amrita Bazaar Patrika*, March 23, 1950.
31. Interview with Chobi Sarkar, 2nd February, 2021, Alipurduar, West Bengal.
32. Sandip Bondyopadhyay, *Deshbhag-Deshtyag*, Kolkata, Anushtup, First Published in January 1994, p. 80.
33. Interview with Ranjit Bhoumik, 18th December, 2020, Alipurduar (W.B.).
34. Hiranmoy Bandopadhyay, *op. cit.*, p. 12.
35. Dipesh Chakrabarty, "Remembered Villages: Representations of Hindu-Bengali Memories in the Aftermath of the Partition" in *Inventing Boundaries: Gender, Politics and the Partition of India*, Mushirul Hasan (ed.), New Delhi, Oxford University Press, 2000, p. 133.
36. Ranbir Samaddar (ed.), *Reflection of Partition in the East*, Calcutta Research Group, Vikas Publishing House Pvt. Ltd., 1997, p. 2.

PART – III

Marginal People: Sports, Environment and Politics

14

Sport as a Tool of Resisting the Marginalization

The Story of the Heroic Emergence of Palwankar Baloo, the First Dalit Indian Cricketer

Suvasish Chakraborty

Marginalization appears to be a global threat to the spirit of diversity and inclusivity within human civilization. It refers to a complex process of relegating the marginal sections of society from the privileged ones, thereby, leading to the destabilization of society. Given this backdrop, in the first section, my article throws light on the concept of 'marginalization'. In the next section, my article endeavours to explore how sport has turned out to be a significant element of society as well as a credible platform through which vulnerable populations have empowered themselves by resisting marginalization in society. In the final section, my article explores the emergence of Palwankar Baloo, the first international Dalit cricketer, in the annals of Indian cricket history who not only proved himself as the greatest Indian cricketer of all times but also as a torch bearer of minority integration in the colonial caste-ridden Indian society.

Marginalization refers to a global mess, a serious threat to the social, cultural, political, or economic stability or equilibrium of society whereby the minorities or sub-groups find themselves in a quagmire of ordeal being constructed upon the predominant majoritarian values. To be more specific, the notion of marginalization can be characterized as follows:

> Marginalization is a complex condition of disadvantage that individuals and communities may experience because of vulnerabilities that may arise from unequal or inequitable environmental, ethnic, cultural, social, political and economic factors.[1]

Considering marginalization as a matter of justice, it can arguably be stated that in several incidents the platform of sport has often turned out to be an emancipator for the unprivileged, marginalized sections of society. Be it as part of intervention programmes like the Sports for Development and Peace programme, being collaborated with the United Nations' Millennium Development Goals, or as a credible medium of empowering vulnerable populations like women and girls, disabled communities, or homeless and migrant people across the world. Sport has become a synonym of equality, integrity, tolerance, and social inclusion. Although in several incidents it has been found that sport persons have often been victimized as the subject of severe marginalization because of the unfair and adverse effect of race, sex, class or caste discrimination within the sporting spectrum itself but it is also undeniable that sporting fields seemed to have been majorly instrumentalized by the oppressed vulnerable communities to challenge and outlaw the prevalent monopolized arbitrary socio-cultural practices, leading to their social deprivation and isolation. Several instances have been glorified in the past for challenging the monopolization and concentration of power by the dominant class which proved that sport can be a domain of empowerment for the downtrodden suppressed minorities. Starting from the impact of the Black lives matter movement against racism or the remarkable rise of Frank Worrel as the first full-time black West Indies or the recent success of France football team in the World Cup 2018 embracing a multi-cultural team, the podium of sport has repeatedly shown its firm commitment to the spirit of inclusivity, diversity and solidarity.

Given the above-mentioned background, my article endeavours to explore how Palwankar Baloo, the first Indian Dalit international cricketer belonging to the 'Chamar' community, has come out to be the most successful cricketer in the history of Indian cricket, resisting all discriminations and humiliations of caste prejudiced oppressive Hindu society in colonial India under British Raj.

The Marginalized History of the Chamar Caste

The word 'Chamar' was historically used to categorise Dalit communities in general who were mostly found in the northern states of the Indian subcontinent and was traditionally subject to the scourge of untouchability which was based on the heinous practice of the Indian caste system. The name 'Chamar' which is being characterized by a derogatory narrative is believed to have originated from the Sanskrit term 'charmakara' (skin worker). Their social existence was intrinsically connected with the word 'charman' or 'charma' which was elicited in the *Yajur Veda*, in the *Rig Veda* and the *Atharva Veda* and other early literature. They belonged to the lower echelon of traditional hierarchical Hindu society and were designated as economically vulnerable sections of the society. Chamars were traditionally worked as tanners and dyers which ultimately resulted in their segregation from and subordination by the higher caste sections in the traditional Hindu social hierarchy. To be more specific, Chamar was "regarded with loathing and disgust by the higher castes. Except when it is necessary, a clean-living Hindu will not visit his part of the village. The author of Hindu Castes and Sects says that the very touch of a Chamar renders it necessary for a good Hindu to bathe with all clothes on. The Chamar's very name connects him with the carcasses of cattle. Besides, he not only removes skins from the cattle that have died but also eats the flesh. The defilement and degradation resulting from these acts is insurmountable."[2] This dominant proposition which equated untouchability with supposedly impure occupation by Chamars was further institutionally reinforced in many reports like the decennial census or the ethnographic reports of the 1870s and 1880s corresponding to the study of untouchability in India. For instance, Caambel, in the 1854 report, has precisely linked the Chamar community with the cattle poising. Briggs in his book '*The Religious Life of India: The Chamars*' has delineated how institutional acts have led to the insuperable oppression by the upper Brahmin caste over the Chamars. For example, the Census Report for 1901 has categorically specified the ground indicating the criteria from which Brahmin can take water, which caste must not be considered untouchable and how the touch of Chamar community defiles the purity of the upper Hindu caste as they eat beef and vermin. This dominant perception has arguably led to the utter degradation of Chamar population in the complex ordering of Hindu social structure.[3] On this point, Dr. Rawat, one of the prominent scholar of Dalit History, has convincingly raised the fundamental point concerning how the occupational stereotypes representing Dalit identity was largely constructed in the colonial and post-colonial time:

> In all these accounts — colonial and post-colonial — we are told that Chamars are "traditionally" leatherworkers and their untouchable status stems from their impure occupation. This is the consistent explanation for why they occupy the lowest occupation. This is the

> consistent explanation for why they occupy the lowest position in Hindu society. Indeed, this formulation has become foundational in Indian historical, anthropological, and sociological writings on Chamars, assuming a status of self-evident truth and providing the starting framework for subsequent studies, be they anthropological or historical. These views have been reinforced by an emphasis on Brahminical texts as primary sources of authority and by colonial reconstructions of knowledge that privileged dominant Hindu social, political and cultural groups of informants. In this sense, then, the representation of the history and society of Chamars and other Dalit groups reflect the often experiences — both past and present — of those defined as "untouchable".[4]

The following statement has sought to discover the sole reason for the continued subordination of Dalits in India which led the Dalit intellectuals and activists to consistently raise markedly different narratives in response to the colonial Puranic sources "to confront colonial and post-colonial Hindu narratives by writing their histories, defining their political agendas, and deploying their self-fashioned identities."[5] However, there is no denying that a very limited amount of research and academic works have been done in the genre of Dalit history of sports in India and are mostly unexplored. Given this backdrop, it is unquestionably important to shed light exclusively on the anecdote of the inspirational uprising of the Dalit Cricketer like Palwankar Baloo, who has revolutionized Indian cricket by his charisma and sheer cricketing talent. Hence, it is imperative to situate Palwankar Baloo's relentless struggling cricketing career within the broader socio-cultural context of his time. Following this background, my article also seeks to portray why Baloo's unsung cricketing journey should be celebrated in the cricketing fraternity who not only proved himself as one of the greatest cricketers of his time by making his presence significant in the domestic cricket as well as in the all-India team touring England in 1911 but also becomes an exemplary figure in the annals of Indian cricket who has waged an uncompromising challenge against all odds of the nascent Hindu hierarchical system in the colonial period.

Chandra Bhanu once stated that 'the British came too late left too early[6] to address the point that British has helped Dalit community to liberate themselves to a large extent from falling prey to the caste-ridden social operations and economic vulnerability due to their untouchable status. Although the upper caste Hindus stayed away from joining ammunition and gun factories fearing that they might have to use the objectionable greased cartage which was made of the flesh of holy cow, this was certainly not the case for Chamars. The Chamar community, who had not maintained such social compliance due to their habitual association with the carcasses, were permitted to work in British cantonments in the western and southern part of India. Moreover, the gradual progression of Dalit education has also been ensured when Dalits continued to have the accessibility of education being undertaken by European missionaries after Britain's established control over India. Their access to primary education consequently strengthened their upward social mobility as well social equalization challenging the biased norms of social stratification in Indian society. Given this broader socio-political scenario Palwankar Baloo, India's first international Dalit cricketer, has begun his career. The extraordinary cricketing journey of Palwankar Baloo as a Dalit icon and his uncompressing struggle with the ugly reality of a caste-driven society was penned down by his younger brother Vithal Palwankar in his autobiography in Marathi entitled '*Maze Crida-Jivan*' (*My Sporting life*).

Baloo's Life and his Battle with the Severity of Caste Discrimination in India

Palwankar Baloo, who was called 'Rhodes' of India,[7] was born in 1875, in the South Indian town of Dharwad in the 'Chamar' caste family. He was brought up with his three brothers — Babaji Palwankar Shivram, Palwankar Ganpat and Palwankar Vithal — all were cricketers. Baloo has started his early life in Poona where his father was employed in the 112th Native infantry regiment of the British army. Baloo and his brothers became well acquainted with the game of cricket when they began to play with the discarded equipment of the European cricketers. He got his first employment to roll and sweep the pitch at the Parsi Cricket Club and also developed his bowling accuracy and technique when he occasionally got to ball to the members in the net. He was paid 3 rupees a month by the local Parsi Gymkhana. But soon Baloo moved to the Poona Club in 1892 which was administered by the Europeans. His rhythmic and smooth bowling, jerky action and immaculate accuracy were noticed by the English Captain of Poona J.G. Grieg (called 'Jungly' Grieg), who was considered as greatest European batsman in India and was renowned as the first Little Master in pre-independent India. Captain Grieg used to pay Baloo 8 annas whenever the latter took his wicket.

Even though Baloo was hardly allowed to bat because batting was under aristocratic preserve in colonial time. Praising Baloo's cricketing brilliance Dr. M.E. Pavri, one of the pioneers of Indian cricket, once regarded the former as "*one of the best native bowlers. A left-handed medium pace bowler with an easy action. Has both breaks and a curl in the air and has a lot of spin on the ball. The most deadly bowler in on a sticky wicket.*"[8] Despite being a distinguished cricketer Baloo's prospect seemed gloomy when he joined the Young Men's Hindu Club because of his connection with 'untouchable' caste status. Even 'Jungly' Grieg sent a letter to the local newspaper condemning the apprehension of Hindus regarding Baloo's inclusion in the team on the account of his caste status and also stated that it would be mindless to ignore Baloo's magical skills on the field. Some of the Telugu speaking, non-Brahmin cricketers in the team also raised voices for Baloo's entry into the team. "Eventually, Baloo and Vithal both were drafted into the Hindus team which can be viewed as a landmark in the nation's emancipation from the old disuniting and denationalizing customs."[9] The admission of Chamar brothers in the Hindu team revealed that "where national interest required, equal opportunity must be given to all of any caste, even though the offer of such opportunity involved the trampling of some old prejudices."[10] In 1906 both Baloo and his brother Shivram have played pivotal roles to clinch the epic victory against the European side. In that match, Baloo's spectacular performance with eight wickets has led to the dismissal of the European Batsman. Baloo's extraordinary achievement against the European Gymkhana in Satara was highly appreciated by the Maharashtrian social reformer Mahadev Govind Ranade who shook hands with the former in a public function appreciating Baloo's praiseworthy contribution to the team. For his achievement, Baloo was also felicitated by Bal Gangadhar Tilak, an ardent nationalist at that time. In 1899 Baloo moved to Bombay. Although even there he also felt severe humiliation for his marginalized identity but being "Fearful of losing the services of a match-winning bowler, the leaders of Hindu Gymkhana were forced, by degrees, to mend their ways and treat Baloo in the same way as they did his upper-caste teammates."[11] Further, the inclusion of a Dalit cricketer in Hindu teams like Poona or Bombay has bolstered the meritocratic essence of the then Indian cricket. Indian Social Reformer, a weekly periodical, which were taking a progressive stance at that time on the burning social issues also highlighted the emergence of the first subaltern spin wizard:

> The champion bowler of the Hindu is Mr. Baloo, a Chamaar. Indeed it is not Bombay that rubbed off this caste exclusiveness. Years back Baloo was a bowler in the Poona European Gymkhana. The Poona Hindus who consisted mostly of upper-caste Hindus found that Chamaar though Baloo was his inclusion in the team would improve matters considerably. With the pluck and spirit, which the Poona Hindus of the 1880s had, they admitted him as their member and so far pollution from touch with a low went, the plucky Brahmins of Poona gave the slip to orthodoxy. . . . The history of the admission of these Chamaar brothers in Hindu Gymkhana is a credit to all and has done far more to liberalize the minds of thousands young Hindus than all other attempts in such spheres.[12]

However, Palwankar Baloo kept battling with heinous caste discrimination in Poona Club. Was he anti-social? No, unfortunately, he was an untouchable downtrodden Dalit. As Guha noted:

> In the event, Baloo was invited to play for the Poona Hindus, but at a price. On the field, the upper-caste cricketers touched the same ball as he observed the ritual taboos. At the tea interval, that ceremony sacred to cricket, Baloo was served the liquid outside the pavilion, and in a disposable clay Matka, while his colleagues drank in white porcelain cups inside. If he wished to wash his hands and face, an untouchable servant of the club took a kettle out into the corner of the field and poured water on from it. Baloo also ate his lunch on a separate plate and a separate table.[13]

In 1899, Baloo has moved from Poona to Bombay. But, as in Poona Baloo also had to face caste discrimination in Bombay by orthodox Brahmins because of his marginal identity. In 1902 Baloo was recruited as a clerk in the BB and CI Railway Company. He is considered to be a star cricketer in the local club matches. Baloo's performance was graceful at Bombay against the English tourist's team Oxford Authentics team. In 1907 and 1910 Baloo also contributed to several memorable triumphs for his team in the Triangular matches. Applauding Baloo's permanence, Kidambi commented:

> We have considered Baloo's life within the political and social context of his times. But what of Baloo the cricketer? Any consideration of his career would be incomplete without reckoning with the specific skills that Baloo displayed in his chosen specialism,

> that of slow, low-arm spin bowling. The best practitioners of this art have certain features in common: they can control the pace and flight of the round, leather-encased projectile they direct at the batsman, deceive their opponent with subtle variations in line and length, and sustain long spells of accurate bowling. Baloo, by all accounts, not only possessed all these qualities in ample measure but had also perfected them to the point where he was indisputably one of the finest practitioners of the art in the entire cricketing world.[14]

Baloo's Connection with Cricketing Nationalism

Cricket in colonial time also developed its connection with the growing nationalism. The winning of a native team against the European sides gave confidence to the former to fight for the cause of India's political emancipation from the imperial bondage. Following this scenario, it is important to unravel the fact that the Natore, a district of the Rajshahi division of Bangladesh, had a close connection with cricket in the colonial period of the undivided Indian subcontinent. The Maharajas of Natore are used to encourage sporting culture with heart and soul. From 1900 onwards cricket was promoted in Natore with the active encouragement of Jagadindranarayan Ray who was determined to launch a cricket team of his own to uplift the status of Natore. Ray was one of the prominent nationalists at that time and an active member of the Indian National Congress. He had built a strong team comprising native cricketers only. The inclusion of native players alone has successfully pulled local support for his team. He also built a cricket stadium composing 45 acres of land at Bondel Road of old Ballygung in South Kolkata. Cricket became a nationalist tool for the team of Natore as Maharaja Ray's ambition was to take an upperhand and to beat the Maharaja of Cooch Behar's team which was mainly dominated by European players like Joe Vine, Frank Tarrant, George Cox and so many others. Jagadindranarayan Ray has articulated the aura of sporting nationalism in the cricket field as he wanted to beat the English at their own game. For that reason, he also recruited players like J.S. Warden, P. Vithal, K. Seshachari, coaches like Sardaranjan Ray, the father of Indian cricket, in his team to promote a strong native cricket team. Palwankar Baloo, one of the finest left-arm Dalit spinner in the first decade of the twentieth century, was recruited in the Natore Team. Recalling his brother Palwankar Baloo's balling brilliance, Vithal regarded that Baloo's incredible cricketing journey made him cemented his place in the Natore XI.[15] While playing for Natore in 1910 Baloo has faced Ranji who was playing for the Maharaja of Jodhpur's team and the former finished off the win gracefully.[16]

The Phenomena of Baloo's Selection in the 1911 Tour: The Making of a Legend

When the Indian team went on a tour to England in 1911 under the captaincy of Bhupinder Singh, the Maharaja of Patiala, both Baloo and Shivram secured their chance in the team as a last-minute replacement. Although the Indian side slumped to defeat, Baloo's performance was outstanding when he registered an astonishing 114 wickets. In the first-class matches of the tour, Baloo took 75 wickets, capturing a best of 8/103.[17] According to Deodhar, the 36-year old spinner proved himself highly impressive by coming at par with Rhodes and Verity.[18] The glory came when Baloo played in some of the prestigious grounds in England like Cambridge and Oxford. He was also reportedly offered to join other country clubs after his bright performance against several university teams and countrysides; 7/83 against Lancashire, 5/87 against Oxford, and 4/96 against the MCC.[19] Most interestingly, when Baloo returned to Bombay after the 1911 tour, he has received a grand felicitation from the Depressed Classes Association of Bombay and the welcome address for the rousing reception at this function was given by Babasaheb Ambedkar. However, despite being the most successful cricketer at that time who has played the pivotal role in projecting India on the world map through his cricketing brilliance, had always been denied the chance of attaining the captaincy. But despite struggling with all those obstacles, mustached Baloo's indomitable journey in the pantheon of Indian cricket history must not be forgotten.

The Controversy Over Baloo's Captaincy

As discussed above that despite being one of the greatest Indian cricketers and finest left-arm bowler of his time, Baloo had always been discriminated against in the Indian cricket circuit because of his social status which belonged to the bottom of the hierarchical Hindu caste system. He emerged as one of the famous Dalit public figures from Deccan Plateau whose skills were even compared with the level of cricketing expertise of an outstanding English cricketer named

W.G. Grace. Although Baloo has shaken the social hierarchy within the social and political milieu of the then India's society by his bowling and earned immense respect in the Indian cricket circuit for his phenomenal cricketing journey he had consistently been deprived of leading the team as a captain. In 1913 Baloo was one of the foremost bowlers in the Hindu team along with his brothers Shivram, Vithal and Ganpat. But the honour of the captaincy of the team was handed over to M.D. Pai, the Gowd Saraswati Brahmin Mitra Mandal. Even Pai himself accepted that the preference of the captaincy must be handed over to Baloo for his on-field experience and intelligence. This injustice to Baloo has triggered several protests between 1910 and 1920 demanding Baloo's selection as the captain of the team. One of the correspondents of the *Bombay Chronicle* also voiced the displeasure concerning that tragic incident:

> Baloo has been the mainstay of Hindu cricket for more than a decade and a half and his services in the cause of Hindu cricket have been invaluable. By every right of ability, of seniority, and the services rendered to his side, he should long be ago has been appointed captain of the team. He has not only been denied that right but now he has been excluded from the team itself.[20]

The most shocking incident happened in the 1920 Quadrangular tournament when Hindu captain Pai fell ill and a young captain from Poona, D.B. Deodhar was appointed as a captain. Most strikingly, Baloo was dropped from the team. The repeated injustice to Baloo has created huge resentment amongst the Hindu Gymkhana players as a reaction of which both Shivram and Vithal withdrew from the team. Their anger and dissatisfaction over the unfair decision were brought to the fore:

> . . . the committees' decision can only be characterized as unsportsman like in the extreme, inasmuch as they have been influenced by the caste and social and educational status of their selection rather than his achievements or seniority in the field of cricket, and as such the Committee's decision can only be taken as part with a bias in favour of caste. . . . In arriving at this decision be it remembered that we feel very strongly the covert and overt insult levelled at us belonging to the so-called depressed class as it amounts to nullification of our claims for recognition for all time. That such matters as caste should be the determining factor in Cricket is more than we can quietly bow down to, hence our decision to stand down from the Hindu Team this year.[21]

However, a result of the growing pressure surrounding the controversy, Baloo was appointed as a vice-captain when the Hindus reached the final. Vithal and Shivram were also selected in the team. However, it would not be an exaggeration to argue that the decision to promote Baloo as vice-captain and not as captain was most likely be instigated by the fear that accepting Baloo as a captain could rattle Brahmin's domination in Indian cricket. However, three years later, Baloo's brother Shivram was chosen as a captain and under his leadership, the Hindus won the Quadrangular for the first time. As Sen noted:

> What Baloo couldn't achieve on the playing field his brother Vithal did. In 1923, for the first time a Dalit, Vithal, was appointed captain of the Hindus. Guha explains that the decision could well have been dictated by pragmatism, since the Hindus had lost in the previous tournaments held in Pune. Now that the tournament was back again in Bombay, where the Banias were more dominant than the Brahmins, the appointment of Vithal as captain was much easier.[22]

Conclusion

The heroic emergence of Baloo as the first Dalit International Indian cricketer is worthy to be remembered for his unending battle with the oppressive caste system in India. The remarkable journey of the greatest cricketer from being cornered as marginalized cricketer who had been treated with disdain and then becoming a national icon is inspirational in the annals of Indian cricket history. As Ahuja put in words:

> In the cricketing folklore of India, some heroes have been immortalized, but some, perhaps with even greater superpowers have been conveniently forgotten by the curators of history. Palwankar Baloo, a name that had once become the symbol of heroic Indian resistance, is one such super hero. . . . This was also the time when B.R. Ambedkar was rising at the political stage and Gandhi was vocally advocating the abolition of untouchability. In a community where there had been no heroes, the Palwankar brothers had truly broken the shackles of prejudice to give hope and a sense of pride to their fellow community members. Cricket had finally triumphed over caste.[23]

Following the above discussion, the critical observation of Ganguly, a cricket historian and scholar, is mention-worthy. According to him, the rise of Baloo requires to be analysed in a stormy context when

Gandhi and Ambedkar were fighting their perpetual battle for the eradication of untouchability in India. It is against this background the impact of Baloo's lifelong struggle with the caste prejudiced Hindu social hierarchy cannot be underestimated. Even his political career as the Congress mediator on the fundamental question of a separate electorate for the depressed class was also significant for his popularized stature amongst the masses. Baloo's extraordinary cricket career and most strikingly, his entry in the 1911 Indian tour to England turned out to be a significant landmark that culminated in the development of egalitarianism in Indian cricket. Thus, it can unequivocally be said that on the one hand when cricket was introduced in India by British regiments as a glorified symbol of Victorian cultural supremacy and subsequently promoted by the natives like Parsees and princely states as a platform of their upward social mobility or for the establishment of their regional supremacy, when cricket was structured upon caste and community lines, on the other hand, Palwankar Baloo's revolutionary voyage on and off the cricket field proved to be instrumental to mark the dawn of a new day for the socially unprivileged downtrodden countrymen. Notwithstanding, Baloo's exceptional contribution in the age of empire also paved the way for the rise of the middle class in the arena of cricket followed by the glory of the Hindu Cricket Club. Hence, the Palwankar brothers' excellence in the Hindu cricket team has vehemently challenged the elitist domination of the Parsi bourgeoisie thereby, helping the game to be embraced by the masses.[24]

However, in the present scenario when Indian cricket has become the superpower of world cricket, few pertinent questions come to the fore — Does India too need caste-based reservations just like South Africa's reservation policy for non-white players in cricket? Does Indian Cricket truly become a meritocratic domain in the era of the 21st century?

Recently, we have also seen how Union Minister Ramdas Athawale was victimized by nasty trolling in social media when he called for reservations for SCs and STs in Team India to ensure the ground of equal opportunity in sport.[25] In 2008, Mr. Niranjan Shah, the ex-Secretary, Board of Control for Cricket in India (BCCI), also has acknowledged the viability of reservation policy in South Africa's cricket and accordingly proposed a similar kind of policy for the sake of the promotion of backward communities in the field of cricket. However, this proposal failed to get approval from the concerned cricket authority.[26] Further, about the question why the representations of Dalit classes' cricketer in Indian team have been adequately low, Kamath, an Assistant Professor of the Mahatma Gandhi University, has addressed the structural impediments and upper-caste homogeneity behind their under-representation:

> How do you people acquire a skill? Is it hereditary? If so, why all your fathers and forefathers became so skilful? You have good access to resources to resources. Whose resources are these? You have accumulated it not even proper way. So do not make me narrate stories of exploitation and creating your so-called skills. It is not to cut short of the length of a screen or runs taken. It is to give opportunity. Then see what is. Even if they fail, there is an aspect of social justice.[27]

Taking into consideration George Bernard Shaw's remark, 'Cricket is a where eleven fools play and eleven hundred fools watch'. He urged for securing the democratic and representative spirit of cricket:

> Cricket is a game where eleven Brahmins and upper caste play and eleven million Sarvajan and Bahujan fools watch and eleven hundred fools in the upper caste media comment and analyse. But, the question of allowing everyone and making it more representative is important to make the nation more democratic in all spheres of life.[28]

However, there is no denying the fact that Indian cricket has become so successful and highly competitive in the new millennium because of its representative nature and inclusive appeal. Had not the Indian team acknowledged the cricketing excellence and contribution of legendary cricketers like Eknath Solkar, Karsan Ghavri, Vinod Kambli, Mohammad Azharuddin, Bhuveneswar Kumar etc. who all came from the background of minority communities, it would have never achieved the glory that Indian Cricket team is holding today, adorning the feathers of 3 World Cups in its crown. Therefore, this transformation of Indian cricket indulging a meritocratic ideology cannot be made possible, if the heroes like Baloo had not fought as a torch bearer for the integration of marginalized population in Indian cricket.

NOTES AND REFERENCES

1. Mehretu, Assefa *et al.*, "Concept in Social and Spatial Marginality", *Geografiska Annaler. Series B, Human Geography*, 82, 2, Development Settlements, 2000, pp. 89-90.

2. Guha, Ramchandra, *A Corner of a Foreign Field: The Indian History of a British Sport*, Penguin Books, 2014 (revised edition), p. 87.
3. Briggs, Geo. W., *The Religious Life of India: The Chamars*, Association Press, 1920, p. 20.
4. Rawat, Ramnarayan S., *Reconsidering Untouchability: Chamars and Dalits History in North India*, Indian University Press, 2010, p. 9. *https://www.academia.edu/40310630/Ram_Rawat_Introduction_Reconsidering_Untouchability*
5. *Ibid.*
6. *Ibid.*, p. 4.
7. See Guha, *A Corner of a Foreign Field*, *op. cit.*, p. 93.
8. *Ibid.*
9. Hindu Cricket, *Indian Social Reformer*, XVI: 25, 18th February, 1906.
10. *Ibid.*
11. Kidambi, Prashant, *Cricket Country: The Untold History of the First All India Team*, Penguin Random House, 2019, p. 166.
12. See "Hindu Cricket", *op. cit.*, pp. 292-294.
13. See Guha, *A Corner of a Foreign Field*, *op. cit.*, p. 90.
14. See, Kidambi, *Cricket Country*, *op. cit.*, p. 166.
15. Caesar, Faisal, "Bangladesh: Natore and Its Relation to Cricket", *cricketsoccer.com*, 8th October, 2018, *https://www.cricketsoccer.com/2018/10/08/bangladesh-natore-and-its-relation-to-cricket/* (Accessed on 10th January, 2019).
16. See Kidambi, *Cricket Country*, *op. cit.*, p. 167.
17. All India in England, June/August 2011, *http://static.espncricinfo.com/db/ARCHIVE/1910S/1911/IND_IN_ENG/* (Accessed on 15th June, 2020).
18. Majumdar, Boria, *Twenty-Two Yards to Freedom: A Social History of Indian Cricket*, Penguin Books, p. 83.
19. See All India in England, June/August 2011, *http://static.espncricinfo.com/db/ARCHIVE/1910S/1911/IND_IN_ENG/* (Accessed on 15th June, 2019).
20. *The Bombay Chronicle*, 3rd September, 1915.
21. *The Bombay Chronicle*, 4th December, 1920.
22. Sen, Ronojoy, *Nation at Play: A History of Sport in India*, Penguin Books, 2015, p. 115.
23. Ahuja, Chandni, "When Cricket Truimphed Over Caste — The Story of Palwankar Baloo, India's Fist Cricket Hero", *Sporskeeda*, 19th August. 2015. https://www.sportskeeda.com/cricket/cricket-triumphed-over-caste-story-palwankar-baloo-indias-first-cricket-hero (Accessed on 1st February, 2020).
24. Ganguly, Sumit, Personal Interview, 1st January, 2021.
25. *The Indian Express*, 2nd July, 2017, *https://indianexpress.com/article/india/ramdas-athawale-demands-reservations-for-scs-sts-in-indian-cricket-team-4731325/* (Acccessed on 10th June, 2019).
26. Komath, Rajesh, "Castes of Cricket in India", *Round Table India*, 23rd September, 2017,*https://roundtableindia.co.in/index.php?option=com_content&view=article&id=9191:castes-of-cricket-in-india&catid=119&Itemid=132%20%20%20/* (Accessed on 3rd May, 2002), *Ibid.*
27. *Ibid.*
28. *Ibid.*

15

Environment *versus* Industrialization and Marginal Coolies in Colonial Bengal Districts

Gopal Chandra Das

Many scholars have done enormous research on the development of the various industries in India, but very few studies have focused on the impact of industrialization on the environment, ecology, society and human life, especially on the marginal industrial coolie class people. It needs to be mentioned at thc outset of the discussion that at present article discusses two industrial sectors in colonial Bengal, namely coal mining and tea plantation industries. Coal mining and tea plantation industries are geographically situated in two separate poles of Bengal — the coal mining industry is primarily located in Asansol-Raniganj of Burdwan district in the south-western part of Bengal and the tea plantation industry is situated in Darjeeling district and contiguous regions of North Bengal. Capitalist industry developed in India as well as Bengal in the second half of the eighteenth century at the hands of colonial imperialist lords. But most of the industrial enterprises were dominated by the British Company rather than Dutch, Portuguese and French Companies. Around the seventeenth and eighteenth centuries, momentous events took place in the entire world. The industrial revolution in England in the middle of the eighteenth century gave birth to a new trend that was influenced by colonialism. With the advent of the industrial revolution came the spread of massive industrialization, factories and urbanization. Simultaneously with the increasing demand for the high quality of human life, the indiscriminate use of natural resources began. The industrial revolution in Britain led to the increase in demand for raw materials for the factories there. At the same time, they also required a market to sell their finished goods. India provided such a platform to Britain to fulfil all its needs. Therefore, the British government in India adopted a number of commercial policies to use the resources of India. Industrialization was one of them. The coal mining and tea plantation industries were some of the most significant commercial landscapes of the British Empire. Needless to say, imperialist industrialization had the most profound effect on the environment and the lower classes of society. Because industrialization causes the balance of various parts of the natural environment such as fauna, flora, water, soil etc. to be disturbed. In addition to this, the arrival of workers in the industrial areas led to the emergence of *bustees* or slums in the industrialized cities, which had a detrimental effect on the natural environment and public health. All of these industrial areas had multiple persistent problems such as unhealthy environment, overcrowded and unplanned housing, lack of adequate pure drinking water, malnutrition, poor health care services, lack of security at hazardous work and low wages etc. On the other hand,in the same way, the industrial owner class and labour class emerged as a new social group. But the industrialist owners and entrepreneurs did not pay much attention to workers' rights. Rather than, the marginalized tribal working class people were the most exploited and deprived by the owner class in the industrial sectors. The discontent of these working classes was manifested through a united resistance against the industrialist owners and contractors. Discussions subject has been discussed based on those issues.

Progress of Industrialization: Impact on Environment and Marginal People

Throughout the seventeenth and eighteenth centuries, the East India Company was the largest and most powerful trading company in Europe and Asia. The company was founded to buy Asian products for the British market. Almost dramatically in the second half of the eighteenth century, the company established an empire in India. In the first half of the nineteenth century, a number of industrial ventures were started by the British capitalists in the Bengal Presidency. Since the last half of the nineteenth century rich coal-based industry and tea plantation industry was grown faster. As a result of enterprise and development of capitalist industries in India had a profound effect on the natural environment, ecology, society and human life especially on the marginal coolie class employed in the industrial zones.

Asansol-Raniganj area was one of the most important mining settlements and rich industrial areas to colonial rulers. In colonial India, the first coal mining was started in Raniganj in Bengal. During the reign of Lord Warren Hastings in 1774, John Sumner and Grant Heatly, two officers of East India Company, took the first initiative to extract coal. Among the native industrial entrepreneurs was Prince Dwarkanath Tagore. Peterson noted in his Burdwan District Gazetteer that the region was rich in sal and various trees, a large number of flora and fauna.[1] But large-scale arbitrary deforestation, indigenous tribal settlements and arable fertile lands were seized for coal mining and subsidiary industries. Large quantities of coal were lifted at that time, which can be deduced from the statistics of Peterson and W.W. Hunter. On the other hand, urbanization and migration also took place in these industrial belts. These huge numbers of marginal ethnic coolies or labour classes came from the adjoining districts such as Bankura, Birbhum, Manbhum, Murshidabad, Santhal Parganas and different parts of India such as Bihar, Patna, Gaya, Bhagalpur, Hazaribagh, Odisha, Central Province, U.P. etc.[2] Gradually these areas became the busiest industrial centres, settlement of the people and workers. Consequently, the arrival of workers in the industrial areas led to the emergence of *bustee* or slums in the industrial cities. The colonial government had to extend the railway to transport coal freely from Asansol, Raniganj, Dhanbad, and Jharia to other places. Such government intervention had taken a heavy toll on the ecosystem and public life. The construction of the railway dams caused the outbreak of lethal malaria fever which was known locally as 'Burdwan fever'.

Apart from the coal mining industry, the unbridled attitude of the imperialist government was also seen in the tea plantation industry. The tea estates of North Bengal were the important field of economic activity of the colonial government. The tea plantation industry gained a special reputation as one of the oldest organized industries in India. It is not unknown to all of us that Darjeeling tea has worldwide fame for its exquisite aroma. For this reason, the colonial rulers became interested in tea cultivation in these hilly areas, keeping in mind lucrative businesses such as the tea industry. The establishment of the tea industry in the Darjeeling district was due to the initiative of Dr. Campbell. By 1856 the industry had begun to develop on a wide scale.[3] The hill regions especially Duars was the largest tea-producing tract to the British. So after the Anglo-Bhutanese War of 1865, the British government annexed the Duars region from Bhutan. From then on, the population of the region began to grow enormously. In 1865 the population of the region was 3,536. But, soon numbers of these immigrants began to increase dramatically. In 1901 its population increased to 41,511. Most of the inhabitants of poor and remote areas destroyed the forest and built new settlements as they could not find good lands anywhere else.[4] Also, *jhum* cultivation (method of destroying the land with fire) destroyed the growth of scrub jungles and herbaceous plants. And heavy rainfall destroyed the Tista, Torsa, Jaldhaka, Raidak, Chel, Sankos and other river plains.[5] The colonial government had to construct railways and roads in Darjeeling and the hilly region as in other parts of the state to transport the raw materials required for the tea industry. Malaria was most prevalent in this district as in other parts of the state. Intensive tea gardens, forests, scrub jungles, wetlands were the source of malaria. However, the incidence of malaria in the Duars region was very high.[6] At the same time, the concept of consolidating the coolies in the tea garden was also involved. Many hired workers were recruited from the surrounding area for the tea industry. This results in pressure on land and the emergence of dense slums. That had a detrimental effect on the natural environment and human life especially marginal lower class people. According to Nandini Bhattacharya, the arrival of immigrant workers in industrial and plantation sites had created a new significance as locations of malarial fever.[7] So, finally, it can be said that the commercial policy of the colonial government was most accountable for this circumstance.

Socio-Economic Condition of Industrial Coolies

Coal mining and tea plantation industries' expansion played an important role in changing socio-economic patterns. From the time of colonial rule, the *arkattis* or *sardars* (contractors) from the remote villages of the neighbouring districts and states used to bring the poor, destitute peasants and working-class people to the colliery and tea plantation areas in the name of giving them lucrative jobs. The employers could easily maintain these jobs day after day due to the low wages of the coolies. Many workers used to came voluntarily in search of work and due to scarcity. Many of them were seasonal workers, during the cultivation they would move to the villages and after cultivation, they would move back to the industrial areas. Even after Independence, working class people continued to come to the industrial zone in search of work and in the hope of earning raw money. Those workers who are the driving force of the society, state continues the trend of production by working tirelessly. But they live in various adversities in society. The capitalists, on the other hand, use their exploitative apparatus indiscriminately for the sake of high profits. As a result, along with the natural environment, the life of the lower people of the society also became miserable.

The development of coal mining and tea industries led to the migration of large numbers of people towards the industrial regions hoping to find work. A large number of marginal tribal communities like *Santhals, Mundas, Bheels, Oraons, Kols, Bauris*, and *Bagdis* came to these areas as labourers. They were generally local agriculture people. In the post-Independence period, people from lower castes were also involved in this work. A large number of migrant labourers started coming from different parts of India like Patna, Gaya and Shahabad (Bihar) to lift the coal in colliery areas.[8] Apart from them, people from *Kol, Gond, Lohar* communities came from Jabalpur, Rewah, Balia, Gaya and *Pasis, Lodhas, Kurmis, Ahirs, Chamars, Bhunyas, Doms, Rajoyaras* were also from U.P., Central Province, Allahabad, Benaras, Rai Bareli, Unnao, Bihar and Patna as labourers. Their physical structure is appropriate for cutting soil and coal. The miners or coolies were usually employed directly by the *sardars* or *jobbers* (contractors). In this way, *Balia bustcc, Oriya dhowrah, Moongheri bustee, Gaya mohalla* were formed due to the arrival of all these coolies in industrial areas like Asansol-Raniganj and Jharia.[9] The massive migration of coolies to the coal mining areas increased the population density and the same time created an unhealthy environment. Colliery owners used to settle miners' slums in the vicinity of the colliery area, which is known as '*dhowrah*' (coolie barracks). Most of the coolies had to live in very small quarters in the coolie lines and *dhoarahs* under swinish conditions.[10] The coolies barracks or *dhowrahs* were completely unhealthy, unhygienic, untidy, unplanned and overcrowded. There was no arrangement of proper ventilation, chimney, bathroom and latrine. These coolie barracks or *dhowrahs* were built in places where there were smelly, cattle beds, pig pens. Adequate lack of sanitary planning hampered the improvement of the health of colliery miners. As a result, these colliery areas soon became breeding grounds for various deadly diseases and epidemics. The chief diseases like cholera, dysentery, diarrhoea, smallpox, malaria, kala-azar, influenza, typhoid, pulmonary etc. were common in the coolies' *bustees* and surrounding regions. Health care services were too meagre. In this way, they become accustomed to living an atrocious life. Prof. Nirban Basu mentions that in the colonial period, the condition of the workers of Asansol, Raniganj was worse than that of the workers of Calcutta.[11] In a word, these barracks were not conducive to living. Due to a lack of protein-rich foods, the coolies or miners often suffered from malnutrition. Lack of pure drinking water in the mining area was another vital issue. The famous sculptor and painter Ramkinkar Baij, who was also a teacher at Ushsgram Boys School, portrayed the scarcity of daily-usage like drinking water of the coal mines people at that time.[12] But unfortunate thing is that, even after independence, there was no significant change in the lives of the coolies living in *dhowrahs*.

Renowned litterateur Sailajananda Mukhopadhyay witnessed the suffering of the coal miners. Through his literature, he has highlighted the painful life of the people working in the mining areas. He wrote, "Those who risk their lives to work everyday in the womb of a coal miner get a small weekly wage at the end of the day. They were constantly oppressed and deprived by the owners. The women coolies of *Santhal, Bauri* and *Bagdi* tribes were the most persecuted by the contractors and the mine owners; they were the object of their desires. Taking advantage of illiteracy and simplicity, the owners, contractors, and moneylenders used to deceive and bankrupt the coolies. Sardars and managers used to torment the workers unspeakably. The moneylenders forcibly snatched the weekly wages of the workers with their finger prints." Sailajananda Mukhopadhyay, in his stories 'Dinmajur' (1932) and 'Kayalakuthi' (1973), shows that the managers and clerks of colliery used to enjoy the same powers as the owner even though they were not the real owner.[13] However, in favour of the government and the mine owners, the working class sometimes got some amenities. So that the coolies' discontent and their movements could not emerge in a gigantic way. Being immersed in the darkness of illiteracy, the coolies were often involved in gambling, drug addiction and illegal activities. Many liquor stores and brothels were sprung up in the vicinity of the colliery areas, where coolies could enjoy their fatigue.

If we look at the tea industries in the Darjeeling district and contiguous regions of North Bengal, the same scene comes to notice. The tea industry is also completely labour-dependent. For this reason, the demand for labour in these regions was huge in the colonial period. Both male and female workers were engaged in the preparation of cultivable land, planting of seeds, spraying of fertilizers and pesticides, clearing the weedicides, pruning, plucking of leaves and buds, sorting, fermentation, drying and packaging etc. works. Tea coolies from Nepal and Chhotanagpur were recruited in the Terai region. The vast majority of the Nepalese were considered suitable in the tea fields for their hard work and enthusiasm.[14] Besides the Napali, the bulk of the emigrant tribal coolies came from the suburbs of Darjeeling and other parts of the lower Bengal. The huge number of workers consisted of *Lepcha, Mech, Rava, Santhal, Kheria, Ghasi, Ho, Savar, Munda, Gond, Mahali* and other ethnic communities. But the role of *Rajbanshis* in tea cultivation was not seen in that way. The workers were usually employed directly by the *sardars*. The coolies depended on the *sardars*, for an advance, and the *sardars* depended on the managers.[15] However, the workers have not bound to any agreement. They could deliberately return to their village from the tea fields and return later if necessary. It was not regulated by any special legislative enactment.[16] And here is the difference between capitalist society and feudal society.

The condition of the tea plantation workers was also the same as that of coal miners. Most of the coolies' quarters in the tea garden were made of brick walls, irons roofs and thatched. In this way, many coolies' huts or coolie lines were built. Sanitation and other facilities were slightly provided. The floors were made of mud and roofs were not more than ten feet high. Ventilation was inadequate; there was no chimney exhaust system. The size of each hut was generally about twenty feet by ten feet. One of the huts was used for cooking and the other for sleeping. Although occasionally a small verandah was also used for cooking. A small plot of land next to the hut was used for cattle rearing and yard except for farming.[17] In a word, the coolies' quarters were extremely unhealthy. The situation was the same in the neighbouring state of Assam. But the houses of the clerks and managers were much more luxurious and expensive than that. Their bungalows were located at the centre of each tea estate and beautiful natural environment.[18] Except in the Terai region, almost all the managers and assistants in the tea fields were Europeans. It is significant that the educated natives were not employed in the region despite being much less cheap than the Europeans.[19] Needless to say, the cool climate in Darjeeling and the hilly areas was much more comfortable and full of natural beauty than other tropical regions of India. For the reason, the British rulers had chosen this region.

There was an insufficient supply of clean drinking water for the coolie lines and there was no latrine facility for the coolies in tea gardens. Coolies often used to succumb to hookworm disease due to their unhygienic environment. Medical equipment and medicines were not always sufficient in tea garden dispensaries. Although there was an indoor hospital in the garden, there were no medical facilities due to the absence of nurses and assistants. Most of the garden owners provided grants for pregnant women and infrequently helped sick workers. Owners occasionally used to donate blankets and umbrellas free of cost to workers. Many garden owners used to bear the expenses of religious festivals and the entertainment of the workers.[20] The tea garden authorities took these nominal initiatives to avoid worker's discontent. The proportion of workers in tea garden industries is often volatile. The percentage of the total population in the gardens decreased slightly between 1939 and 1944. During the Second World War, many amateur workers left the tea garden in search of lucrative jobs. Of the working people in 1939, 39 per cent were males, 43 per cent females and 18 per cent children. But in 1943 it became 34 per cent males, 49 per cent females and 17 per cent children.[21] The plight of the women workers in the tea gardens was as dire as in the coal-mining region. Many female workers were oppressed and deprived by male workers and owners in tea plantation industry sectors. In the neighbouring state of Assam, women workers were similarly tortured and harassed. Female workers were paid less than male workers. They were often victims of sex. *Sardars* and managers were in favour of the permanent settlement of workers in the tea sector. Royal Commission on Labour in India reported that other factories emphasize individual recruitment but the tea gardening industry focus on family-based employment.[22] So *sardars* and managers gave more importance to the recruitment of family-based workers including husband, wife and children. For this reason, unmarried and married male workers were often married to unmarried and widow workers. Mita Bhadra argues that marriage was much flexible in the tea plantation society and there was no restriction. Women used to enjoy a lot of freedom and the participation of women workers was also much higher. That she did not see such a scene in the case of jute and other industries.[23] It can be said that this kind of freedom was given keeping in mind the needs of a large number of women workers in the tea industry.

Marginal Coolies and their Agitation

The advancement of capitalist industries in colonial India gave birth to significant and complex diversities such as the industrial owner-labour class relationships as a new social group. Needless to say, the symbiotic relationship between the two classes existed also in the pre-capitalist, i.e. feudal era, but their character was somewhat different. Pertinent to mention, in colonial India, the coolie classes had to fight against the imperialist rule and exploitation as well as against the exploitation of Indian and British capitalists. In the colonial period, coal mining and tea plantation industrial areas had multiple persistent problems such as unhealthy environment, overcrowded and unplanned housing, lack of adequate pure drinking water, malnutrition, poor health care facilities, lack of security at hazardous work and low wages etc. But the industrialist, owners and entrepreneurs did not pay much attention to workers' rights. Rather than, the marginalized tribal working class people were the most exploited and deprived by the owner class in the industrial sectors. Besides, women especially young girls were sexually abused by the owners, managers and planters. The discontent of these working classes was manifested through a united resistance against the industrial owners and contractors.

After the First World War, the coolie or labour movement began to take a gigantic shape. The All India Trade Union Congress was established in 1920. From that time the consciousness of the labour movement was awakened. Wages that were paid during the First World War were reduced at the end of the war, leading to increased labour unrest.[24] The trade union movement was very weak in the Asansol-Raniganj colliery area. According to Deshpande's report, there were no trade union in Raniganj.[25] However, according to Sunil Basu Roy, this information is not accurate. He argues that the leftist ideology was getting stronger among the workers at that time.[26] Indeed, the labour movement did not happen that way before the First World War. The Report of the Committee in Industrial Unrest in Bengal reported that, in 1920-21, there were six strikes in the Asansol-Raniganj coal mine region, namely Victoria Colliery, Narasmuda Colliery, Babuishol Colliery and Baraboni Colliery.[27] After independence, from the 1950s and 60s of the twentieth century, labour organizations and trade union movements led by the Communist Party began to take militant form in the colliery region. Deshpande's report further states that there was no strike in the five years after 1943. The India Coalfields Committee was formed in 1946. Coal conservation and rationalization were the main issues of this Committee. In this context, the Committee was asked to discuss and decide on labour issues and needs.[28]

Diwan Chaman Lall, a prominent trade union leader at that time, said that coolies were forced to leave their gardens only due to starvation and torture. There was no political reason behind it.[29] Although no workers' union was found in Duars, the workers were not silent, they protested against the oppression of tea owners, administrators, police etc. These protest movements ran from 1895-1918 on the path of their movement. Unfortunately, no political party or union, or intellectual group supported their agitations.[30] It took a long time for political trade union consciousness and organization to develop among the tea garden workers. There were many reasons behind this. Illiteracy, ignorance, fear as well as alienation from their territory, lack of political propaganda in the tea fields, barriers to the entry of political leaders and other workers into the tea garden and vindictive activity of the owners.[31] Besides, the National Congress pursued a moderate policy to appease the industrialists and capitalists. That is why the labour movement could not develop in that way. The pre-Independence period did not create much of an atmosphere for labour moment in these two industrial areas, despite the frustration and discontent among the workers. However, after the rise of the Leftists, the labour movement sprung up in many places of Bengal. But it is unfortunate that before and after independence, women did not form any trade union movement to express their demands in these two industrial areas.

Conclusion

In conclusion, it can be said that, just as capitalist industrialization has brought about drastic changes in socio-economic life, it has also had a lasting effect on the balance of the ecological environment and human life. On the other hand, the labour class people who keep the flow of industrialization alive through production are in turn oppressed, humiliated and deprived of the necessities of life by the industrial owners and contractors. Although industrialization has brought happiness to a section of the people in the society, especially in civic life, the life of the poor and marginalized people has not changed much. Many marginalized people used to come to these industrial zones for the purpose of poverty and livelihood. Poor families did not have easy financial means so that men, women and children also used to work hard in coal mines and tea gardens. The condition of tribal coolies in these industrial areas was very deplorable. Coal miners and tea plantation coolies still live precarious life. In all these industrial employers, managers, and owners were reluctant to improve workers' quality of life, the safety of life, health care facilities, fixed working hours and increase in wages. Therefore, in all these industrial areas, the coolie or labour movement was formed on a large scale from time to time. Needless to say coolies of lower classes tried to sustain their existence through resistance and violence. But they could not do that due to a lack of strong organization and various adversities.[32]

NOTES AND REFERENCES

1. Peterson, J.C.K., *Bengal District Gazetteers: Burdwan*, Calcutta: Bengal Secretariat Book Depot, 1910, pp. 14-15 and 128-130.
2. *Deshpande Report*, p. 22.
3. O'Malley, L.S.S., *Bengal District Gazetteers: Darjeeling*, Calcutta: The Bengal Secretariat Book Depot, 1907, p. 72.
4. *Ibid.*, p. 99.
5. *Ibid.*, p. 100.
6. Bhattacharya, Nandini, "The Logic of Location: Malaria Research in Colonial India, Darjeeling and Duars, 1900-30", *Medical History*, 2011, No. 55: 183-202, p. 187.
7. *Ibid.*, p. 191.
8. Peterson, *op. cit.*, p. 43.
9. Dasgupta, Priobrata, "Bardhhaman Jelar Koyla Shilper Bikasher Dhara, (Adiparba)", in *Bardhhaman Jela Sankhya*, edited by Tarun Bhattacharya and Dibyajoyti Majumdar, Kolkata: Tathhya O Sanskriti Bibhag, Paschimbanga Sarkar 1977, pp. 104-05.
10. Dutta, Achintya Kumar, *Economy and Ecology in Bengal District: Burdwan 1880-1947*, Kolkata: Firma KLM Private Limited, 2002, p. 190.
11. Basu, Nirban, "Industrialization and Emergence of Labour Force in Bengal during Colonial Period: Its Socio-Economic Impact", *Vidyasagar University Journal of History*, 2012-13, Vol. 1, pp. 17-38.
12. Basu, Samaresh, *Dekhinai Phire*, Kolkata: Ananda Publisher.
13. Biswas, Santosh Kumar, *Sailajananda Mukhapadhyay Jeebon O Sahitya*, Kolkata: Patra Bookstall, 2002, pp. 22-24.
14. O'Malley, *op. cit.*, p. 84.
15. *Ibid.*
16. *Ibid.*
17. Dash, Arthur Jules, *Bengal District Gazetteers: Darjeeling*, Alipore, Bengal: Superintendent, Government Printing and Bengal Government Press, 1947, pp. 120-21.
18. O'Malley, *op. cit.*, p. 85.
19. *Ibid.*, p. 84.
20. Dash, *op. cit.*, p. 121.
21. *Ibid.*, p. 119.
22. *Royal Commission on Labour in India*, London: Majesty's Stationery Office, 1931, Vol. VI, Part 1.
23. Bhadra, Mita, *Women Workers of Tea Plantations in India*, New Delhi: South Asia Books, 1992, pp. 140-156.
24. Bandyopadhyay, Sekhar, *From Plassey to Partition: A History of Modern India*, New Delhi: Orient Black Swan, 2004, p. 375.
25. *Deshpande Report*, pp. 105-06.
26. Basu Roy, Sunil, "Raniganjer Koyla Khani Shramik in Bengali", in *Bardhhaman Jela Sankhya*, edited by Tarun Bhattacharya and Dibyajoyti Majumdar, Kolkata: Tathhya O Sanskriti Bibhag, Paschimbanga Sarkar, 1997, p. 72.

27. Mukhopadhyay, Falguni, "Koyla Shilpe Shramik Andolan-1", in *Asansoler Itihas O Sanskriti*, edited by Nanda Dulal Acharya, Calcutta: Mitram, 1998, p. 171.
28. Basu Roy, *op. cit.*, p. 72.
29. Chaman Lall, Dewan, *Coolie: The Story of Labour and Capital in India*, Lahore: Oriental Pub. House, 1932, p. 17.
30. Sutradhar, Kartik Chandra, "Tea-Labour Movements in the Northern Bengal since 1947", *SSRG International Journal of Humanities and Social Science (SSRG-IJHSS)*, 2018, Vol. 5 (September to October), p. 29.
31. Sen, Sukamal, *Bharater Shramik Andoloner Itihas (History of the Labour Movement in India 1830-1970)*, Kolkata: Nabajatak Prakashani, 1975, Vol. I, p. 104.
32. *Ibid.*

16

Marginal People and Politics in West Bengal, 1947-1971

Krishna Kanta Dhali

A large number of Marginal or Indigenous people are living in India and all over the World. They are always victimized. So UN has organized a lot of programmes under the 'Declaration of the International Decade of the World's Indigenous People', aimed at strengthening international cooperation on redressed crises in the areas of human rights, development, education and health. The World Health Organization has given the importance that indigenous people have higher rates of infant mortality, lower life expectancy and more cases of chronic illness than the non-indigenous populations in their home countries. It is a common phenomenon that the indigenous people have always been victimized and their socio-economic condition deteriorated all-over the World.[1] In this connection Marginalization describes the position of individuals, groups, or populations outside of 'mainstream society', living at the margins of those in the centre of power, of cultural dominance and economical and social welfare. It is defined as, a process by which a group or individual is denied access to important positions and symbols of economic, religious, or political power within any society of a marginal group may constitute a numerical majority and should perhaps be distinguished from a minority group, which may be small in numbers, but has access to political or economic power. "To be marginalized, or is to be distanced from power and resources that enable self-determination in economic, political, and social settings. . . . It is an inherent characteristic of 'those in the margin', that they have poor access to economical and other recourses like education and social services, meanwhile, participation and self-determination are on a low level. However, definitions of what is regarded as marginalized are highly depending on the historical and socio-economical context of a society."[2] The marginal man . . . is one whom fate has condemned to live in two societies and in two, not merely different but antagonistic cultures . . . his mind is the crucible in which two different and refractory cultures may be said to melt and either wholly or in part, fuse.[3] According to Stonequist, psychological marginality results from living in two or more different cultural milieux. All these cultures are generally arranged in a hierarchy of these levels, one of which carries prestige and power, while the other is evaluated as peripheral and inferior to the first. Hence immigrants in different countries and indigenous minorities such as West Bengal in India traditionally the so-called Marginals were seen as unclean in a religious sense and presumed to defile others by their touch or presence. It is understood that they had to live in separate areas, at some distance from others. It is retrieved that they were born to serve others, it was believed that they carried out the occupations dealing with ritually defiled materials. Moreover, education and other kinds of reading and writing were not proceeding for those who lack a Varna the scriptures stated in India.[4] It has integrated rich, affluent and educated classes, but has fractured working classes of marginalized sections such as Dalit who do not have the skills and economic clout to profit from open markets.

Hundreds of millions of marginal people across the country, the actual effects of neo-liberal policies have been inequality, poverty, hunger, increased susceptibility to disease and sickness, and economic and political marginalization. There is a real difference between Bengal's idea of the marginal man and the concept of marginal man in a greater context. The idea of marginal people is intrinsically linked with the historical context of the Partition of India and Bengal. The tragic history of refugees who migrated from East Bengal to West Bengal after the Partition of Bengal and their struggle for rehabilitation constitutes the biography of a marginal people. The problems of refugees and the idea of marginal people are coalescent. The idea of marginal people is used to justify the unbearable life struggles and the movement of refugee people of West Bengal. However, the real problem lies in the indifference of the State machinery towards the question of food, clothing and shelter for the marginal people and the opportunistic politics involving them.

The migration of Bengali Hindus from East Bengal started in October 1946, after the communal riot in Noakhali.[5] Although the migration from East Bengal started in 1946 it continued in the same way up to

1970. The greatest number of migrations happened in 1971 but the context was a little different then. Till 1956, the number of people coming from East Bengal and registering as refugees at check-posts was 41.17 lakh. In 1970 this number rose to 52.14 lakh.[6] The book '*The Story of Rehabilitation*' published by the Refugee Rehabilitation Ministry notes that apart from the registered refugees from East Bengal lakhs of refugees came to India without any registration. This number of illegal refugees is huge.[7] Social and political anarchy followed by communal violence led to an unprecedented rise in the number of illegal refugees in 1946-47. The situation got more complicated in 1947 after the Partition of India. After Partition, the mass immigration of Hindus from Pakistan as marginal people was caused not only by communal violence but also by the psychological oppression that the minority Hindu community had to suffer. Statistical data collection on migration started to solve the problems of refugees who emigrated from Pakistan.

Table 16.1: Migration Statistics from 1946 to 1951 will make the Picture Clear

Place of migration	*Year and number of migration (%)*						*Total number of migration*
	1946	*1947*	*1948*	*1949*	*1950*	*1951*	
India	2.3	18.2	19.2	12.8	46.0	1.5	25,49,390
East India	2.3	17.7	19.2	12.9	46.4	1.5	25,23,115
West Bengal	2.1	18.3	20.2	13.2	44.7	1.5	20,76,338

Source: Kanti, Pakrasi, *The Uprooted: A Sociological Study of the Refugees of West Bengal*, India, Calcutta, 1971, p. 25.

From the above data, it is clear that the Bengali refugee marginal people gathered in the states that shared a border with East Bengal, i.e. West Bengal, Assam and Tripura. A majority of refugee marginal people migrated on foot from East Bengal to the border adjacent areas of West Bengal where they lived under terrible conditions in government refugee camps. In a speech, in Parliament, Mr. Laxmikanta Maitra clearly explained that these people did not come to this country as refugees and marginals voluntarily. He said that extortion in the name of collecting subscriptions for Azam Fund, higher taxation rates for Hindus, confiscating firearms from non-Muslims and giving them to the National Guard, rape of women, loot and arson of Hindu homes and many other ways of exploitation, torture and humiliation forced these people to escape by leaving their homes and properties to become refugees and lead marginal lives.[8] These people became marginal and sought shelter at various refugee camps. These refugee camps slowly evolved into colonies. Notable refugee camps include — Salt Lake, Kashipore,

Ultadanga, Ghushuri, Titgarh, Kartikpur, Ranaghat, Banshdroni, Habra, Ashoknagar, Bongaon, Shalboni, Piyardoba, Rotibati, Basudebpur, New Barrackpore and Dhudhulia. Camps are like these find mention.[9] There were certain differences among these camps. The refugee camps were differentiated according to the parameters of rehabilitation of the families residing there. For instance: (1) Some refugee camps were made where families suitable for rehabilitation were placed. It was decided that they would remain there until it is possible to transport them to rehabilitation grounds. Examples include Cooper's camp, Dhudhulia, Kanga, Nababgarh etc. Even if the first two camps were closed in 1950 after shifting the refugees, they were reopened later after the number of refugees increased. (2) There were a number of camps for those families in which the guardian was disabled or old and therefore, incapable of rehabilitation efforts. These were named Permanent Liability Camps because the government had to provide for these families for an indeterminate time. Some of these were Rupashree camp, Chandmari and Beltala. (3) The third type of refugee camps were those designated for families which did not have a male guardian, mainly constituting widows and their children. They were determined to be completely unsuitable for rehabilitation. These included Titagarh, Karthikpur, Ranaghat, Banshberia, Bhadrakali etc.[10] The first group of refugee marginal people was transported to the Andaman Islands for rehabilitation in 1949. There were no well-defined government policies regarding the selection of refugee families in this case. As a result, there were many educated middle-class families in this group. The plan of rehabilitation by making them clear out forest areas and establish agricultural livelihoods failed.[11]

Table 16.2: Marginal People in Refugee Camps in 1948 and 1950

1948 — Month	*Total marginal refugee people*	*1950 — Month*	*Total marginal refugee people*
July	8,408	January	1,150
August	19,109	February	1,002
September	18,638	March	75,596
October	9,182	April	14,960
		May	27,440

Source: These statistics August and September of 1948 and March of 1950 saw the highest number of migrations.

Refugee marginal people had to leave East Bengal in groups and live helpless lives in West Bengal and various parts of India. During this time a number of newspapers and magazines and organizations showed individual interest in the living conditions of refugees and their rehabilitation. Anxious about the problems of refugee marginal people and the responsibility of the Central Government, the editor of *Anushilan Samiti*, Mr. Nalini Ranjan Bhattacharya wrote if the border problem and East Pakistan problem is not resolved it is suspected that the minorities in East Bengal may face extinction. In East, Pakistan life-property-dignity is under attack from all sides. The minorities cannot find hope anywhere in these troubled times. Those who could afford it left their homes to find themselves in precarious situations on the other side, while those who were incapable of leaving had to stay in Pakistan and become weaker and poorer.[12] In a meeting for refugee marginal people on 11th January, 1948 organized by United India Properties Ltd. presided over by Mr. Bidhubhushan Sarkar, sympathy was expressed over their plight and it was said that creating space for housing these people was the duty of all Hindus in West Bengal.[15] Immigration of refugees did not stop in 1950. The wave continued well beyond. A record of the number of refugees, setting up of refugee camps and rehabilitation efforts in 1950-1958 will show that people migrated from East Bengal continuously.

Table 16.3: Number of Refugees from 1950 to 31st December, 1958

Sl.No.	*Year*	*Total refugees*
1.	According to the census of December 1950	23,04,514
2.	From January 1951 to April 1952	85,457
3.	From May to October of 1952	1,93,668
4.	From November 1952 to December 1953	13,044
5.	Till 31st December, 1954	65,918
	Total	**26,62,601**

Source: Hiranmay Bandopadhyay, *Udbastu*, Dip Prakashan, 2013, Kolkata, pp. 433-434.

Table 16.4: Number of Refugees Living in Refugee Camps from 1948 to 1958

Sl.No.	*Year*	*Total place in refugee centre*
1.	1948 (July-December)	64,788
2.	1949	41,303
3.	1950	2,54,564
4.	1951	79,805
5.	1952	55,816
6.	1953	10,474
7.	1954	50,838
	Total	**5,57,544**

Source: Hiranmay Bandopadhyay, *Udbastu*, Dip Prakashan, 2013, Kolkata, pp. 433-434.

Table 16.5: Number of Refugees Sent from Refugee Camps to Rehabilitation Centres from 1949 to 1958

Sl.No.	*Year-wise rehabilitation*	*Total number of rehabilitation*
1.	1949 total number of Rehabilitation	90,075
2.	1950 total number of Rehabilitation	85,907
3.	1951 total number of Rehabilitation	1,81,950
4.	1952 total number of Rehabilitation	20,125
5.	1953 total number of Rehabilitation	18,016
6.	1954 total number of Rehabilitation	12,477
	Total	**4,08,550**

Source: Hiranmay Bandopadhyay, *Udbastu*, Dip Prakashan, 2013, Kolkata, pp. 433-434.

The above statistics prove that this inhuman and intolerable event that happened in the heart of Bengal almost led to the Bengali people drowning under the tides of history. However, while the migration of refugee marginal people continued, some efforts at solving this problem were also made. Providing refuge and rehabilitation to these marginal people and changing their tragic lives involved various factors like the Bengal government and Central Government's attempts as well as indifference, the individual efforts of many benevolent persons, and the efficient actions taken by many organizations according to their capabilities. There were some obligations and constraints as well. For instance — West Bengal is a densely populated state and it was hard to find land for rehabilitation; the West Bengal government did not take any step for economic rehabilitation of the marginal people; instead of rehabilitation efforts the government evicted those who earned livelihoods through business; the acquisition of arable land for rehabilitation also led to people protesting against the refugees and the government which created further problems.[13]

Table 16.6: Percentage of Refugees Coming from East Bengal in 1951, 1961 and 1971

Year	*Total population of West Bengal*	*Number of refugees from East Bengal*	*Percentage of refugees out of the total population*
1951	2,62,99,980	21,04,241	8.00
1961	3,49,26,279	30,68,750	8.78
1971	4,43,12,011	42,93,000	9.68

Source: Census Report of India, 1951, 1961, 1971.

Helpless refugee people emigrated from East Bengal in phases and because of the Bangladesh Muktijuddho in 1971 immigration from East Bengal to West Bengal increased to a much greater scale. Migration continued, primarily from East Pakistan to India mainly in West Bengal, right up to the liberation of Bangladesh in 1971, both on an ongoing basis and with spikes during periods of particular communal unrest such as the 1964 East Pakistan riots and the 1965 India-Pakistan War, when it is estimated that 6,00,000 refugees left for India.[14] Estimates of the number of refugees up to 1970 are over 5 million to West Bengal alone. This includes around 4.1 million coming between 1946 and 1958 and 1.2 million coming between 1959 and 1971.[15] Another major influx into India came in 1971 during the *Bangladesh Liberation War* when Hindu refugees escaped systematic *mass killings, rapes, lootings* and *arson*. It is estimated that around 10 million East Bengali refugees entered India during the early months of the war, of whom 1.5 million may have stayed back after Bangladesh became independent.[16] After leaving their homeland the rootless people became not only economically, socially and culturally exhausted, they were also devoid of political representation. They felt battered by the state machinery. From 1947 to 1971 various political parties tried to solve the problem of food-shelter-clothing for the refugees. As a result, these marginal people became victims of party politics. After Partition when refugees started coming in large numbers neither the West Bengal state government nor the Central Government paid much heed to the problem. This is evidenced by a report the then Chief Minister Prafulla Chandra Ghosh sent to Prime Minister Jawaharlal Nehru saying that after the situation calms down most of these refugees will return to their countries.[17] However, the migration of marginal people to this country as refugees did not stop and neither did they have the mindset of returning to their homeland. The Prime Minister was quite disturbed by this phenomenon as evidenced by his letter to Dr. Bidhan Chandra Ray. Although both the Central Government and West Bengal State Government were ruled by Congress, Bengali refugees received very little help from the Centre. Enraged by this, Dr. Ray informed Prime Minister Nehru in a letter that in the years 1947-48 and 1950-51 the state received only ₹ 300 crore from the Centre, an amount which is insignificant compared to the needs. He also said that upper-class and middle-class Hindus have been forced to come to this country hungry and destitute, looking for a livelihood. The Central Government did not give them any recognition or take any responsibility even after so many months.[18] In 1951 Bidhan Chandra Ray informed the Vidhan Sabha that in West Bengal 29084 acres of land was requisitioned and 20,106 refugee families were rehabilitated there, 20,000 houses were acquired where 1,00,530 refugees were sheltered, 10,000 acres of land was distributed among them, and 53,825 acres of agricultural land and 68,335 acres of non-agricultural land was being used for refugee rehabilitation.[19] In spite of this, the Central Government's unyielding attitude and the state government's obligations and limitations resulted in these marginal people not receiving the rehabilitation efforts they hoped for. The then Rehabilitation Minister said that in the future the Central Government will follow the report of the Minister's Committee and this report will be acceptable to both the Central and State Governments. The Central Government's Rehabilitation Minister Mr. Ajit Prasad Jain inspected different refugee rehabilitation colonies in West Bengal and said, "The work of refugee rehabilitation in West Bengal has progressed a lot and as a result, the refugees have found new hope — I have no qualms about saying this."[20] Therefore, there was a continual effort by the Central and State Government to provide food, clothing, and shelter to the marginal people.

After Partition the way the refugee marginal people started pouring in, the Congress, the Leftists or the other political parties of West Bengal did not understand how to combat the problem. At first, the Congress and the Leftists were quite enraged about refugee marginal people coming to this country. Both parties assumed that these people would return to their homeland. No proper relationship developed between the Leftists and the refugee marginal people from the beginning. The upper-class people like zamindars and influential lawyers from East Bengal who immigrated to this country were Congress supporters. The Communist Party's support was limited to middle-class Hindus. Although there were some Communist influence among the farmer class who emigrated from certain regions of East Bengal. However, certain events before Independence like the people's war theory, opposing the August revolution, labelling Netaji anti-national, supporting the British, led to anti-leftist sentiments among all classes of Hindus.[21] The Leftists felt that if these marginal people came under the influence of the Congress or some other right-wing communal party, they would become dangerous tools in the hands of the enemies of the Communist Party and become the chief weapon for breaking up labour strikes. In 1948 factory owners in Maniktala used them to break up strikes. Thus Left leadership realized that to get their support in the future, this is the time to start a movement supporting their claims. However, there were disagreements among Left leaders about the claims and rehabilitation needs of these people. At last on 4th June, 1950, due to the efforts of CPI leader Anil Singha the United Central Rehabilitation Council (UCRC) was established with 200 representatives from 43 organizations. Yet, in the 1952 general elections, it was seen that the refugee people put their hopes and trust in the Congress party.

After 1952 the Leftists realized that they must work to eliminate communal attitudes towards the refugee marginal people and lead them towards Leftist ideas without actually bringing them within the folds of the Party. So Bijoy Majumder was made a Party member and given the responsibility to work amongst these people. Gradually increase in the population of refugees and the consequent problems like shortage of food and space, price hike, lack of work opportunities led to the administrative machinery nearly breaking down and the Leftist movement slowly taking shape. At this time Leftist leadership worked with United Central Rehabilitation Council (UCRC) leadership to hold confidential meetings in refugee camps and colonies and create 'secret cells' to bring the refugees under their influence.[22] In the meantime UCRC stood in favour of the refugees during the 'forcible colony creation' based on CPI leader B.T. Ranadive's programme of absolute revolution, Nehru's stepmotherly policy, the refugee satyagraha movement for various claims and rights, and revealed itself as a powerful organization while the Leftist Movement also became strengthened. However, when the Central and State Governments unitedly decided to rehabilitate refugees at Dandakaranya section of the Leftists supported the programme of rehabilitating refugees who are willing to go. The refugee marginal people did not understand these acute political motives and during the 1960s under the rule of Chief Ministers Bidhan Chandra Ray and Prafulla Sen, the Leftists executed various agitation programmes like hunger, marches, strikes, food revolutions etc. with the help of the refugees that the Congress government found impossible to control.

Through these movements in the 1960s for the sake of the refugee people, the Communist Party itself became almost refugee-centric. Nevertheless, the importance of class struggle and food movement should not be diminished and 'the relationship between refugees and Leftists' should not be seen as political opportunism. Due importance must be given to the complex equation involving rights, the State and Leftist politics. From the 1960s onwards educated Bengalis also came closer to Leftist politics because the indomitable working capacity, strict work ethics and industriousness of the refugees led to the expansion of the Kolkata Metropolitan district which in turn influenced Leftist politics in West Bengal. In the 1960-1970 decade the rise of Leftists in West Bengal's political landscape following different movements for these marginal people and movements based on Leftist ideology for all marginal people from factory workers to farmers beyond communal limits was reflected in and centred upon the urbanization and growth of Kolkata. As a result of urbanization there was a rise in employment, a gradual increase in the population of marginal people and radical new metropolitan politics, language and organizations. These changes and rearrangements led to a new vision of society. Reverberations of these changes were felt not only on refugee marginal people but also urban middle-class people, their ideas and perspectives, cultural activities and even their use of political language. These factors increased the city-centric marginal refugee population as can be seen in the following statistics.

Table 16.7: East Bengal and the Percentage of City-Centric Refugees from the Census of 1951, 1961 and 1971

Year	*Total urban population of West Bengal*	*Urban refugee population*	*Percentage of the refugee population of the city out of total urban population of West Bengal*
1951	62,81,642	10,52,121	16.74
1961	85,40,842	15,61,530	18.28
1971	1,09,67,033	27,24,936	24.84

Source: Census Report of India, 1951, 1961, 1971, Ed. Semonti Ghosh, *Deshbhag Smriti Aar Stobdhota*, Publisher Gangchil, first publication, Kolkata, 2008, p. 81.

A large section of the marginal refugee population consisted of Dalit Namashudra people. Most marginal people who came to this country in 1950-1971 belonged to the 'general caste' category, but the majority of refugee marginal people who immigrated within late 1960s to early 1970s, i.e. during and after the Bangladesh Liberation War belonged to the Scheduled Caste Namashudra community. There was a lot of caste-based politics involving these people also. The saviours of Namashudra refugee marginal people Pramatha Ranjan Thakur, Jogendranath Mondal, Manindranath Biswas and Mahananda Halder joined the Indian National Congress in 1956 to solve the problems of the extremely unfortunate Dalit refugees in government and non-government camps like unhygienic atmospheres, problem of rehabilitation and lack of employment etc. P.R. Thakur actually put more importance on proper and fair rehabilitation of these marginal people through providing them adequate housing and arable land, rather than trying to gain political power himself. The attitudes of Communist leader Bankim Mukherjee and SUC leader Subodh Mukherjee towards the residents of refugee camps were clear from their speeches in the Vidhan Sabha. Bankim

Mukherjee had said, "Eating in the camps has given them beggar-like attitudes. Being averse towards work has made them lose their ability to work. This aversion towards work should be changed and ways to increase the will to labour must be found."[23] By then the UCRC and Leftist leadership with their movement involving refugee marginal people had made their everyday lives prone to protest and unrest. Meanwhile, Pramatha Ranjan Thakur kept at his attempts to solve the problems of these people and even pleaded with the Chief Minister Dr. Prafulla Ghosh, but he was labelled as a creator of communal problems by Dr. Ghosh and told that he exaggerated refugee problems and he should go to Bangladesh because there were no problem faced by refugees in West Bengal. After many conflicts, he left Congress on 6th March, 1964. The same year he joined Ajay Mukherjee's Bengal Congress and became Co-President. As a result in 1967, the number of seats for Scheduled Castes decreased in the Vidhan Sabha and Lok Sabha elections simultaneously. The number of winning candidates came down from 33 in 1962 to 25 in 1967.[24] The result of interim elections in 1969 saw a decrease in the number of Scheduled Caste candidates at a drastic rate. Out of the 58 seats, 11 were won by Congress, 10 by Bengal Congress and 25 by CPI(M).[25] Again in the 1971 West Bengal Vidhan Sabha election CPI(M) won 113 seats, New Congress won 105, CPI won 13 and Bengal Congress won 5 seats.[26] However, nobody won an absolute majority of 139 seats and political turbulence in Bengal kept rising. During this time a new wave of refugees caused by the Bangladesh Liberation War complicated the situation further. In the 1967-77 time period because of various complexities in West Bengal's Congress and Leftist party politics, party influences and infightings, problems over control and divisions etc., P.R. Thakur was unable to achieve his goal of developing the conditions of Dalit marginal people and bringing them to mainstream society. In 1977 he retired from active politics.[27]

Marginal people who came from 1950 to 1971 started living in different legal and illegal colonies, on both sides of railway lines and in forcibly occupied colonies. Most of these settlements grew under the umbrella of some political parties. In those cases following the policies of that political party became their chief purpose. They had to participate in local political actions, marches and demonstrations and even join bigger gatherings in Kolkata when required. In exchange, they received small favours like voter cards or ration cards. They ended up becoming captive voters or political slaves. Thus Bengal saw a new wave of 'politics of giving and getting'.

NOTES AND REFERENCES

1. Sarkar, Anil Kumar, *Tribes of Sub-Himalayan Region (Meches, Rabhas, Totos and Garos)*, Mittal Publications, New Delhi, 2021, p. 1.
2. Schiffer, Kartin and Schatz, *Evberhard, Marginalization, Social Inclusion and Health*, (Daniel, Fletcher, Linder, 2002, 3); Amastedam, 2008, p. 6.
3. Park, Robert Ezra, "Human Migration and the Marginal Man," *American Journal of Sociology*, p. 192.
4. Hardtmann, Eva-Maria, *The Dalit Movement in India* (Local practices, Global connections), Oxford University Press, New Delhi: Oxford, 2009, p. X.
5. Ed. Semonti Ghosh, *Deshbhag Smriti Aar Stobdhota*, Pub. Gangchil, 1st Publication, Kolkata, 2008, p. 52.
6. *Ibid.*
7. Editor Chandrasekhar, MP, Member of Congress Working Committee, *Weekly Young Indian Special Independence*, 1st Publication in journal, Number, New Delhi, 1972.
8. *Anandabazar Patrika*, 17th January, 1948, Arpita Basu edited *Udbastu Andolan O Punorbasati: Samasamayik Patra Patrikay*, Gangchil Publishers, Kolkata, 2013, p. 18.
9. Hiranmay, Bandopadhyay, *Udbastu*, Dip Prakashan, Kolkata, 2013, pp. 126-160.
10. *Ibid.*, pp. 126-160.
11. Semonti, Ghosh, ed,, *Deshbhag Smriti Aar Stobdhota*, Pub. Gangchil, Kolkata, 2014, p. 55.
12. Hiranmay, Bandopadhyay, *Udbastu*, Dip Prakashan, Kolkata, 2013, pp. 127, 142.
13. *Anandabazar Patrika*, 17th January, 1948, Arpita Basu edited *Udbastu Andolan O Punorbasati: Samasamayik Patra Patrikay*, Gangchil Publishers, Kolkata, 2013, p. 17.
14. *Ibid.*, p. 18.
15. *Dainik Basumati*, 22nd November, 1953, Arpita Basu edited *Udbastu Andolan O Punorbasati: Samasamayik Patra Patrikay*, Gangchil Publishers, 2013, Kolkata, pp. 231, 241, 243.
16. Chakravartty, Gargi, "Coming Out of Partition: Refugee Women of Bengal". *http://www.weeklyholiday.net/2006/050506/cul.html*, Archived from the original on 6 January, 2007.
17. "The East Bengal Refugees", *www.catchcal.com*. Archived from the original on 25 September, 2009, Retrieved 4 July, 2016.
18. Nakatani, Tetsuya, "Away from Home: The Movement and Settlement of Refugees from East Pakistan in West Bengal, India", *Journal of the Japanese Association for South Asian Studies*, 2000, 12: 73, *doi:10.11384/jjasas1989.2000.73*, Chakraborty, Prafulla, *Prantik Manob*, Dip Prakashan, Kolkata, 2019, p. 27.
19. Prafulla,Chakraborty, *Prantik Manob*, Dip Prakashan, Kolkata, 2019, p. 29.
20. Biswas, Monashanta, *Banglar Matua Andolan Somaj Sanskriti Rajneeti*, Setu Prakashani, Kolkata, 2016, p. 277.
21. *Jugantar*, 16th and 17th July, 1958, Arpita Basu edited *Udbastu Andolan O Punorbasati: Samasamayik Patra Patrikay*, Gangchil Publishers, Kolkata, 2013, pp. 356, 355, 356.
22. Prafulla, Chakraborty, *Prantik Manob*, Dip Prakashan, Kolkata, 2019, p. 42.
23. Singha, Anil, *Poschimbonge Udbastu Uponibesh*, Book Club Publishers, Kolkata, 1995, p. 12.

inadvertently excluded. Persons with disabilities (PWDs) are one such type of group. This is because much of the advocacy on how to stay safe during the pandemic has not factored in the inability of people who are immobile or living with mental illnesses to follow these instructions.

Types of Disability

There are many types of disabilities like Locomotor Disability, Visual Disability, Mental, Illness, Speech, and Hearing Disability, Learning Disability, Multiple Disability.

Key Aspects of Disabled Persons

Table 17.1: Distribution of Total Population, Disabled Population and Percentage of Disabled Population to Total Population by Sex for Malda District as per 2001 Census Report

Sex	*Population 2001*			*Disabled population 2001*			*Percentage of the disabled population to the total population*		
	Total	*Rural*	*Urban*	*Total*	*Rural*	*Urban*	*Total*	*Rural*	*Urban*
Persons	32,90,468	30,49,528	2,40,940	61,379	56,822	4,557	1.87	1.86	1.89
Males	16,89,406	15,65,654	1,23,752	34,646	32,086	2,560	2.05	2.05	2.07
Females	16,01,062	14,83,874	1,17,188	26,733	24,736	1,997	1.67	1.67	1.7

Source: Government of West Bengal Health & Family Welfare Department.

Table 17.1 shows the total population of disabled persons and percentage sex-wise, relative to the total population of Malda District. This table makes clear that as per Census 2001, the total number of the disabled population in Malda District was 61,379 and the disabled male population was 34,646 that was 2.05 per cent and the female population was 16,01,062 were 1.67 per cent relative to the total population of Malda District.

Table 17.2: Total Population of Disabled Persons (comparative study between West Bengal and Malda District)

	West Bengal	*Malda*
Total PWDs	20,17,406	84,158
Seeing	4,24,473	20,005
Hearing	3,15,192	13,631
Speech	1,47,336	5,678
Movement	3,22,945	12,820
MR	1,36,523	5,820
MI	71,515	2,806
MD	1,96,501	7,870
Others	4,02,921	15,528

Source: 2011 Census Report of West Bengal.

Table 17.2 shows, according to Census Report 2011, in West Bengal 20,17,406 persons with disabilities constitute 2.21 per cent of the total population of West Bengal. This table shows the population of many types of disabled persons like persons with visual, hearing, speech, locomotor, mental retardation, mental illness and multiple disabilities. Here I tried to point out the comparative study between West Bengal and Malda District by the population of disabled persons.

Government Initiatives

In India, the Union Ministry of Social Justice and Empowerment came up with the nodal agency for Disability Services through various projects such as the Regional Rehabilitation Training Centre (RRTC) till 1985, National Information Centre on Disability and Rehabilitation (NICDR), National Council for Handicapped Welfare, National Handicapped Finance and Development Corporation etc. The main objective of the ministry was to promote services for disabled persons through government and non-government organizations. And disabled people are encouraged to become functionally independent and productive members of the nation through this type of opportunity like education, vocational training, medical rehabilitation, and socio-economic rehabilitation of the disabled.

Some initiatives are taken by Malda District for disabled people. Few activities have gained importance over the years:

- Name of the scheme: Manabik Pension (> 50% disability)
    - District Quota: Unlimited
    - Amount (₹): 750
- Name of the scheme: Disability Scholarship
    - District Quota: 200
    - Amounts (₹): 300
- Name of the scheme: Disability Identity Cards
    - District Quota: Unlimited
    - Amounts (₹): .....
- Name of the scheme: Disability Pension
    - District Quota: 2136
    - Amount (₹): 750

After Digital India, Clean India, Skill India our government launched the Accessible India Campaign which will focus on making India a disabled-friendly country, this is a joint venture by the Department of Empowerment of Persons with Disabilities and Ministry of Social Justice and Empowerment. Here are the seven key initiatives which will be a part of the Accessible India Campaign.

Considering the above, the study strongly suggests that the above projects and plans should be more protected to work towards their social, educational and economic empowerment and especially for the betterment of the socially disabled. As it turns out, poverty is the main cause of disability which is a vicious circle that increases the incidence of disability in India. Considering the existing framework and strategies, the department's concern is to note the results of the current study and come up with programmes for the overall improvement of the country's disabled population.

While the initiatives are commendable and welcomed for the long-neglected part of our society, there are a few charitable issues that need to be addressed in the overall integrated establishment of a social system for the protection of the disabled. It is argued that non-governmental organizations can be encouraged and that the government should take a more watchful and supervisory role. Rehabilitation of the disabled is called for corporate culture. Evaluation and approval of qualified professionals are also important.

In addition to special provisions for persons with disabilities in general schools, children with disabilities should be encouraged to focus on formal education options. The efforts of different departments of the government need to be coordinated to avoid similarity. The legal rights of the disabled also need to be addressed urgently.

NOTES AND REFERENCES

1. Ghai Anita, *Disability in South Asia Knowledge and Experience*, Publications India Pvt. Ltd., 2018, pp. 44-59, 60-74, 75-91, 189-205.
2. Davis J. Lennard, *The Disability Studies Reader*, Fourth Edition, Routledge Taylor and Francis Group, New York and London, 2013, pp. 214-221, 308-315.
3. Clements Luke and Read Janet, *Disabled People and the Right to Life: The Protection and Violation of Disabled People's Most Basic Human Right*, Routledge Taylor and Francis Group, New York and London, 2008, pp. 1-29.
4. *People with Disabilities in India: From Commitment to Outcomes*, Human Development Unit South Asia Region, the World Bank Report, July 2009, pp. 1-22, 57-79, 83-105.
5. Naraharisetti Ramya and C. Castro Marcia, *Factors Associated with Persons with Disability Employment in India: A Cross-sectional Study*, Research Article, BMC Public Health, 2016.
6. *Social Welfare at a Glance — Schemes and Activities*, Official Website of Malda District, *https://www.malda.gov.in/node/48*
7. Census 2011 Report, *wbcommissionerdisabilities.gov.in/user/census*

18

Political Impacts in the Society and Culture of the Marginal Autochthon Communities of the Western Duars since Colonial Period

Ananta Das

Tribal is called 'Adivasis' (Autochthon) in India who have been living in the subcontinent from unrecorded time and possibly driven them into the forests by more aggressive newcomer acts. The Constitution of India contains elaborate provisions for protecting the rights of tribal communities and for the promotion of their interests. The Constitution envisages a two-way approach to the tribal question: one is to protect them from various levels of exploitation and the other is to promote their development at all levels. However, despite all Constitutional guarantees and legislative measures, the tribal communities continued to remain marginalized. Marginalization is a complex phenomenon in the present-day world and a critical concern of international, national and regional communities. Its widespread occurrence is a consequence of several interrelated factors in society and culture which gain significance in the era of globalization. In many Third World countries like Indian society's people of the lower classes or castes such as Dalit and Adivasi (tribal) communities are pushed to the margins of society as a result of various historical and developmental factors. Tribal communities in India have been alienated not only from the development processes but even from their dwellings. As mainstream development processes tended to create social spaces of inequality, Dalit and tribal communities face marginalization virtually in every sphere of social life. In so far as the marginalized groups sustain a unique point of view shaped by their long-standing social position, the question of their 'self-representation' has become relevant in social research. Since 1900s many tribal groups have emerged in India and tried to become effective instruments for political articulation and mobilization. Consequently, a new political consciousness has been underway among the tribal, which is often referred to as 'identity consciousness' or 'identity politics'. Although, they were raised by such groups in the context of increasing marginalization and alienation. Conceptually, identity politics is linked with marginalization. However, the term identity politics is widely used in social sciences to describe phenomena as diverse as multi-culturalism, women's movements, Dalit or Adivasi movements, civil rights, Lesbian and gay movements, separatist movements and violent ethnic and nationalist conflicts in different parts of India. Politics of the identity is assumed to be cultural because identity groups advocating for recognition of and respect for their cultural differences derive their distinct group identities from their cultural matrix. The emerging theories of new social movements (NSMs) provide a framework for understanding the phenomenon of marginalization among the tribal communities. It would be of great interest to study how the tribal movements in India have introduced a number of tactical and organizational innovations using the power of the media and the expanded circuits of communication, and how they speak to a new audience differently with a different voice.

Political Impacts on the Traditional Society and Culture

The introduction of tea plantations in northern parts of Bengal during colonial rule and served the Western capitalist revenue interest in the Terai and Duars region. The European conquest and colonialism not only expanded their commercial empire but also had created a distinctive social space altering the economic and environmental history in the non-European world. One of the ways was the commercialization of agriculture and the second was the establishment of large-scale plantations which served the Western capitalist and revenue interest. Along with the large-scale cultivation of cash crops like jute, the tea plantations in British India. During the nineteenth century British colonial rule in India, the introduction of tea plantations in northern parts of colonial Bengal had changed the economic base and the demography. In that time tea-growing districts of present-day West Bengal, namely Darjeeling, Kalimpong, Jalpaiguri and Alipurduar. Erstwhile, this region was divided into two districts, namely Darjeeling and Jalpaiguri (undivided). In 2014, the Alipurduar subdivision of Jalpaiguri became a separate district and in 2017 Kalimpong subdivision of Darjeeling district became a separate district. This region is divided into three physiographic zones, namely Darjeeling Himalayan, Terai and Duars. We will look into the Duars region through my study. The foothills of the Darjeeling Himalayan region located on the eastern bank of the Teesta River is known as Terai which also includes the Siliguri subdivision of Darjeeling and the western bank of the Teesta River is known as Duars. Subsequently, in 1869 the Jalpaiguri district was formed with the amalgamation of Terai, Duars and the Tertulia subdivision of Rangpur district of present-day Bangladesh (Debnath, 2010). In this tea plantation period, the resident like "Lepchas at Darjeeling and the Mache's and Rajbanshi at the foothills were the people who claimed to be lived in these regions and practiced subsistence agriculture" (Das Gupta, 1992). At that time the tea planters want to provide huge tea labourers for the tea plantation in Duars and Terai region, primarily the tribes of Chhotanagpur and Santhal Parganas (like Oraons, Mundas, Santhals and Kharias) were recruited as Immigrant labourers. On the other hand, most of the indigenous (Toto, Mech, and Rabha) tribes were deprived of tea workers in the British period. If we say the reason for the incident that they (planters) know indigenous people will demand and protest against them and build unity. Since the colonial period, both communities suffering and suppressed in the name of development. Both suppressed in every sphere of life such as the right of the people, health, education, standard housing and jobs. This is not the end, they are still seen as a backward class or backward people in the whole society. Many times, politically or in other ways they are suffering from suppression in the name of development across the country.

Immigrant tribe was isolated from the local people or indigenous tribe and British were provided the all-separate treatment among them. Sometimes they suffered from fever and disease. But Indigenous Tribe also are facing the same problems. Marginality is a living condition that affects millions of people throughout the world. People who are marginalized have relatively little control over their lives and the resources available to them. "This results in making them handicapped in earning their share from the society. A vicious circle is set up whereby their lack of positive and supportive relationships means that they are prevented from participating in local life, which in turn leads to further isolation. This has a tremendous impact on the development of human beings, as well as on society at large" (Ray, 1998). As the objective of development is to create an enabling environment for people to enjoy a productive, healthy, and creative life, it is important to address the issue of marginalization.

Marginalization is a complex and multi-layered concept since the beginning. Nations can be marginalized at the global level, while classes and communities can be marginalized from the dominant social order within nations. Likewise, ethnic/caste/religious groups, families, or individuals can be marginalized within localities. Marginalization is also a changing phenomenon linked to many socio-economic factors and conditions. For instance, individuals or groups/communities might enjoy high social status at one point in time, but as social change takes place, so they would lose this status and become marginalized. Peter Leonard defines social marginality as "being outside the mainstream of productive activity and/or social reproductive activity". Leonard characterizes these people as remaining outside "the major arena of capitalist productive and reproductive activity" and as such experiencing 'involuntary social marginality'. The experience of marginality can also arise in a number of ways. For some people, those severely impaired from birth, or those born into particularly marginal groupings this marginality is typically life-long and greatly determines their lived experience. In such situations, a serious combination of cultural, economic, political and social exclusion with the possibility of significant consequences at the personal level in terms of a lack of self-esteem and a confused self-identity means that the individual withdraws into a world of his/her own. Marginalization is thus a complex as well as a very serious phenomenon. It can effectively push people to the margin of society, where their sense of security is in every way a threatened one.

People who are marginalized have relatively little control over their lives and the resources available to them; they may become stigmatized and are often at the receiving end of negative public attitudes. Their opportunities to make social contributions may be limited and they may develop low self-confidence and self-esteem. If they do not have work and live with service supports, for example, they may have limited opportunities for meeting with others and may become isolated. A vicious circle is set up whereby their lack of positive and supportive relationships means they are prevented from participating in local life, which, in turn, leads to further isolation. Social policies and practices may mean they have relatively limited access to valued social resources such as education and health services, housing, income, leisure activities, education and work. The impacts of marginalization, in terms of social exclusion, are similar, whatever the origins and processes of marginalization, irrespective of whether these are to be located in social attitudes (such as towards impairment, sexuality, ethnicity and so on) or social circumstance such as the closure of workplaces, absence of affordable housing and so on. In sociological literature, marginalization is defined as the situation in which people sit on the borders of two cultures existing within a society but are full members of neither culture. This is cultural marginalization. More recently, the phenomenon of social exclusion is also understood alongside this. It means people who have been socially excluded have no significant role in society. They tend to be excluded from the regular productive systems within society and are problematic consumers of the benefits of society as a result of their economic situation and minority status within. This exclusion may take the form of a lack of acceptance by the members of the majority social groupings but, even more significantly, it may give rise to discriminatory behaviour and violence.

In the tea plantation, the immigrant tribes and the indigenous tribes are treated by a different system. Most of the immigrant people were isolated by the British. They inhabited the remote is of the Duars. Both the tribes are pressurized that time by the Government and also lost their traditional culture by the European power. Most of the tribes converted to Christianity, and obey the new Christian culture. "Christianity of Sub-Himalayan Bengal and Lower Assam is deeply rooted with the colonial expansion including the growth of Western Education and conversion of the tribal communities of this region. The indigenous tribal community (specially Meches, Boro and Rabha), as well as the immigrant tribal communities (Santhals, Oraons, Mundas, Mahalis etc.), have embraced Christianity in the Duars regions" (Barman, 2019). In spite of their conversion, the tribal communities have still retained their own religious culture. The Koch-Rabhas have their religious traditions of worshipping Jog-Rishi. However, some of the Rabhas of the Duars are followers of the Jan-Jogi order and Christianity (Barman, 2019). Government schemes have changed the perception and attitude of tribes towards their cultural practices. Indigenous culture is overpowered by modern culture (Bhosale, 2019). The denial of civil and political rights, social repression, exclusion, and economic inequality was the defining conditions of most tribal communities in India. The tribal communities in West Bengal also continued to face marginalization over decades. The fact that more than three-fourth of the tribes are landless and that their social conditions in areas such as livelihood, housing, health and sanitation, education, welfare etc. remained very much below the state average shows the extent of marginalization.

The situations of marginalization are many and varied in the contemporary scene. One situation is clear that results from migration in its various forms. The immigrant tribes are habited under the tea areas, most of the settlements are in the Indo-Bhutan border of the western Duars. Those people are suffering from various problems like education. The almost total habited area is remote, they deprive of the education or higher education facilities. Settlements of the people, like Hamilton Ganj, Madhu Tea state, Bandha Panni, Dhekla Para tea state, and Toto Para, if they got primary education but deprived of higher education (college education) because of the huge distance of the college from the home of the learner. If someone trying to get higher education, they dropped from the college due to lack of money. "Some people are earning their money by selling firewood which is collected from the forest, if the descendents want to get the degree, then how to bear the expenses of the higher study. . . ." said Sukhdev Oraon. Among all these communities habited far from the town, they trouble lack of good roads, this is another problem to push backward them, government is silent. In the political depredation or other issues, if they want to learn Hindi from primary to college they could not since the British rule. But some places have seen the school, college but the little number, or huge far from the home. Not only in the education they also deprive of the government facilities. The politician always promises to do everything. They will provide better education facilities, will make the road, will provide the houses etc., but all the promises are still under dreams. Marginalization is related to the social conditions emerging from the status of specific castes or classes. Members of these castes or classes are born into a situation of inferior status and are, therefore, in danger of being marginalized. The caste system of India is an example, while in many other countries, ethnic identity, education, living standards etc. are being perceived as the criteria of exclusion. The degree and seriousness of the exclusion vary from these areas.

Social development is the expansion of people's choices or options in life and, here globalization can have a positive influence too. Certainly, many would glorify the actual and potential benefits of globalization. However, others would bring to light the negative consequences of globalization. As it is, the global economy is based on the desire of companies to make profits within a highly competitive market place. Essentially, globalization is presented by many commentators as a situation where liberalization policies are removing state's protection against domination and exploitation by more powerful states and forcing the weaker states to compete with all other states within a set of conditions that are, in effect, controlled by the most powerful states. The well-documented inequality between nations and sub-regions has shown that the powerful will grow wealthier. An economically unequal world has resulted in an increasingly unequal political world and this continues to be the situation in many parts of the world having their impact on the life of poor and marginalized people in all countries, both developed and developing. The context of the discourse on the indigenous, initiated by the ILO and later accepted by the UNO thus basically hinged on the twin concepts of 'need right' and 'power right' of a certain social category of people all over the world. This category of people was progressively being marginalized and dispossessed from their sources of livelihood and was vulnerable to cultural shock and decimation of their collective identity (Xaxa, 1999). Thus, three aspects are central to the conceptualization of the indigenous people. First, the indigenous are those people who lived in the country to which they belong before colonization or conquest by people from outside the country or the geographical region. Secondly, they have become marginalized as an aftermath of conquest and colonization by the people from outside the region. Thirdly, such people govern their life more in terms of their own social, economic and cultural institutions than the laws applicable to the society or the country at large. What is important here is that the notion of indigenous people, despite sharing attributes in common with the people described as the tribal and semi-tribal population. It is only with the internationalization of the rights and privileges associated with it that the use of the term indigenous has come to be critically examined or even challenged in the Indian context. The sense in which the term was used earlier and the sense in which it has come to be used today are not identical though they overlap in some sense. Today, aspects of marginalization are built into the definition of indigenous and immigrant people.

Current concerns about the potentially catastrophic consequences of climate change within the region further reinforce the role of the state in protecting its most vulnerable and marginalized populations from the most extreme impacts of changes in the natural world. Associated with this is the continued challenge of creating the conditions for inclusive economic and political citizenship within a region characterized by high levels of absolute poverty and ethnic and social diversity. While the twenty-first century will continue to provide new economic, political, social and environmental problems that confront the state in the Asia

Pacific region, it is unlikely to mark the untimely demise of this abiding political concept. Marginalization is a process that denies opportunities and outcomes to those 'living on the margins,' while enhancing the opportunities and outcomes for those who are at 'the centre'. Caste and class prejudice, in many societies across the globe, exclude many communities and hinder their effective participation in economic and social development. It directly affects the attainment of effective endowments in the spheres of education, occupation and livelihood. A vicious circle is set up whereby their lack of positive and supportive relationships means that they are prevented from participating in local life, which in turn leads to further isolation.

Conclusion

In the conclusion, we must say that marginal people are deprived of the period to period. They are far from modern society and culture now time is to merge them. Based on social groups, the educational level of the males among the marginalized section is worse than that of the females belonging to the other category. If the government takes charge to set up the number of colleges, most of the girl/boy students who want to get higher education, they can get. Most of the tea gardens were remained closed for a long time, if the government look into it and provide the job then they have to remove their little suffering. Though I had an ambition to analyse why under development higher education in the remote areas and Tea belt area or Duars area. I could not reach my goal because of the pandemic. I hope some other scholars and researchers would come forward to continue this type of study in near future.

NOTES AND REFERENCES

1. Ghosh, Ananda Gopal and Sutradhar, Kartick Chandra, *Marginal Identities and Environment: Perspective of (Sub-Himalayan) North Bengal*, Towards Freedom, 2018.
2. Debnath, S., *The Dooars in Historical Transition*, Siliguri: N.L. Publishers, 2010.
3. Das Gupta, Ranajit, *Economy, Society, and Politics in Bengal: Jalpaiguri 1869-1947*, Delhi: Oxford University Press, 1992.
4. Barman, Rup Kumar, *The Practice of Folk Medicine in Sub-Himalayan Bengal: A Study on the Folk Medicinal Practices of the Rajbanshi's in Historical Perspective*, Abhijeet Publication, New Delhi, 2019.
5. Bhosale, Prashant S., *Tribal Herbal Practitioner*, Orange Books Publication, Delhi, 2019.

6. Ramakrushnudu, B., *Social Economic and Cultural Status of Marginalized Groups in Andhra Pradesh*, Thesis submitted in the Department of History at Sri Krishnadevaraya University, Anantapur, Andhra Pradesh, 2015.
7. Xaxa, V., "The Tribes as Indigenous People of India", *Economic and Political Weekly*, December 18-24, 1999, Vol. 34, No. 51, pp. 3589-3595.
8. Milligan, J.A., *Final Report on the Survey and Settlement Reports in the Jalpaiguri District, 1906-1916*, Calcutta: APAC, 1919, p. 16.
9. Ghosh, S., *The History of Medical and Health Care Systems of North Bengal from 1869 to 1969*, Ph.D. thesis submitted in the Department of History at University of North Bengal, Darjeeling, 2011.
10. Ray, Kabita, *History of Public Health: Colonial Bengal 1921-1947*, Calcutta: K.P. Bagchi & Company, 1998.
11. Grunig, J.F., *Eastern Bengal and Assam District Gazetteer*, Allahabad: Pioneer Press, 1911.
12. Hunter, W.W., *A Statistical Account of Bengal*, Vol. X., Districts of Darjeeling and Jalpaiguri, & State of Kuch Behar, London: Trubner, 1876.
13. Risley, H.H., *The Tribes and Castes of Bengal*, Printed at Bengal Secretariat Press, 1892.
14. Sarkar, Anil Kumar, *Reflections on the History of North Bengal*, Abhijeet Publication, New Delhi, 2020.
15. O'Malley, L.S.S., *Bengal District Gazetteer: Darjeeling*, Logos Press, 1907.
16. Sarkar, Amitabha, *Toto: Society and Change: A Sub-Himalayan Tribe of West Bengal*, Generic, 1993.

19

Colonial State and Homophobia
Criminalization of Homosexuality in Colonial India

Apurba Ghosh

Homophobia is not new in India rather if it has been existing since the ancient period of times. However, the state-sponsored homophobia and legislations against homosexuality were introduced in India for the first time by the colonial authority which made homosexuality a criminal offence under the Section 377 of the Indian Penal Code (IPC). Post-Colonial Indian State has adopted the colonial tradition for a very long time. Though recently the Supreme Court of India in its verdict has declared the law (IPC Section 377) as unconstitutional in case of its implementation to the consensual sexual acts between adults of same-sex, the society and state's rigid attitude has not changed much yet. To trace the State-sponsored homophobia, therefore, we must have to look at the Colonial state's policy towards homosexuality in India. This article would try to focus on the ideology and considerations of colonial state played fundamental roles in making homosexuality a criminal offence in India. It would also try to find out the answer to the question that did the colonial state make the Indians homophobic on such a strong foot that it has been continuing?

Section 377 of the Indian Penal Code was authored by Lord Macaulay, the President of the Indian Law Commission, in 1860, as part of Britain's effort to impose Victorian values on its biggest colony. Similar laws were imposed on most of its colonies, including the United States. It reads as follows: "Section 377: Unnatural offences — whoever voluntarily has carnal intercourse against the order of nature with any man, woman, or animal shall be punished with imprisonment for life, or with imprisonment of either description for a term which may extend to 10 years, and shall be liable to fine."[1] Although not explicitly defined, the 'carnal intercourse against the order of nature, has been taken by the Indian Courts in the intervening years to include anal sex, oral sex and in some cases other non-procreative sexual acts, such as mutual masturbation.[2] Even when such sex is consensual, the 'voluntary' provision in the law makes it illegal. In most Western democracies, such kind of laws like Section 377 has been banned. Britain, the inventor of Section 377 during the colonial era, decriminalized homosexuality in 1967. During the 1980s, the European Court of Human Rights ruled that criminalizing same-sex sexual behaviour was a violation of the protection of private life.[3] Although the Section 377 has been banned by the Supreme Court and homosexuality is no more a criminal offence in India, Indian State's role in giving the rights of marriage, child adoption and so on to homosexuals is very rigid. The colonial mentality in state's policy is a prolonged phenomenon; and due to that reason for understanding such colonial mentality, it is necessary to overlook the policies of colonial authority in India towards homosexuals.

Criminalization of Homosexuality in Colonial India

During the ancient period in India homosexuality was not completely an accepted social phenomenon. However point to be noted that, though in ancient India homosexuality was not completely an accepted social phenomenon, there was no uniform category of forbidden sex (such as sodomy).[4] Apart from it, there has been no evidence found so far of anyone being executed or punished in ancient India for having same-sex relations. There has been no evidence or reference that the state making the law to forbid homosexuality.[5] But, it is the colonial law that made homosexuality a criminal offence.

The question comes why did the British government or the colonial state take such policy? Victorian morality or 'Victorian fanatical campaign' played an important role in the policies of the colonial government in case of criminalizing homosexuality.[6] In Victorian England notions of patriarchy and masculinity got importance. Therefore, Victorians considered homosexuality as a threat to masculinity as homosexuality could destroy the patriarchal structure. A new kind of sexual moral code emerged in Europe from the 18th century onwards, especially during the 19th century and this also came in India with the British. In the field of sexual morality the Victorian Moral codes established a belief that except for the sexual acts between men and female genitals, all other sexual acts (like sodomy, mutual masturbation etc.) were to be considered as 'unnatural'. It established that the need for sex is just to produce the child, not for the pleasure. In the words of Foucault: "Sexuality was carefully confined; it moved into the home. The conjugal family took custody of it and absorbed it into the serious function of reproduction. . . . A single locus of sexuality was acknowledged in social space as well as at the heart of every household, but it was a utilitarian and fertile one: the parents' bedroom."[7] Therefore, all the people engaged in non-procreative sexual acts identified as deviants.

However, Victorian morality, new sexual culture played important role in criminalizing or making homosexuality a criminal offence by the colonial authority that is very clear, but the issue is that India was not the mother country of colonisers, then why they became so conscious about the sexual morality or social vice of India? The fact is that colonial authority was very much apprehensive about the existence of sexual freedom and homosexuality in the society and culture of the Orient. Robert Aldrich has shown that "Colonial islands included most of the Africa, South and Southeast Asia and the islands of the Pacific and Indian oceans and the Caribbean, provided a haven for many Europeans whose sexual inclinations did not fit neatly into the constraints of European society."[8] It made the colonial government apprehensive that British colonies including India would become the centre for queer acts where British citizens would be indulged in homosexual acts. Therefore, the colonial government introduced such laws (like Section 377 of IPC) in different colonies including India. And few British officials got engaged in sodomy or homosexuality that also colonial authority had noticed. For example, in 1845 Sir Richard Burton, a British officer in the colonial Sindh province, under the instruction of Charles Napier, Governor of Sindh, surveyed the brothels of Karachi where significant numbers of male or homosexual prostitutes used to work. And after a detailed survey, Burton wrote a report which was known as *Karachi Report.*[9] In the report Burton wrote that many British officials in Sindh province used to go to the Karachi brothels to satisfy their sexual needs from the male prostitutes. The report later on destroyed, but the reference of it can be found in Burton's work titled *Terminal Essays.*[10] However, it was very alarming for the colonial government and it became necessary to stop such possibilities in the British colonies including India by imposing laws. One thing should be remembered that in the countries where homosexuality is or was illegal, most of them have a history of

British colonial domination. For that reason, it would be very true to argue that British colonialism is largely responsible for the criminalization of homosexuality around the world. Another thing is that British authority often tried to project various institutions, customs of Orient as 'oriental vice'. They used to claim that they were civilized and East or Orient was uncivilized, and the civilized race had the right to rule over the uncivilized races. Homosexuality was also projected by the colonial authority as 'Oriental vice'. Now colonisers realized that if their people would indulge in such vices, the colonial claim of the British race as superior would come under question. Therefore, the colonial authority had to stop such possibilities anyhow by imposing laws like Section 377.

The Colonial state was also very apprehensive about the influence of homosexuality on the colonial army. British authority thought that due to the long distance from their wives/female partners British white army personnel posted in India might have indulged in homosexual acts, more specifically sodomy. Therefore, there was a probable need to declare homosexuality as a criminal offence officially. Interesting thing is that the colonial government under the provision of *Contagious Diseases Act* (1868) allowed prostitution in cantonment cities which was completely against the Victorian social morality. In each cantonment city, separate regimented red light areas or regimental bazaar (*lal bazaars*) were established from where the soldiers could satisfy their sexual needs from the prostitutes.[11] The idea was to control the movement of soldiers beyond the controlled environment of the cantonment which made them more susceptible to contracting diseases. Lock Hospitals were opened where suspected women were examined and infected women were admitted by force, if necessary, for treatment. The medical examinations, as they involved the genital area, were embarrassing and came to be resented. There was also the fear of both chaste as well as unchaste women being treated like prostitutes based on mere suspicion. The objective here was not the health of the women; rather the purpose was to provide safe pleasure for the soldiers and European residents in India. Ronald Hyam in his text has shown the existence of innumerable instances of masturbation, homosexuality and sodomy as the forms of sexuality among the army personnel which later in the Victorian era came to be dreaded. The provision of safe pleasure (through the prostitutes in cantonments) was a solution to this.[12] Therefore, it can be argued that though prostitution was against the Victorian notion of 'ideal women', the colonial government allowed it just to save their white army personnel from the 'danger' of homosexuality and also to provide safe pleasure for the soldiers.

This research has tried to go deeper into the issues around sexualities and body politic taking into consideration of alternative sexualities. To do so, it is necessary to look after the colonial archival documents. But the problem is that colonial archives provide very little information about this theme. Anjali Arondekar has termed it as "the politics of archives for there has been a deliberate omission and invisibility of alternative sexualities."[13] The archives that could prove the engagements of British residents (in India) in homosexual acts were consciously destroyed by the colonial authority as that might destroy the image of colonial heterosexual masculinity. However, despite the deliberate omission in the archives, few traces of homosexuality have not gone unnoticed; but it is worth mentioning that the available archival documents only put light on the engagement of Indians in alternative sexualities.

Basically, the law reports and judicial reports are important among the colonial archival sources for this theme. From Indian Law Reports (Allahabad) a famous case came into the light which is known as *Queen Empress* vs. *Khairati*.[14] In 1884 this case came up in the then colonial Allahabad High Court. For months, the police had been tailing a person named Khairati on the suspicion that he was a 'eunuch' or homosexual and after being tipped off that on a visit to his ancestral village, he was found dancing and singing dressed as a woman. The police arrested him on the suspicion that he was a 'habitual sodomite' and subjected him to a medical examination, which recorded that the examinee showed the characteristic mark of a catamite (a Victorian term for a man kept for homosexual desires) and noted that the anal orifice was 'shaped like a trumpet'.[15] He was prosecuted under Section 377 of the Indian Penal Code (IPC), and became the first recorded case under the law and set the ground for numerous similar convictions in colonial stemming from suspicion, rumours and anonymous tip-offs. Thus, with criminalization of homosexuality also entered the realm of medical interrogation and treatment.

In the case of *Noshirwan* vs. *Emperor*,[16] having seen two young men, both adults, walking into the house of one of them, Solomon, the neighbour, peeped 'through a chink in the door panels' and noticed that the two were attempting to commit sodomy. He walked into the house and forced them both to the police station. The two accused were released and their conviction set aside as the act of the sodomy was never completed, although the judge did reprimand one of the men, Ratansi, as a 'despicable' specimen of humanity for being addicted to the 'vice of catamite' on his admission.[17]

In the case of *DP Minwalla* vs. *Emperor*,[18] Minwalla,a young man was caught in doing the act of oral sex with another man in the back of a truck, in a semi-public place. Minwalla, in a desperate attempt to redeem himself, submitted to a medical examination to convince the court that his anal orifice was not shaped like a 'funnel', which is a sign of a habitual sodomite. The court confirmed the conviction of Minwalla with a reduced sentence, mindful of the importance of the physical attribute.[19]

In *Government* vs. *Bapoji Bhatt*[20] case, the appellate charged with Section 377 of IPC who was caught doing oral sex with a minor. As such case has to be dealt with under child abuse but it was trialed under Section 377. The court held according to the definition of 'carnal intercourse against the order of nature does not include oral sex and thus the case was dismissed. But in *Khanu* vs. *Emperor*[21] case the wide scope of Section 377 of IPC has been explained. In this case, a minor was forced for oral sex by an old man. In the judgment of this case, the court declared that Section 377 is not limited to '*coitus per annum*'[22] and it can be extended to '*coitus per os*'[23] and the court said that the sin of Gomorrah is no less carnal intercourse than the sin of sodomy. Thus Section 377 got its mature form, and till September 2018 this mature form of Section 377 had been active in India.

Homophobia and the Responsibility of Colonial State

Now the question comes whether the colonial law suddenly made Indians homophobic or not. Homophobia cannot be enforced in long run by law only. For a very long time, colonial law (Section 377) was active due to the already existing prejudice and strictures of Indian society against the queer community. However, though the level of homophobia became more intense during the colonial period, traces of homophobia can be found in the ancient texts. Vanita and Kidwai in their famous book argue: "[Ancient texts] tend to take a somewhat derogatory view of those who are homoerotically inclined. The range of terms used for such persons suggests a groping for words rather than complete social integration. Many of these terms bring from heterosexual assumptions ascribing effeminacy, impotence, or some sort of inadequacy to non-heterosexual persons."[24] The role of society in regulating sexuality is best illustrated by S. Gurumurty (RSS ideologue) through his statement.

According to him, "the Indian discipline was always built around unenforced social and family norms, not state laws. Self-restraint and shyness were the tools to regulate the deviants from the norms, not the police or courts. Even today, it is this non-formal moral order — read dharma — not the laws of parliament or state assemblies, that largely govern this society. . . . In the Indian tradition, homosexuals, as elsewhere, were thus regarded as deviants. . . . Yet no one can argue here or elsewhere that homosexuality is a virtue. No law or court of law can declare it as a virtue."[25] And from this above statement one can understand that how society is more powerful than law in India to some extent. For example, '*sati*' custom was abolished through the law in 1829, but despite that, it continued for a long time, even the news of '*sati*' came from Rajasthan during 1980s. Homophobia is still prevalent in Indian society despite the abolishment of Section 377 (in the case of consensual sexual intercourse between the adults of the same sex) just because of the rigidity of society. Therefore, the role of society is always important in India. If there has been no pre-existing homophobia in Indian society, it would not have been possible to survive by law. Homophobia has been continuing in India from very early times, and it would not be approprite, therefore, to blame the colonial government or state solely.

Conclusion

In conclusion, it can be argued that British colonialism or colonial rule was not the fundamental factor for making the Indians homophobic. Homophobia is a prolonged phenomenon that has been continuing in India since the ancient period. Homophobia is very much related to patriarchy. It (homophobia) exists where patriarchy is powerful. As homosexuality somehow gives the challenge to the patriarchal notions of family and procreation, patriarchy cannot accept the existence or visibility of any alternative sexuality and gender. From the later Vedic period to date, patriarchy has been maintaining its significant position in India and consequently, homophobia is very much prevalent here. However, it is true that due to the legal procedures and legislation against homosexuals, or the sexual minorities and their sexual acts (like sodomy) in colonial India, the phobia and anxiety of Indians towards sexual minorities including homosexuals had increased significantly. Homophobia is so much engulfed in our society that even after the abolishment of Section 377 or the decriminalization of homosexuality, the situation has not changed much yet in case of societal acceptances. Therefore, instead of blaming the colonial rule, the liberal section of society should come together and try to bring changes in the primitive perceptions of society.

NOTES AND REFERENCES

1. Indian Penal Code. Section 377: Unnatural Offences, 1860, *http://www.vakilno1.com/bareacts/indianpenalcode/S377.htm;www.indiankanoon.org.*
2. Alok Gupta, "Section 377 and the Dignity of Indian Homosexuals", *Economic and Political Weekly*, Vol. 41, Issue No. 46, 18 November, 2006.
3. Geetanjali Mishra, "Decriminalising Homosexuality in India", *Reproductive Health Matters*, Vol. 17, No. 34, November 2009, pp. 20-28, at: *http://www.jstor.org/stable/40647442*
4. Ruth Vanita and Saleem Kidwai, (eds.), *Same Sex Love in India: Readings from Literature and History*, New York: Palgrave, 2000, p. xviii.
5. *Ibid.*
6. Suparna Bhaskaran, "The Politics of Penetration: Section 377 and the Indian Penal Code", in Ruth Vanita (ed.), *Queering India: Same Sex Love and Eroticism in Indian Culture and Society*, London: Routledge, 2002, pp. 15-29.
7. Michel Foucault, *The History of Sexuality: An Introduction*, New York: Pantheon Books, 1976, Vol. 1, p. 3.
8. Robert Aldrich, *Colonialism and Homosexuality*, London: Routledge, 2003, p. 3.
9. For the details about the *Karachi Report*, see Anjali Arondekar, *For the Record: On Sexuality and the Colonial Archive in India*, Durham and London: Duke University Press, 2009, pp. 27-59.
10. *Ibid.*
11. Mridul Megha, "Body Politic: Sexuality, Health and Hygiene in Colonial India (1860-1930)", *South Asian Journal of Multidisciplinary Studies*, Vol. 4, Issue. 3, 2018, pp. 286-310.
12. Ronald Hyam, *Empire and Sexuality: The British Experience*, New York and Manchester: Manchester University Press, 1991, pp. 121-123.
13. Anjali Arondekar, *op. cit.*, 2009, p. 2.
14. *Queen-Empress* vs. *Khairati*, 1884 ILR (Indian Law Report) All 204.
15. *Ibid.*
16. *Noshirwan* vs. *Emperor*, AIR 1934 Sind 206.
17. *Ibid.*
18. *DP Minwalla* vs. *Emperor*, AIR 1935 Sind 78.
19. Alok Gupta, *op. cit.*, 2006.
20. *Government* vs. *Bapoji Bhatt*, 1884(7), Mysore LR 280.
21. *Khanu* vs. *Emperor*, AIR 1925 Sind 286.
22. Sexual intercourse or oral intercourse performed by male inserting his penis into the anus of a male or female partner.
23. Oral Sex.
24. Ruth Vanita and Saleem Kidwai, *op. cit.*, 2000, p. 26.
25. S. Gurumurty, "Shy Society: Shameless Debate", *Organiser*, 12-18 July, 2009 (Organiser is the official publication of the Rashtriya Swayamsevak Sangh).

INDEX

CONCEPT
1041/2 | 10/9/22
AJ AJ